BLAKE AND SWEDENBORG

Opposition Is True Friendship

SWEDENBORG FOUNDATION, INC.
NEW YORK

TO ALL THOSE WHO REST NOT
FROM THE GREAT TASK

Blake, *Jerusalem* **95 (detail)**

BLAKE AND SWEDENBORG

Opposition Is True Friendship

AN ANTHOLOGY

Compiled and Edited by
Harvey F. Bellin and Darrell Ruhl

in conjunction with
George F. Dole, Tom Kieffer
and Nancy Crompton

With an Introduction by George F. Dole

The Sources of William Blake's Arts
In the Writings of Emanuel Swedenborg

SWEDENBORG FOUNDATION, INC.
NEW YORK

Cover illustrations from William Blake's *Jerusalem* are reproduced by the courtesy of the Collection of Mr. and Mrs. Paul Mellon.

LEFT: Frontispiece (partial)
RIGHT: Plate 97 (partial)

BLAKE AND SWEDENBORG
Opposition Is True Friendship

First Edition
10 9 8 7 6 5 4 3 2 1

Contents and compilation
Copyright © 1985 by The Swedenborg Foundation, Inc.
Except where otherwise noted.

Library of Congress Card Catalog Number 85-050060
ISBN: 0-87785-127-1

Design by Nancy Crompton

The Swedenborg Foundation, Inc.
139 East 23rd Street
New York, N.Y. 10010

Printed and bound in the United States

Contents

Abbreviations

WORKS BY WILLIAM BLAKE

A	*America, a Prophecy* (1793)
BA	*The Book of Ahania* (1795)
BT	*The Book of Thel* (1789)
BU	*The (First) Book of Urizen* (1794) (sometimes cited as *Ur*)
DC	*A Descriptive Catalogue* (1809)
E	*Europe, a Prophecy* (1794)
EG	*The Everlasting Gospel* (c. 1818)
FZ	*Vala, or the Four Zoas* (1795-1804)
GA	*The Ghost of Abel* (1822)
GP	*For the Sexes: The Gates of Paradise* (c. 1818)
GP ch	*For Children: The Gates of Paradise* (1793)
J	*Jerusalem* (1804-20)
Job	*Illustrations of the Book of Job* (1823-26)
L	*The Book of Los* (1795)
Laoc	*Laocoön* plate (c. 1820)
M	*Milton, a Poem in 2 Books* (1804-08)
MHH	*The Marriage of Heaven and Hell* (c. 1790-93)
NNR	*There is No Natural Religion* and *All Religions are One* (c. 1788)
SI	*Songs of Innocence* (1789)
SE	*Songs of Experience* (1794)
SL	*The Song of Los* (1795)
VDA	*Visions of the Daughters of Albion* (1793)
VLJ	*A Vision of the Last Judgement* (1810)

Quotations from Blake's works are frequently referenced with an abbreviated title and, occasionally, plate and line numbers: thus, *J* 16; 61-9 is *Jerusalem*, plate 16, lines 61 through 69. Manuscripts, letters, annotations and letterpress editions of Blake's works are generally cited by page number and often appended with or substituted by a page reference to a compilation of Blake's writings: thus, *VLJ* p. 94; *E.* 565 is *A Vision of the Last Judgement*, page 94, and can be found on page 565 of Erdman's *Poetry and Prose of William Blake*. The two compilations used by authors in this anthology are:

E *The Poetry and Prose of William Blake*, ed. David V. Erdman (Garden City, New York: Doubleday & Co., 4th printing, 1970)

K *The Complete Writings of William Blake*, ed. Geoffrey Keynes (London and New York: Nonesuch Press, 1957; Oxford: Oxford University Press, 1966)

WORKS BY EMANUEL SWEDENBORG

AC	*Arcana Coelestia (Heavenly Secrets)* (1749-56)
AE	*Apocalypse Explained* (1759)
AK	*The Animal Kingdom (The Soul's Domain)* (1744)
AR	*Apocalypse Revealed* (1766)
CL	*Conjugial Love* (also called *Marital Love*) (1768)
DLW	*Divine Love and Wisdom* (1763)
DP	*Divine Providence* (1764)
EAK	*Economy of the Animal Kingdom (The Dynamics of the Soul's Domain)* (1740-41)
Faith	*Doctrine of Faith* (1763)
HH	*Heaven and Hell* (1758)
I	*Intercourse Between Soul and Body (Soul-Body Interaction)* (1769)
JD	*Journal of Dreams* (1743-4)
Life	*Doctrine of Life* (1763)
LJ	*Last Judgement* (1758)
Lord	*Doctrine of the Lord* (1763)
NJHD	*New Jerusalem and Its Heavenly Doctrine* (1758)
PRIN	*Principia* (Vol. 1 of *Philosophical & Mineralogical Works*) (1734)
SD	*Spiritual Diary* (1747-65)
SS	*Doctrine of Sacred Scripture* (1763)
TCR	*True Christian Religion* (1771)
WE	*The Word Explained* (1746-7)

Quotations from Swedenborg's works are frequently referenced with an abbreviated title followed by a paragraph number, in conformity with Swedenborg's own numbering system, which has been reproduced in all translations and editions of his writings: thus *AC 68* is *Arcana Coelestia*, paragraph 68. The standard reference for biographical documents is:

Docs.	*Documents concerning the Life and Character of Emanuel Swedenborg*, 2 vols., collected, translated and annotated by R. L. Tafel (London, 1875 and 1877)

Acknowledgements and Sources

ILLUSTRATIONS

Our special thanks is extended to Mr. Paul Mellon for allowing us to reproduce several unique, tinted engravings by William Blake from the Collection of Mr. and Mrs. Paul Mellon. These include our cover illustrations from the Mellon copy of Blake's *Jerusalem*, and illustrations on pages ii, 37, 54, 65, 99, 131 and 156.

Blake engravings reproduced from the Lessing J. Rosenwald Collection of the Library of Congress occur on pages 39, 43, 49, 57, 60, 63, and 64.

Blake's engraved *Illustrations of the Book of Job*, reproduced from originals in the Glencairn Museum of the Academy of the New Church, Bryn Athyn, Pennsylvania, occur on pages 55, 91, and 101.

Plates from Emanuel Swedenborg's books and portrait of Swedenborg are from the Swedenborg Foundation Image Archive, Robin Larsen, curator.

Other illustrations and marginalia are from facsimiles created by April Howlett, Nancy Crompton and Harvey F. Bellin for the Swedenborg Foundation television docu-drama, *BLAKE: The Marriage of Heaven and Hell*, a Global Concepts/The Media Group, Inc. production, and from nineteeth century sources in private collections.

TEXT

Morton D. Paley provided his "A New Heaven is Begun: Blake and Swedenborgianism," which originally appeared in *Blake: An Illustrated Quarterly* (Vol. 12, No. 2; Fall, 1979), a journal of which he is co-editor.

Quotations in Harvey F. Bellin's "Opposition Is True Friendship" have been reprinted with permission from the following: Crown Publishing, Inc., for excepts from Albert Einstein's *Ideas and Opinions*, translated by Sonja Bargmann (New York: Dell Publishing Co., 1973), copyright © 1954 by Crown Publishing, Inc.; Princeton University Press for excerpts from *The Collected Works of C.G. Jung*, translated by R. F. C. Hull, Bollingen Series XX, Vol. 12: *Psychology and Alchemy* Princeton: Princeton University Press, 1968, copyright © by Princeton University Press; and Farrar, Straus & Giroux, Inc. for excerpts from Czeslaw Milosz's *The Land of Ulro*, translated by Louis Iribarne (New York: Farrar, Straus & Giroux, Inc., 1984), translation copyright © 1981 by Farrar, Straus & Giroux, Inc.

Dr. Kathleen Raine has graciously provided two articles, including her previously unpublished text of an address entitled "The Human Face of God," which was delivered in May 1985 at l'Université St-Jean de Jérusalem in Paris (on the occasion of an annual conference established by Henry Corbin). She has granted permission to reprint excerpts from her book, *The Human Face of God*, (London: Thames and Hudson, 1982), copyright © 1982 by Kathleen Raine, and "The Swedenborgian Songs," which originally appeared as Chapter One in Volume I of *Blake and Tradition*, Bollingen Series XXXV-11, published for the Bollingen Foundation by Princeton University Press, copyright © 1968, by the Trustees of the National Gallery of Art, Washington, D.C. Reprinted by the permission of the National Gallery of Art.

Patrick Gregory of Boston University Scholarly Publications provided Raymond H. Deck, Jr.'s "New Light on C. A. Tulk, Blake's 19th Century Patron," which originally appeared in *Studies in Romanticism*, 16, no. 2, copyright © 1977, Trustees of Boston University.

Excerpts from Alexander Gilchrist's 1863 edition of *The Life of William Blake*, and from Robert Hindmarsh's 1861 edition of *The Rise and Progress of the New Jerusalem Church in England, America and Other Parts*, are reprinted from books in the libraries of Harvey F. Bellin and the Swedenborg Foundation, respectively.

The Reverend Donald Rose alerted the editors to Donald Fitzpatrick, Jr.'s article, "William Blake's New Church Crit-ics" (from *New Church Life*, January 1959), and to "William Blake and the Writings of Emanuel Swedenborg," the text of an address by the Reverend Peter M. Buss, delivered at the Olivet Church of the New Jerusalem in Ontario, Canada, on 28 January 1984. The third of our "Swedenborgian Postscripts," H. N. Morris's "Blake and Swedenborg," excerpted from the British publication, *New Church Herald* (Vol. XXX, 1949), was provided by the Reverend Brian Kingslake of London.   —The Editors.

Preface

EMANUEL SWEDENBORG (1688-1772)
SWEDISH SCIENTIST/THEOLOGIAN

WILLIAM BLAKE (1757-1827)
BRITISH POET/ARTIST

I can venture to assert that as a moralist, Swedenborg is above all praise; and that as a naturalist, psychologist and theologian, he has strong and varied claims on the gratitude of the professional and philosophical student.

Samuel Taylor Coleridge (1827)

He is a genius—and I apprehend, a Swedenborgian—certainly, a mystic emphatically. You perhaps smile at my calling another poet, a mystic; but verily I am in the very mire of commonplace commonsense compared with Mr. Blake.

Samuel Taylor Coleridge (Letter, 2/2/1818)

With rare exception, every major study of William Blake's life and arts includes at least passing mention of the influences of Emanuel Swedenborg's theological writings. Although literary criticism abounds with similar references to Swedenborg's impact on Balzac, the Brownings, Coleridge, Emerson, Goethe, Strindberg, Whittier, and 1980 Nobel Poet Laureate, Czeslaw Milosz, Swedenborg has remained an elusive, often overlooked figure in the history of literature and ideas.

A leading authority on Blake, Kathleen Raine stated in her 1982 book, *The Human Face of God*, "No Blake scholar has yet done justice to the extent and importance of Swedenborg's influence on Blake." In a 1985 address, published for the first time in this anthology, Dr. Raine concludes:

> Wonderful as are Blake's poems, his visionary paintings, his aphorisms, it is, in essence, the doctrines of Swedenborg that Blake's works embody and to which they lend poetry and eloquence.

This anthology is intended as a comprehensive exploration of Emanuel Swedenborg's influences on the poetry, visual arts, ideas and life of William Blake, examined from a spectrum of literary, art historical, philosophical, religious and historical perspectives.

The Introduction is by the Reverend George F. Dole, a foremost modern translator of Swedenborg.

This is followed by brief historical and philosophical overviews, composed by the editors: "Biographical Notes" highlights striking similarities, and dissimilarities, in the lives of Swedenborg and Blake; "Correspondences" highlights corresponding ideas from their writings on issues of mutual, and universal concern.

In "A New Heaven is Begun: Blake and the Swedenborgians," Morton D. Paley, co-editor of *Blake: An Illustrated Quarterly*, traces Blake's complex and shifting attitude toward Swedenborg, and defines Blake's relationship to the dynamic Swedenborgian milieu of late eighteenth and early nineteenth century England.

"Opposition Is True Friendship: Emanuel Swedenborg and His Influences on William Blake," by Harvey F. Bellin, an editor of this anthology and co-author/producer of television docu-dramas on both Swedenborg and Blake, presents an overview of Swedenborg's career and of the Swedenborgian roots of the mythology Blake created in his illuminated poems.

Two studies by Kathleen Raine show Swedenborg's imprint on both the formative and late stages of Blake's work. In "The Swedenborgian Songs," she finds Swedenborg's theories of "correspondence" and "influx" shaping Blake's emergence as a symbolist poet in his popular early poems, *Songs of Innocence and of Experience*. In "The Human Face of God," Dr. Raine notes even stronger Swedenborgian influence in the religious and psychological themes of Blake's final poems and engravings.

Additional historical perspectives are contained in a whimsical excerpt from Alexander Gilchrist's 1863, *The Life of William Blake*; in Raymond H. Deck's "New Light on C.A. Tulk: Blake's Nineteenth Century Patron," about a prominent Swedenborgian Member of Parliament who introduced Blake to Coleridge; and in Robert Hindmarsh's eyewitness account of the 1789 General Conference to establish a new religious denomination based on Swedenborg's writings—an event attended by Blake and his wife, Catherine.

The reciprocal interest in Blake among Swedenborgians is represented in three articles by New Church writers, reprinted in the "Swedenborgian Postscripts" of this anthology.

The editors also wish to acknowledge the invaluable contributions to the evolution of this anthology made by the Directors of the Swedenborg Foundation. Without their encouragement and guidance, this book would never have existed.

Ultimately, this book is a tribute to Emanuel Swedenborg and William Blake—two seemingly "opposite" men, who probably never met, but who forged a "true friendship" by dedicating their respective lives and talents to understanding and articulating what it means to be a human being.   —The Editors

I rest not from the great task!
To open the Eternal Worlds, to open the immortal Eyes
Of Man inwards into the Worlds of Thought, into Eternity
Ever expanding in the bosom of God, the Human Imagination.

William Blake, *Jerusalem*, 5:17-20

Introduction

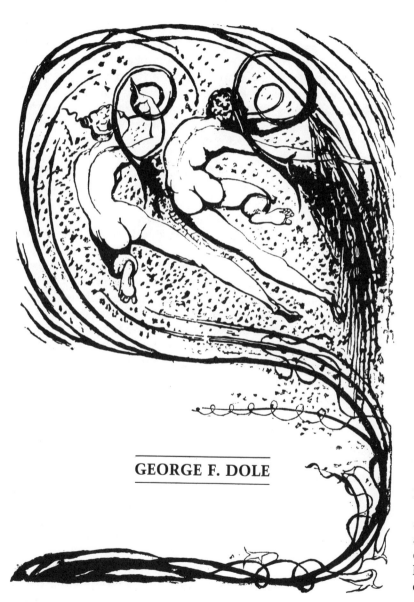

GEORGE F. DOLE

REV. George F. Dole, recipient of a B.A. from Yale in Greek and Latin, an M.A. from Oxford in Hebrew, and a Ph.D. from Harvard in Assyriology, is an ordained minister of the General Convention (Swedenborgian) and a foremost translator of Swedenborg. His published translations include *Emanuel Swedenborg: The Universal Human & Soul-Body Interaction*, from the Paulist Press series, Classics in Western Spirituality, as well as modern translations of *Heaven and Hell* and *Divine Love and Wisdom*. He edited and compiled *A View From Within: A Compendium of Swedenborg's Theological Thought*, and is author of *An Introduction to Swedenborg's Theological Latin*, and the award-winning television program, *Images of Knowing*, narrated by Anne Baxter. His latest filmscript is *The Other Side of Life*.   —Ed.

Emanuel Swedenborg (1688-1772) was not just a mysterious "someone who influenced Blake." He was a man who could have had a life of elegance, but who chose instead to embark on a quest, with totally unexpected results.

His father was a man of rising importance in the Lutheran church of Sweden, eventually to be ennobled. His mother and stepmother were both from families prominent in the mining industry, the mainstay of Sweden's economy. The connections were there, especially for a talented young man, for a career of wealth and power, either in the church or in the world of technology. All he had to do was precisely what everyone would expect him to do.

Swedenborg chose instead to face the duality of his parentage. Since the time of DesCartes, Swedish science and religion had diverged, and were now competing for young minds. In his university education, Swedenborg chose the scientific route, but with the conviction that this was simply a new avenue to the eternal truths maintained by religion. He would later recognize a large measure of youthful arrogance in his assumption that he, unlike the rest of his contemporaries, could reconcile the two.

His quest led him through engineering and the physical sciences to cosmology, anatomy, and psychology; and his ability and energy were such that he advanced the frontiers of virtually every discipline he undertook. But as he entered his fifties, he was increasingly aware of the futility of his efforts. Every answer raised deeper questions. He began to pay more attention to himself as the searcher—to listen to his dreams, to attend to his own mental and emotional processes. He had started to find "the" soul: he was beginning to find his own.

His years of scientific discipline proved invaluable. Through a period of profound inner turmoil—during which he continued a thoroughly competent life as scientist and government official—he retained his habit of precise observation, recording, and reflection. Profound inner experiences, culminating in a Christ-vision, brought him through to a lucid consciousness of spiritual realities; and he spent the last third of his life commissioned as a "spiritual scientist," trying to convey both his experience and its implications to a materialistic world.

The energy he brought to this task was impressive. In approximately twenty-five years, he wrote and published a theological corpus that comprises twenty-two substantial volumes in English translation. The wealth of detail is formidable, and it is perhaps for this reason that few Blake scholars have really taken the plunge.

Swedenborg's youthful arrogance was now gone, obliterated by his direct encounters with meaning. Now he struggled rather with a daily awareness that he and his language were inadequate to express the vibrant reality of spirit. Time and again, he would tell the reader that he could say no more, that the rest was ineffable.

What he did manage to express caught Blake's attention. It is demeaning to Blake to describe the relationship in terms of "influence," as though Swedenborg were the master and Blake the student, the one active and the other passive. It is truer to human experience simply to say that Swedenborg's descriptions helped Blake to understand his own experience, that in a way, Blake recognized himself in *Divine Love and Wisdom*. He would not have been Blake had he not also rebelled against Swedenborg, had he allowed his own creative integrity to be violated by submission to authority.

It seems that Blake affirmed particularly some of Swedenborg's most basic and pervasive assumptions, which will be outlined below. The reader needs to bear in mind that Swedenborg worked these ideas out in considerable detail, usually within specifically Biblical and Christian boundaries.

First of all, I would stress the concept of "distinguishable oneness." Swedenborg seems to have been neither a dualist nor a monist in the classical sense, but to have believed that while ontologically all reality was one, it was both valid and necessary for epistemological purposes to "draw lines." He used the example of physical substance and form. These can be usefully distinguished mentally, but no object can exist in which they are not wholly united.

For Swedenborg, the ultimate substance, the ground of all being, is love, and the ultimate form is wisdom, with love providing both the energy and the oneness of reality, and wisdom providing its structure and distinguishability. As substance and form "make" an object, love and wisdom "make" actions. Love-and-wisdom is inherently self-expressive. So the divine love-and-wisdom is inherently creative; and since it is the nature of love to love others, the divine creates "otherness."

There are observable degrees of this "otherness," degrees of the extent to which distinguishability occupies the foreground, and oneness recedes. At the furthest remove from oneness is the realm of matter, where things seem fundamentally self-existent and discrete from each other, subject only to mechanical interactions. Yet even here the oneness is present. Every stone is an ongoing creation of the divine and therefore an ongoing expression of the divine.

We as people are for the most part in a sort of lower middle range of otherness. We have (or are) both love and wisdom, the ability to unite and the ability to distinguish; and each is meaningless without the other. Each of us, as a focus of consciousness in the total field of being, is a microcosm of the whole, needing boundaries in order to be other, and having only the boundaries that we ourselves draw.

Because our consciousness is predominantly physical, we tend to make sharp distinctions between self and other; and since we tend actually to feel life only within ourselves, this means that we objectify the other. Separated from the empathy of genuine love, the intellect renders everything lifeless, bleak, and harsh. United to love, the intellect both discriminates clearly and identifies with the other. The congruent soul experiences distinguishable oneness. The divine is everywhere present, everywhere the same, and everywhere differently expressed.

Ours is not a world of congruent souls, however, and the road to congruence can be difficult. We do not unite love and wisdom in ourselves by drifting off into some romantic and uncritical feeling of oneness. Love and wisdom are united through our experiencing the full force of alienation and the full force of oneness, and by accepting both.

The more we refuse this integration or avoid the confrontations it requires, the narrower and more rigid are the boundaries we draw around ourselves. The ambiguity of this world supports either integration or alienation, whichever we choose. But Swedenborg maintains that ultimately we reach a point of no return, meaning a point at which there is no longer any desire for the unchosen attitude. This is the point of transition to the relatively unambiguous spiritual world; and the only judgment there is the removal of ambiguity.

After physical death, that is, we steadily lose the power to pretend. Our environment is directly responsive to our fundamental attitudes, so there is nothing to pretend with. Swedenborg's heaven is a heaven of personal transparency, of lively perceptiveness and mutual trust and affection. His hell is a hell of self-deception and self-concealment, of mutual alienation and suspicion. It is not a matter of reward or punishment according to some moral scorecard, but a matter of what we have decided to be.

In each case, the whole environment actually reflects the personalities who inhabit it. It is not simply projection, since that environment has its basis in the divine. It is more as though the selectivity of our earthly perception, our tendency to see only our side of this ambiguous world, now operates on a responsive spiritual field rather than on an unresponsive physical one. This means, incidentally, that hell does not normally look ugly to its inhabitants. It is, after all, an embodiment or representation of their own preferences.

In this life, then, we are to begin to grasp our relationship to the world around us. We can begin to see more spiritually. Whatever "the world as it really is" may be, our perception of it reflects our values and our discriminations. The world becomes symbolic rather than merely literal.

For Swedenborg, the same necessarily held true for the Bible. It was a kind of epic parable, in which Israel's struggles for an earthly kingdom reflected the soul's strivings for independence. In this story, the coming of Jesus marked that pivotal point at which one does in fact start to see spiritually, when the longing for an earthly kingdom is transformed into a longing for a heavenly one.

All the meaning of human history, whether collective or individual, comes into sharpest focus at this point. In the figure of Jesus, Swedenborg saw the definitive intervention of the divine. Here, if you will, were infinite love and wisdom embroiled in our own human process, wrestling with our own ambiguities. There is in Swedenborg's theology no trace of vicarious suffering, no notion of appeasement. The essence of redemption is the self-expression of divine love and wisdom in our own human terms. In a sense, in Jesus we are shown how to see, which as already stated involves the union of empathy and discrimination in action.

Swedenborg was aware, however, that no two people would follow precisely the same path. While he insistently regarded the Christian experience as normative, he was equally insistent that the omnipresent divine provided the means of salvation everywhere. He had no use for church institutions that claimed the power to save. In fact, he was more tolerant of "good Gentiles" than of people who accepted a distorted Christianity.

Still, there is ample material in his theology for the institutional mind. His insistence on clarity offers a fertile field for the dogmatist, and his followers have rarely been able to combine tolerance and precision as consistently as he did. His *True Christian Religion* is particularly susceptible to codification; and the meeting of "receivers of the doctrines" which the Blakes attended in 1789 used it to draw sharp theological boundaries around a fledgling organization.

'. . . And Priests in black gowns, were walking their rounds,/ And binding with briers, my joys & desires."* Blake would not accept the "mind-forged manacles" even of thoughts congenial to his own; and it seems likely that the discovery that ideas so like his own could be dogmatized precipitated a new struggle within him.

Swedenborg had not written with Blake in mind. He was not there to respond to Blake's reactions. The battle "between Swedenborg and Blake" was carried on within the poet's own consciousness, and its persistence testifies to the strength and rootedness of "Swedenborgian" ideas in that consciousness.

---

*William Blake, "The Garden of Love," *Songs of Innocence and of Experience*, pl. 44:11-12

Biographical Notes

Emanuel Swedenborg		William Blake
Born in Stockholm, January 29, 1688. Father, a Bishop of the Swedish Church. Family ennobled in 1718.	**Birth & Family**	Born in London, November 28, 1757. Father, a hosier of Broad Street, Carnaby Market. Family of modest means.

Honors student at Sweden's Upsala University (1699-1709); studied medicine, astronomy, mathematics, sciences, Latin, Greek, music and poetry.
  Independent study with leading scientists and scholars in Sweden, England, Holland, France, Germany, Italy and Bohemia.
	Education & Travels	No formal schooling. Studied at Pars School of Drawing (1767-1772); apprenticed to engraver James Basire (1772-9); student at Royal Academy Schools (1779).
		  Never left London, except for a stay at Felpham, Sussex, on the English Channel (1800-03).

Church of Sweden (Lutheran). Seldom attended formal worship in adult life, but considered himself devoutly Christian. All his writings after the mid-1740s concern theology.	**Religious Affiliation**	Family affiliation unclear. Attended 1789 General Conference for establishing the Swedenborgian New Jerusalem Church, but never returned. Seldom attended church, but considered himself devoutly Christian.
Lifelong bachelor.	**Marriage**	1782 marriage to Catherine Boucher, a market-gardener's daughter whom he taught to read, write, draw, paint, and make prints. No children.
Appointed Royal Assessor of Mines (1716); helped development of Swedish mining, smelting and steel production. Unpaid scientist, philosopher and theologian. Independently wealthy.	**Profession**	Engraver. Occasional commissions for book illustrations and paintings, mostly from friends. Unpaid poet, illustrator, engraver and printer of his own books. Remained poor most of his life.
Active member of the House of Lords of the Swedish Diet. Initiated legislation on fiscal reform, international trade, finance, peace, and development of the mining industry.	**Political Activities**	Caught up in the Gordon Riots (1780). Associated with progressive political groups advocating social justice, democracy, abolition of slavery and civil rights (1780s–1790s). Supported American and French Revolutions.

Emanuel Swedenborg

William Blake

Trials

1768-71 Gothenburg heresy trial, initiated by local clerics, resulted in the banning of his theological works in Sweden.

Tried for sedition, Chichester, England (1804), upon charges brought by a British soldier. Acquitted.

Inventions & Discoveries

Numerous early inventions include glider aircraft (1716), mercurial air-pump and airtight stove.
   Theoretical writings laid foundations for the sciences of metallurgy and crystallography, and anticipated modern theories of molecular basis of magnetism, nebular formation of planetary systems, and nature of the atom.
   Discovered functions of endocrine glands, cerebellum and cerebro-spinal fluid; discovered memory and thinking localizations in cerebral cortex, and the integrative action of the nervous system.

Discovered an acid-etching process for creating relief-type, copper printing-plates. These enabled him to combine his words and pictures on a single plate, which he could then print on his own small proofing-press.
   Also experimented with multi-color printing.
   Created new forms of poetry and visual arts which became prototypes for the Romantic Era.
   Invented a new mythology, personifying aspects of consciousness as "Giant Forms," the protagonists of the illuminated poems in his "prophetic books."

Visionary Experiences

Developed a form of meditation in childhood.
   Experienced flashes of light (photism) during moments of insight (1736).
   Frequent transcendent experiences—dreams and waking visions—began in 1743-4, and peaked in a life-transforming vision in 1745. Thereafter, he discontinued study of physical sciences and focused on psychology and theology.
   Visionary experiences (which continued until the end of his life) and Bible studies were the primary sources of his theological writings.
   Also demonstrated remarkable clairvoyant talents (1759-61), which he discounted as unimportant.

Visions of angels, prophets, and the face of God began in childhood; similar visions occurred throughout his lifetime.
   The spirit of his dead brother Robert appeared to him many times, as did apparitions of angels, demons, saints and historical personages. Often, ordinary objects, such as plants or grains of sand, transformed into spirits before Blake's eyes.
   Visionary experiences were a primary source of his poems and visual arts. During seances with the painter/zodiacal physiognomist John Varley, Blake drew a notebook full of "Visionary Heads" (1818-20).
   Also demonstrated some clairvoyant abilities.

Publishing Method

Self-published, often anonymously, at great personal expense. Usually printed his Latin texts in Holland or England, which enjoyed a freedom of the press lacking in his native Sweden.

Self-published, at the cost of nearly all his meager resources. Assisted by his wife, Catherine, he wrote, designed, engraved, printed and tinted his books in his humble rented rooms.

First Publication

Scientific theories and inventions, in *Daedelus Hyperboreus*, Sweden's first scientific journal, which he co-edited (1716).

Poetic Sketches (1783). One of the rare instances of typeset printing of his works during his lifetime. Publication was financed by friends.

Death

London, March 29, 1772.

London, August 12, 1827

Emanuel Swedenborg

Scientific-Philosophical Writings

Motion & Position of the Earth & Planets (1719)
Principles of Chemistry (1720)
Philosophical & Minerological Studies:
    Vol. 1, *Principia;* Vol. 2, *On Iron;*
    Vol. 3, *On Copper* (1734)
On the Infinite (1734)
The Cerebrum (1738-40)
Economy of the Animal Kingdom
    (The Dynamics of the Soul's Domain)
    (1740-41)
Rational Psychology (ms. 1742)
The Brain (ms. 1743-4)
The Animal Kingdom
    (The Soul's Domain) (1744)

Journals

Journal of Dreams (ms. 1743-4)
Spiritual Diary (ms. 1747-65)

Theological Writings

Worship & Love of God (1745)
The Word Explained (ms. 1746-7)
Arcana Coelestia
    (Heavenly Secrets) (1749-56)
Earths in the Universe (1758)
The Last Judgement (1758)
The New Jerusalem & Its Heavenly Doctrine
    (1758)
The White Horse of the Apocalypse (1758)
The Apocalypse Explained (ms. 1759)
The Four Doctrines (1763)
Divine Love & Wisdom (1763)
Divine Providence (1764)
Apocalypse Revealed (1766)
Conjugial Love (1768)
Intercourse of the Soul & Body
    (Soul-Body Interaction) (1769)
True Christian Religion (1771)

Major Works

William Blake

"Illuminated Books" & Major Engravings

There is No Natural Religion (c. 1788)
All Religions are One (c. 1788)
Songs of Innocence (1789)
Tiriel (c. 1789)
The Book of Thel (1789)
The Marriage of Heaven and Hell (c. 1790-93)
For Children: The Gates of Paradise (1793)
Visions of the Daughters of Albion (1793)
America: a Prophecy (1793)
Songs of Innocence and of Experience (1794)
Europe: a Prophecy (1794)
The (First) Book of Urizen (1794)
The Song of Los (1795)
The Four Zoas (Vala) (ms., unfinished; 1795-1804)
Milton, A Poem in 2 Books (1804-08)
Jerusalem: The Emanation of the Giant Albion
    (1804-20)
For the Sexes: The Gates of Paradise (c. 1818)
The Ghost of Abel (1822)
Illustrations of the Book of Job (1823-6)

Other Writings (Selected)

An Island in the Moon (ms., c. 1784)
The French Revolution (1791)
A Descriptive Catalogue (1809)
A Vision of the Last Judgement (1810)
The Everlasting Gospel (ms. 1818)

Other Paintings & Engravings (Selected)

Engravings for Stedman's *Narrative of a Five Year*
    Expedition Against Revolted Negroes of
    Surinam (1792)
Engravings for Wollstonecraft's *Vindication of*
    the Rights of Woman (1792)
Designs & engravings for Young's *Night Thoughts*
    (1796-7)
Biblical watercolor paintings (1803-05)
Illustrations for Blair's *Grave* (1805)

"Correspondences"

The visible universe is nothing else than a theatre, representative of the Lord's kingdom.

—Emanuel Swedenborg
Arcana Coelestia, 3483

There Exist in that Eternal World the Permanent Realities of Every Thing we see reflected in this Vegetable Glass of Nature.

—William Blake
A Vision of the Last Judgement, 69

"Correspondences" was Emanuel Swedenborg's term for psychological-spiritual archetypes—images from outer realities ("the visible universe") which correspond to inner realities ("the Lord's kingdom"). Blake was greatly influenced by the "correspondences" Swedenborg had deciphered from the image-language of dreams, the Bible and arts of antiquity; and Blake used similar imagery in his own arts to reveal "that Eternal World" in which there exists "the Permanent Realities of Every Thing we see reflected in this Vegetable Glass of Nature."

Many of Blake's other ideas about the Eternal World correspond to those of Swedenborg, and are discussed in detail in this anthology. The following selection is presented as a brief overview.   —Ed.

Emanuel Swedenborg

William Blake

Life

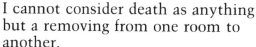

Every created thing . . . is an image of God in a mirror.

— *Divine Love and Wisdom*, 56

For everything that lives is Holy.

— *Marriage of Heaven and Hell*, 27

Death

Death is not an extinction, but a continuation of life . . . merely a transition from one state to another.

— *True Christian Religion*, 792

I cannot consider death as anything but a removing from one room to another.

— from a conversation with Crabb Robinson, 12/7/1826

Emanuel Swedenborg   William Blake

God

God is Very Man.
— *Divine Love and Wisdom*, 11

God becomes as we are, that we may be as he is.
— *There is No Natural Religion*, b:12

The Bible

Such is the style of the Word that it is holy in every sentence, in every word, sometimes in the very letter.
— *True Christian Religion*, 191

The Hebrew Bible and the Gospel of Jesus are not allegory but Eternal Vision or Imagination of all that Exists.
— *A Vision of the Last Judgement*, 68

Heaven & Earth

Man is both a heaven and an earth in microcosm.
— *Heaven and Hell*, 90

. . . In your Bosom you bear your Heaven and Earth, & all you behold, tho it appears Without, it is Within.
— *Jerusalem*, 71:17-18

Spirits & Visions

A person is guided into a particular state which is halfway between being asleep and being awake. . . . All his senses are as alert as when he is fully awake physically . . . more acutely sensitive than ever in physical wakefullness. In this state, spirits and angels have been seen . . . heard . . . and, remarkably, touched. Then virtually nothing of the body intervenes.
— *Heaven and Hell*, 440

I am not ashamed, afraid, or adverse to tell you what ought to be told: That I am under the direction of Messengers from Heaven, Daily and Nightly. . . .

I write when commanded by the spirits, and the moment I have written I see the words fly about the room in all directions. It is then published and the spirits can read it, and my manuscript is of no further use.

— from a letter to Thomas Butts, 12/10/1802, and a conversation with Crabb Robinson, 2/18/1825

On Seeing Angels with the Inner Eye

Emanuel Swedenborg

Angels are not visible through men's physical senses, only through the eyes of the spirit within man. . . .

The eye is so crude that it cannot see the smaller elements of nature except through a lens, as everyone knows. So it is less able to see the things above the realm of nature, like the things of the spiritual world.

However, these things are visible to a man when he is withdrawn from physical sight and his spiritual sight is opened. . . .

This is the way Abraham, Lot, Manoah, and the prophets saw angels. . . .

Bringing about such sight is called "opening the eyes," as happened to Elisha's servant, of whom we read, "In prayer Elisha said: 'God, open his eyes, please, so that he may see.' And once God had opened the servant's eyes, he saw that behold, the mountain was full of horses and chariots of fire about Elisha." (II Kings 6:17)

— *Heaven and Hell*, 76

William Blake

I question not my Corporal or
Vegetative Eye any more than I
would question a Window concerning
Sight, I look thro it and not with it.
— *A Vision of the Last Judgement*, 95

This Lifes dim Windows of the Soul
Distorts the Heavens from Pole to Pole
And leads you to Believe a Lie
When you see with not thro' the Eye.
— *The Everlasting Gospel*, 97-100

If the doors of perception were
cleansed, everything would appear to
man as it is: Infinite.
— *The Marriage of Heaven and Hell*, 14

The Prophets describe what they saw
in visions as real and existing men,
whom they saw with their imaginative
and immortal organs. . . .
— *A Descriptive Catalogue*, 37

I rest not from the great task! . . .
to open the immortal Eyes of man
inwards . . .
— *Jerusalem*, 5:17-19

Bring me my Bow of burning gold:
Bring me my arrows of desire:
Bring me my Spear: O clouds unfold!
Bring me my Chariot of fire!
— *Milton*, 1:9-12

ANALYSES OF BLAKE'S CONNECTIONS TO SWEDENBORG

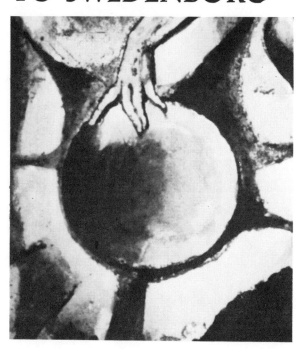

"A New Heaven Is Begun": Blake and Swedenborgianism

MORTON D. PALEY

"ALTHOUGH much has been written about Swedenborg's influence on Blake, Blake's complex and shifting attitude toward Swedenborg has not yet been adequately described. My purpose here is both to reconstruct that attitude in its several phases and to define Blake's relationship to the Swedenborgian milieu of his own day."

That is the intent of this finely crafted overview of Blake and Swedenborg by the noted scholar, Professor Morton D. Paley of the University of California, Berkeley, English Department. Author of *The Continuing City: William Blake's Jerusalem* and several other works on Blake's arts and life, Professor Paley is also co-editor of *Blake: An Illustrated Quarterly*. – Ed.

PREFATORY NOTE: I began work on this subject in 1974 and delivered a paper on Blake and Swedenborg at the University of Lund. In the summer of 1978, thanks to a grant from the Nordenskjöld Fund of the Royal Swedish Academy of Sciences, I was able to complete my research. I presented the results at a graduate seminar at the University of Stockholm in September 1978. In undertaking this task, I was greatly assisted by librarians at the Royal Library, Stockholm; the British Library; and Swedenborg House, London. I am also grateful for information and advice from G. E. Bentley, Jr., Ray H. Deck, Jr., Morris Eaves, Robert N. Essick, Paster O. Hjern, Inge Jonsson, Peter Lineham, and Edward P. Thompson.

I

The formative influence of Emanuel Swedenborg on William Blake was once an article of faith among Blake scholars and enthusiasts. Blake was supposed to have come from a family of Swedenborgians: William Allingham imagined the fourteen-year-old Blake meeting the eighty-four-year-old Swedenborg in the streets of London; Alexander Gilchrist declared "of all modern men, the engraver's apprentice was to grow up likest to Emanuel Swedenborg."[1] We now know that the story of Blake's Swedenborgian background is a myth supported by no verifiable facts,[2] yet there can be no doubt that Swedenborg's writings and doctrines are of unusual importance in relation to Blake's. Although much has been written about Swedenborg's influence on Blake, Blake's complex and shifting attitude toward Swedenborgianism has not yet been adequately described. My purpose here is both to reconstruct that attitude in its several phases and to define Blake's relationship to the Swedenborgian milieu of his own day.

What we know factually about Blake's Swedenborgian interests may be summarized briefly. Blake owned and annotated at least three of Swedenborg's books: *Heaven and Hell*, *Divine Love and Divine Wisdom*, and *Divine Providence*; he mentions two others in such a way as to suggest that he read them: *Earths in Our Universe* and *Universal Theology* [*True Christian Religion*]. He and his wife attended the first General Conference of the New Jerusalem Church in 1789. Then, turning sharply against the Swedenborgians, he satirized them and their Messenger in *The Marriage of Heaven and Hell* (1790-93). After that he mentions Swedenborg twice in his published writings—in *A Descriptive Catalogue* (1809) and in *Milton* (1804-10). At first this may not seem like the chronicle of a major intellectual relationship, but the General Conference of 1789 is the only meeting of any organization that Blake is known to have attended, and only thirteen books annotated by him have survived. So when we consider these facts in relation to the amount of information about Blake available, they bulk relatively large, and it cannot be doubted that Blake found Swedenborg a

---

It cannot be doubted that Blake found Swedenborg a figure of unusual interest.

---

figure of unusual interest. The nature of Blake's interest in Swedenborg can, moreover, be divided into four distinct periods. From the late 1780's until 1790, Blake's attitude was studious and respectful; even in disagreeing with Swedenborg during these years, Blake expresses himself so as to put the most optimistic construction upon Swedenborg's doctrines. In 1790 Blake repudiated Swedenborg vehemently in the marginalia to *Divine Providence*, and he wrote at least part of the satire of *The Marriage of Heaven and Hell*. From 1793, when *The Marriage* was completed,[3] to about 1800 there is little to indicate interest in Swedenborg on Blake's part: but after 1800 Swedenborgian concepts and references began to reappear in Blake's works, and in 1809 he exhibited a picture on a Swedenborgian subject. In this late period, Blake's view of Swedenborg tends to be ambivalent, as typified by the exclamation of Rintrah and Palamab-

ron in *Milton*: "O Swedenborg! strongest of men, the Samson shorn by the Churches!"[4] Working with the documentary information that we have, and making reasonable inferences from what we know of the history of English Swedenborgianism, we can account for some of these changes in Blake's attitude. At the same time, we can hope to illuminate one aspect of the development of Blake's thought which was insufficiently discussed in my book on the subject.[5]

II

We do not know precisely when Blake became interested in Swedenborg, but a date c. 1787 seems likely. Blake's annotation to *Heaven and Hell* include a reference to Swedenborg's *Earths in Our Solar System*,[6] first published in English in 1787; and in that year John Flaxman, who could have introduced Blake to Swedenborgian circles, left for a seven-year stay in Italy. An even earlier date is possible, for in 1779 a William Blake was among the subscribers to Jacob Duché's *Discourses on Several Subjects*, and Duché was a Swedenborgian, although he had not yet declared his allegiance publicly.[7] (Another Swedenborgian, William Sharp, engraved the frontispiece after Benjamin West, showing male and female angels.) Duché became Chaplain and Secretary of the Society for the Reception of Orphan Girls in 1782, and opened his house in Lambeth to meetings of a Swedenborgian group which became known as the Theosophical Society. "As public worship had not yet been established in the New Church," says Robert Hindmarsh, "many of our friends attended his ministry on the Sundays."[8] It is possible that Blake attended some of Duché's meetings, and Blake's reference to what "was asserted in the society"[9] about the nature of influx may refer to a meeting of the Theosophical Society. However, Blake's first specifically datable contact with the Swedenborgians was at the General Conference of April 13-17, 1789, when William and Catherine Blake entered their names in the Conference's Minute Book and so implied assent to the forty-two theological propositions which were unanimously approved by the participants.[10]

Among the propositions (all taken from Swedenborg's works) which clearly agreed with Blake's own expressed views were those affirming free will, condemning predestination, and declaring that "all have a capacity to be regenerated, because all are redeemed, each one according to his state." Blake would also have agreed with Proposition 33: "Now it is allowable to enter into the Mysteries of Faith." (The words "Now it is allowable" were inscribed over the door of the New Jerusalem church in Eastcheap, in contrast to the "Thou Shalt Not" to be written over the door of the Chapel in Blake's "Garden of Love.") The Conference's reaffirmation of Swedenborg's declaration that a Last Judgment had taken place in 1757 must have particularly interested Blake, as that was of course the year of his own birth. Blake would have sympathized with the Conference's endorsement of Swedenborg's statement that the things seen by the visionary "are not fictions but were really seen and heard in a state in which I was broad awake," for the Swedenborgians had to defend their Messenger, just as Blake had to defend himself, against charges of "enthusiasm" and madness. Furthermore, many Swedenborgians shared another of Blake's deepest concerns—opposition to slavery. Swedenborg taught that the inhabitants of the interior of Africa had preserved a direct intuition of God, and as a result the first abolitionist society was founded by Swedenborgians in Norrköping in 1779.[11] The founder of that group was one of the most active of European abolitionists, Charles Bernhard Wadström; and Wadström with another Swedish Delegate, Augustus Nordenskjöld, attended the 1789 General Conference. Wadström and Nordenskjöld were deeply involved in a plan to set up a free community of whites and blacks on the west coast of Africa, and Blake can hardly have been unaware of (or uninterested in) this well publicized project. A spirit of millenarian expectation was abroad, and even the pedestrian Hindmarsh was moved to something like poetry: ". . .The tree of life, whose roots are planted in the gardens and streets of The New Jerusalem, as well as on either bank of its river, spontaneously sprung up before our eyes, luxuriant in foliage, and laden with the sweetest fruits of paradise in endless variety and abundance."[12] It must have seemed to Blake as if there were a possibility of sharing his own prophetic vision with a community of kindred spirits—as if, indeed, the New Jerusalem were descending.

For more concrete evidence of what attracted Blake to Swedenborg's doctrines, we must go to the marginalia to *Heaven and Hell* and to *Divine Love and Divine Wisdom*. Those to *Heaven and Hell* are brief.[13] They begin with a defense of the imagination, addressed not to Swedenborg but to a previous owner of the volume. In addition, two paragraphs about the state of little children in heaven are scored in a margin, #513 has Blake's note "See N 73 Worlds in Universe for account of Instructing Spirits" (E 591), and # 588 has Blake's note concerning the relationship of heavens to hells. According to Swedenborg, "Both Heaven and the World of Spirits may be considered as convexities, under which are arrangements of those infernal mansions." This Blake elucidates: "Under every *Good* is a hell. i.e. hell is the outward or external of heaven. & is of the body of the lord. for nothing is destroyed" (E 591). Here we see Blake hopefully pushing Swedenborg's idea toward a conception of unity according to which Hells are only mistakes for Heavens; for Blake Hell (not yet having acquired the subversive sense it bears in *The Marriage*) is merely negative and therefore redeemable. Later, Blake would have to admit that this was not the meaning Swedenborg had intended, and Blake would accordingly condemn Swedenborg's view as predestinarian.

Blake's chief concern is the same as Swedenborg's: The relationship of the spiritual and the natural worlds, and hence of the spiritual and natural man.

Blake's notes to *Divine Love and Divine Wisdom*[14] once more show Blake working out his own ideas through the medium of Swedenborg, finding as many areas of agreement as possible, and reasoning away differences. In these marginalia Blake's chief concern is the same as Swedenborg's: the relationship of the spiritual and the natural worlds, and hence of the spiritual and the natural man. As Blake's tractates of c. 1788 show, Blake believes that although the two can be distinguished there is a unity underlying them, and that this unity is perceived by the imagination or Poetic Genius.[15] Blake hopefully glosses Swedenborg's "spiritual idea" (#7) as "Poetic idea," and where Swedenborg writes of the Angels' reception of Love and Wisdom from the Lord (#10), Blake writes: "He who Loves feels love descend into him & if he has wisdom may perceive it is from the Poetic

Genius which is the Lord" (E 592). The idea of Poetic Genius enables Blake to take Swedenborg's statements as metaphors. "The Negation of God constitutes Hell," Swedenborg writes, "and in the Christian world the Negation of the Lord's Divinity"(#13); Blake notes: "the Negation of the Poetic Genius" (E 593). If Swedenborg's God can be seen as a manifestation of the indwelling human imagination, then Blake can regard himself as in agreement.

On the larger subject of the relations between spiritual and natural worlds, Swedenborg's characteristic view is that they "are so distinct, that they have nothing in common with each other; but nevertheless are so created, that they communicate, yea are joined together, by Correspondences" (#83). Blake is quick to seize upon passages which emphasize the link, implicit in such a view, between spiritual and natural. For example, Swedenborg says that the human mind can only shake off appearances by an investigation of the cause, which in turn cannot do "without keeping the Understanding in spiritual Light" (#40). "This Man can do while in the body"—notes Blake (E 593). According to Swedenborg, there are "three degrees of Altitude" (#237)—Natural, Spiritual, and Celestial: the man in whom the spiritual Degree is open comes into divine Wisdom when he dies, "and may also come into it by laying asleep the Sensations of the Body, and by Influx from above at the same Time into the Spirituals of his Mind" (#257). Blake comments: "this is while in the Body/This is to be understood as unusual in our time but common in ancient" (E 596). Here and in similar passages Blake takes Swedenborg's view to be that natural man can be irradiated by spiritual light in this life. This is of course Blake's own view, as is the idea, also shared by Swedenborg, that ancient men had a greater capacity for spiritual vision than their modern counterparts.

At some times, however, Swedenborg emphasizes the discrete natures of the two worlds, and then Blake is distinctly uneasy. In the Swedenborgian universe there are two suns, a living sun in the spiritual world and a dead one in the material world. "It follows that . . . the dead Sun itself was created by the living Sun from the Lord" (#164). "How," Blake objects, "could life create death" (E 594); "the dead Sun is only a phantasy of evil Man." As with suns, so with souls. Swedenborg explicitly denies the existence of portions of divinity in man, regarding such a belief as a sort of spiritual narcissism: "for if there was. . .any Thing Divine in them, then it would not be beloved by others, but it would love itself" (#49). Blake objects to this because it rules out the divine in man—"for if a thing loves it is infinite" (E 593). Still he hopes that the difference is merely a semantic one: "Perhaps we only differ in the meaning of the words Infinity & Eternal."

In fact, Swedenborg's view of the two worlds as discrete but connected by correspondence and influx can at times accommodate Blake's desire for a synthesis of both and at other times appear to contradict it. All depends on which aspect of the Swedenborgian psychic model of the universe is stressed. If the emphasis is on correspondence and influx, then Blake can enthusiastically agree, as in his series of "Mark this" notes in Part V, where the influx of Love is the subject. Such wide areas of agreement prompted Blake to explain away some very real differences between Swedenborg's world view and his own. Characteristically, he does so by attempting to assimilate Swedenborg's doctrines into his own: "Heaven & Hell are born together" (E 598); "Good & Evil are here both Good & the two contraries Married" (E 594). As this marriage was in part imposed by Blake upon Swedenborg, divorce, as can be expected in such a case, was imminent.

In Blake's works of the late 1780s and early 1790s, the effects of Swedenborg's doctrines can only be described as pervasive.

In Blake's works of the late 1780s and early 1790s, the effect of Swedenborg's doctrines can only be characterized as pervasive.[16] Blake freely borrowed from Swedenborg's system of correspondences, adapting it to the purposes of his own poetry. Thus, as is widely recognized, Swedenborg's characteristic symbolic imagery appears throughout the *Songs of Innocence and of Experience*, and certain characteristic Swedenborgian themes are given expression there.[17] One of these themes is the insufficiency of man's "Proprium," a term glossed by John Clowes as "his own Propriety, or all that he is of himself, when separated from Divine Influence. . . ."[18] In "The Clod & the Pebble," for example, the Pebble's view that "Love seeketh only Self to please" is that of the Proprium. A society based on such a view, according to Swedenborg, can maintain only a spurious order masking its own essential destructiveness:

> But the dominion of Self-Love, which is opposite to the Dominion of neighbourly Love, began when Man alienated himself from the Lord for in proportion as Man doth not love and worship the Lord, in the same Proportion he loves and worships himself, and in the same Proportion also he loves the World: Then it was that, compelled by Motives of Self-Preservation and Security from Injustice, Nations consisting of Families and Houses cemented themselves into one Body, and established Governments under various Forms, for in Proportion as Self-Love increased, in the same Proportion all kinds of Evil, as Enmity, Revenge, Cruelty, and Deceit increased with it, being exercised toward all those who opposed that Love. . . .[19]

Similarly, Blake writes in "The Human Abstract":

> And mutual fears bring peace;
> Till the selfish loves increase,
> Then Cruelty knits a snare,
> And spreads his baits with care. E 27

Swedenborg's view of the body politic thus agrees with Blake's, just as his view of the "vastated" state of the Christian churches does. Other Swedenborgian themes to be found in the *Songs* include the Africans' direct intuition of the Divine Humanity ("The Little Black Boy")[20] and the manifestation of God in a human form as opposed to the idea of a "vapour." Such similarities as these occur equally in *Songs of Experience*, written after Blake had rejected Swedenborg, as in *Songs of Innocence*; as Schorer puts it, "The striking fact about his use of Swedenborg is that he derived. . .the materials for his myth from the dogma that he rejected."[21]

Even the idea of two contrary planes of existence, each with its appropriate world of images, can be found in Swedenborg as well as in Blake. Yet there is a significant difference between Swedenborg's conception of Heaven and Hell and Blake's of Innocence and Experience. Many of the correspondences employed in Blake's poems appear, for example, in Swedenborg's description of Hell:

> None of the pleasing Scenery of Heaven is to be seen there, but all things in direct opposition thereto, inasmuch as the

Affections of Love in its inhabitants, which are the Concupiscences of Evil, are directly opposite to the Affections of Love that prevail in the Angels of Heaven. Wherefore amongst the inhabitants of Hell, particularly in their Deserts, there appear Birds of Night, as Bats, and Owls, and likewise Wolves, Leopards, Tigers, Rats, and Mice, with venomous Serpents of all kinds, as Dragons and Crocodiles; and where there is any appearance of Grass, there grow Thorns, Thistles, Briars, and Brambles, and some poisonous Herbs, which at times disappear, and then nothing is to be seen but huge Heaps of Stones, and large Fens full of croaking Frogs. These things also are Correspondences, but then, as was observed, they are Correspondences agreeable to the Affections of Love in the Inhabitants, which are the Concupiscences.[22]

This paragraph seems like a catalogue of the flora and fauna of *Experience*, but where Swedenborg sees the Affections of Love and their Correspondences to be permanent in Hell, Blake presents his images as symbols of the state of the self at a given point in its development. In "The Little Girl Lost" and "The Little Girl Found," "Lovely Lyca" wanders through a landscape of Innocence "hearing wild birds song," becomes lost in a "desart" at night, and falls asleep; then "the beasts of prey,/Come from caverns deep"; and she is surrounded by lions, leopards, and tygers which carry her naked to their caves. In Swedenborgian terms this lapse from singing birds to beasts of prey, from day to night, from "southern clime" to "desart" would mean a fall from Heaven to Hell. But in Blakean terms Lyca has entered a transitional state in which the passions are experienced and then discovered to be part

of a psychic unity. So Lyca's parents find that there is nothing to fear: the lion is really "a spirit arm'd in gold" and their daughter is safe "among tygers wild." Accepting the life of instinct and emotion,

> To this day they dwell
> In a lonely dell
> Nor fear the wolvish howl,
> Nor the lions growl.[23]

Thus, in accordance with his belief that "Good & Evil are here both Good & the two Contraries Married," Blake deliberately corrects Swedenborg. This contrast between their respective uses of correspondences indicates the basis of Blake's quarrel with Swedenborg's thought.

III

The third, and to our knowledge the last, book by Swedenborg that Blake annotated was *Angelic Wisdom Concerning the Divine Providence*.[24] Throughout his annotations to this volume, Blake accuses Swedenborg of believing in predestination, and perhaps owing to the vehemence of Blake's remarks, some critics have assumed that he was correct.[25] Yet a reading of *Divine Providence* hardly bears out Blake's accusation that Swedenborg's view concerning predestination is "more abominable than Calvin's" (E 600). Swedenborg's view, on the contrary, is that "All who are born Men, in whatever Religion they may be principled, are capable of being saved" (#253) and that *"They are saved who acknowledge a God and lead a good Life"* (#325, italics in the original). Indeed, the section comprising #322-30 is headed *"That every Man may be reformed and that there is no such thing as Predestination"*; and Swedenborg even declares *"That thus all are predestined to Heaven, and none to Hell"* (#329). In order to accuse Swedenborg of being a predestinarian, Blake must interpret *Divine Providence* in a deliberately hostile sense.

For Blake the essential problem in Swedenborg's view is the failure to reconcile man's free will and God's foreknowledge. Thus when Swedenborg writes, "But the Man who doth not suffer himself to be led to, and enrolled in Heaven, is prepared for his place in Hell" (#69), Blake asks "What is Enrolling but Predestination?" (E 599). Yet Swedenborg's "enrolled" is intended to distinguish between divine intention and human will; God intends that all men go to heaven, but some choose Hell. Again, Blake asks of #185 "What could Calvin say more than is said in this Number" (E 599), but Swedenborg's point here is that honored, worldly men may bring hell on themselves notwithstanding their success in this life. Blake accuses Swedenborg of being a "Spiritual Predestinarian" in #277 because Swedenborg says that "every one also is judged according to his actions, *not that they are enumerated* [emphasis mine], but because he returns to them. . . ." Blake's objection seems not to be predestination as that idea is usually understood, but rather to the disposition of spirits after death. Swedenborg teaches that while a man is alive in the world he also has an "internal"

existence in Heaven or Hell and an "external" existence in the world of Spirits between Heaven and Hell. During his life on earth, as a man changes he is correspondingly "translated" by the Lord from one Society to another or "led out of hell and introduced into Heaven"; but after his death, "he remains in that [Society] in which he is according to his Life; wherefore when a man dies, he is inscribed in his own Place" (#307). This is what Blake terms "Predestination" (E 600).

It is interesting that one of the Swedenborgians' most formidable critics, Joseph Priestley, far from accusing Swedenborg of Predestinarianism, regards him as an ally who opposes Calvinism as the Unitarians do. Priestly says:

> "[Calvinism is] a system which represents the whole human race as so fatally injured by the sin of Adam, that they retain no natural power of doing the will of God. . . .a system which teaches us that, in order to effect the redemption of a few, God was under a necessity of reversing the known maxims of his conduct, in punishing the innocent instead of the guilty; changing his character of *gracious* and *merciful*, into that of an inexorable tyrant. . . .Whereas it is justly observed by Mr. Swedenborg, in his *Doctrine concerning the Lord*, p. 95, "there is nothing of vindictive justice in God."[26]

If Swedenborg's Unitarian opponent could say this, how could Blake assert that Swedenborg's doctrine was "more Abominable than Calvins"? Did Blake misunderstand *Divine Providence*?

The answer of course is that he did not: Blake's annotations to *Divine Providence* are a rhetorical assault upon Swedenborg, who Blake knows was as far from believing in predestination as any Christian who yet affirms the existence of heaven and hell can be; the whole point is that that is not far enough. Blake is saying that Swedenborg, who opposed the doctrine of predestination, is from a *Blakean* perspective as much a predestinarian as Calvin. The belief in an omniscient God who created human beings knowing that some of them would choose hell is the common denominator. *Any* Christian theodicy is to be rejected according to such a view, and Blake is consistent in the early 1790s in rejecting not some but all churches. It is not a view that he would retain consistently—in *Milton* the Arminian Wesley and the Calvinist predestinarian Whitefield are paired as the Christian witnesses foretold in Revelation; presumably Whitefield's good works and his emphasis on inner regeneration outweighed his theology for Blake at that time.[27] But in 1791 Blake was disposed to find the worst in Swedenborg's doctrines, where previously he had tried to accommodate the differences between his views and Swedenborg's. One reason for this re-evaluation was no doubt Blake's growing realization that Swedenborg's views were in some respects incompatible with his own; at the same time events within the New Jerusalem Church c. 1790-91 almost certainly contributed to Blake's rejection of Swedenborgianism.

Events within the New Jerusalem Church c. 1790-1 almost certainly contributed to Blake's rejection of Swedenborgianism.

Perhaps the most obvious inference we can draw is that the Revolution that occurred in France just three months after the General Conference sent Blake and the majority of English Swedenborgians in different directions. Blake's pro-Revolutionary sympathies are too well known to need restatement here,[28] while the New Church was anxious to disassociate itself from political radicalism. At the General Conference of 1791, says Hindmarsh, "a Protest was entered in the Minutes. . .against all such principles of infidelity and democracy as were then circulating in this country,"[29] and Paine was specifically attacked. In Birmingham the Church-and-King mob that had destroyed Priestley's Unitarian chapel (as well as his laboratory and library) went on to the Swedenborgian church; but there the minister, Joseph Proud, told them "that the minister and worshippers were not Unitarians, nor inimical to the Government. A shout was raised—the New Jerusalem for ever, and the crowd dispersed."[30] At the same time the Church was incorporating liturgical practices quite opposite to Blake's view that "The Whole of the New Church is in the Active Life & not in Ceremonies at all" (E 595). At the Second General Conference in April 1790 a catechism for children was prepared, and Joseph Proud's hymn book was approved along with a form and order of worship. The necessity of living according to the Ten Commandments was also affirmed. At the next year's General Conference, minister's garments were approved: "an inner purple silken vest, and also an outer garment of fine white linen having a golden girdle round the heart."[31] Also in 1791 the New Church petitioned Parliament for the right to perform all religious ceremonies, saying they were ready to take the oaths of allegiance and supremacy but "without being required to describe themselves as Protestants or Dissenters."[32] Furthermore, two dramatic events of 1789-90 must have contributed to Blake's ironical view of the Swedenborgians as "Angels". . .the concubinage dispute and the opening of Swedenborg's tomb.

The concubinage dispute has had a shadowy existence in the history of the New Jerusalem Church, for there was an attempt, very nearly successful, to cover up its very existence. The entries for the period 4 May 1789 to 11 April 1790 were torn out of the Minute Book of the Great Eastcheap Society;[33] and the subject is not mentioned in Hindmarsh's *Rise and Progress* although Hindmarsh himself was expelled from the Society as a result. We know about the dispute only because in 1839 a controversy about which Swedenborgian congregation was the oldest led the Reverend Manoah Sibley to publish his recollections of the early New Jerusalem Church. In the course of his argument, Sibley relates that in 1789

> a very sorrowful occurrence befell the infant New Church, whereby the flood-gates of immorality were in danger of being thrown open to her inevitable destruction. The Church held many solemn meetings on the occasion, which ended in her withdrawing herself from six of her members, viz. Robert Hindmarsh, Henry Sevanté, Charles Berns Wadstrom, Augustus Nordenskjöld, George Robinson, and Alexander Wilderspin.[34]

Sibley says no more about the matter except to add that "this grievous circumstance I kept locked up in my own bosom for years." The dispute must nevertheless have attracted considerable attention in Swedenborgian circles at the time, since at least four of the expelled members were prominent, active Swedenborgians. The gist of the controversy concerned Swedenborg's view of concubinage, as incorporated by Augustus Nordenskjöld into a comprehensive plan of church governance. Nordenskjöld's complete plan is extant only in Swedish in a little book entitled *För-samlings Formen uti det Nya Jerusalem* (Copenhagen, 1790).[35] Part of Nordenskjöld's proposal was also published in the *New Jerusalem Magazine* (of which Wadström and Servanté were the editors) in 1790; but the parts about con-cubinage were left out. The Nordenskjöld plan was presented to at least two meetings of English Swedenborgians and re-jected by both, though whether the matter of concubinage was presented is not clear. John Clowes, perhaps the best known of the Swedenborgians who remained within the Church of England at this time, later recalled an occasion when "two Swedish gentlemen" presented to the New Jerusalem Church in London a plan of worship which Clowes found "opposed to every sentiment of propriety, decorum, and common sense of mankind."[36] And the minutes of a provincial conference held at Kighley, near Halifax, in 1791 record that "a printed plan for organization, recommended by Frederic Nordenskjöld, Esq." was read and discussed but not accepted.[37] Thus the Nordenskjöld plan gained little sup-port in Britain.

It must not be thought that Nordenskjöld was primarily concerned with the subject of concubinage—this was only one subject of the many taken up in *Församlings Formen*. Nordenskjöld's proposal is a broad plan of religious practice and governance for the New Church and for civil society as well. It seems to have had its inception in connection with the proposed African colony. Wadström was careful, in pre-senting his projects to the public, not to mention the Sweden-borgian concerns behind the project; no doubt he wished to attract the broadest basis of support possible. But those con-cerns certainly existed, and *Församlings Formen* appears to be the constitution that the African colony would have had if the Swedenborgians alone had possessed the resources to found it.[38] The plan is a relatively democratic one, with all adult members (including women) enfranchised to elect rep-resentatives. The body of the presentation comprises first fifty-four numbered paragraphs (pp. 2-34), then "Observa-tions" (pp. 35-52). The section concerning marriage com-prises paragraphs 46-54 (pp. 28-34), and the discussion of concubinage forms only part of this section. It was, then, only a small part of Nordenskjöld's proposal that led to inter-nal dissension in the New Jerusalem Church and sub-sequently to the the expulsion of Nordenskjöld, Wadström, and four others.

Marriage, according to Nordenskjöld, would always be the foundation of the New Jerusalem. The married would be considered as two-thirds of the whole group and would pos-sess five-sixths of the franchise. However, only those mar-riages in which both man and wife accepted Swedenborg's doctrines were lawful. If a man were to be baptized into the community and were then to marry a woman who did not accept its beliefs, that man would have to be expelled. Where there was no spiritual union before the Lord, there was no marriage, according to Nordenskjöld, but merely concubin-age; yet such merely external unions might be permitted under certain circumstances. Likewise there were situations in which concubinage without marriage was acceptable:

> As it will happen, of course, that for a long time to come there will be unmarried men in our Church who are not able to marry, and married men who have been received among us, but who have unchristian wives, rejecting the New Doc-trine, and who thus must live in a disharmonious marriage, it follows that when such men are driven so strongly by the inborn *amor sexus* that they cannot contain themselves, it is inevitable, for the sake of order, that they be permitted, the former to take a mistress and the latter a concubine. But no one is permitted to live thus in our Church who does not report it to the Bishop or the Marriage Priest. These are to examine, according to Swedenborg's rules, *De Fornicatione et de Concubinato*, if his case is truly such as he presents it. After this he is to receive their written permission, in which the conditions are to be carefully stated, and he may live with his mistress or concubine. If this be observed, he may still be received among us as a dear member and brother, and his life will be no reproach to him. But if he does not report it he must be punished, and this in the degree that his life is disorderly; for no kinds of adulteries or anti-conjugial life can be tolerated in the New Jerusalem if the Church is to continue and the LORD to find an habitation among us.[39]

Nordenskjöld's views were, as he says, based on those of Swedenborg. At the time of the concubinage dispute, the Swedenborgian source, *Conjugial Love*, was available in complete form only in Latin; the first complete English trans-lation (by John Clowes) was published by Hindmarsh in

1794.[40] According to Swedenborg, the "legitimate causes" of concubinage are the same as those of divorce (#488). These causes can be physical, mental, or moral—including among others disease, madness, difference of faith, and adultery. Recognizing that in some instances divorce for these reasons may not be practical or even possible, Swedenborg maintains "That they, who from causes legitimate, just, and really conscientious, are engaged in this concubinage, may be principled at the same time in conjugial love" (#475). This applies only to those who really prefer marriage to concubinage and enter into concubinage for the causes Swedenborg describes as legitimate.[41] (Marital intercourse must of course be abandoned.) Thus it can be seen that Nordenskjöld's views on concubinage are precisely those of Swedenborg, with the introduction only of an institutional mechanism. Many respected followers of Swedenborg in Sweden shared these views, at least in theory; indeed it is hard to see how they could do otherwise, since Swedenborg is so explicit on the subject.[42] This no doubt accounts for the presence among those expelled of the conservative Hindmarsh, who certainly did not share Nordenskjöld's ideas about other aspects of church governance.[43]

Less than a year after the event, the French surgeon Benedict Chastanier, who had been active in Swedenborgian circles since the early days of the Theosophical Society, protested: "No, no, men and brethren, they will never send there [in Heaven's societies] any letter of exclusion or dismission among them to any of their fellow members, as did not many years ago a certain society, not one hundred miles distant from the monument, to some of its dissentient members, for no other reason than that they were a few degrees deeper grounded in the truth than the rest.[44] We can easily conceive how Blake would have regarded the affair. In *The Marriage of Heaven and Hell*, at least part of which was etched in 1790, the year of the concubinage dispute, Blake proclaims an ethos of libidinal freedom which goes far beyond the narrow doctrinal issues involved in that parochial argument. "The nakedness of woman is the work of God" (E 36) and "He who desires but acts not, breeds pestilence" (E 35) are assertions of the positive goodness of the fulfillment of desire. And in *Visions of the Daughters of Albion* (1793) Blake, through his heroine Oothoon, specifically addresses the question of whether sexual love ought to be limited to the institution of marriage:

> *I cry, Love! Love! Love! happy happy Love! free as the*
> *   mountain wind!*
> *Can that be Love, that drinks another as a sponge drinks*
> *   water?*
> *That clouds with jealousy his nights, with weepings all*
> *   the day:*
> *To spin a web of age around him. grey and hoary! dark!*
> *Till his eyes sicken at the fruit that hangs before his sight.*
> *Such is self-love that envies all! a creeping skeleton*
> *With lamplike eyes watching around the frozen marriage*
> *   bed.*
>
> *But silken nets and traps of adamant will Oothoon spread,*
> *And catch for thee girls of mild silver, or of furious gold;*
> *I'll lie beside thee on a bank & view their wanton play*
> *In lovely copulation bliss on bliss with Theotormon:*
> *Red as the rosy morning, lustful as the first born beam,*
> *Oothon shall view his dear delight, nor e'er with*
> *   jealous cloud*
> *Come in the heaven of generous love; nor selfish blightings*
> *   bring. (E 49)*

Doctrines such as these sharply distinguish Blake's views about sex even from those of the expelled Swedenborgians, with one possible exception: Augustus Nordenskjöld was reputed to have carried out in life what the others merely maintained in theory, and is said to have maintained as his justification that Swedenborg himself had had a mistress while in Italy.[45] Blake himself was the subject of an unattributed story that, according to Mona Wilson, "he proposed to add a concubine to his household."[46] Whether or not the story has any basis, the concubinage dispute must have made Blake all the more aware of the gap that separated him from the majority of English Swedenborgians.

A second dramatic event occurred among Swedenborgians c. 1790—the opening of Swedenborg's tomb. The most detailed source of information about the first opening—for the tomb was opened a second time shortly afterwards—is an account by Gustav Broling, a Swedish metallurgist and a member of the Royal Academy of Sciences who lived in England from 1797 to 1799. [47] His account is second-hand but it agrees in most respects with shorter reports by Robert Hindmarsh and by J. I. Hawkins. According to Broling, an American physician who was enthusiastic about Swedenborg's writings came to London for the purpose of proving that Swedenborg was not really in his coffin but rather "must have been removed thence in some extraordinary manner." With the help of "a follower and countryman of SWEDENBORG, still famous at that time,"[48] the American, accompanied by ten or twelve "New Jerusalemites," penetrated the vault of the Swedish Church. Swedenborg's casket was opened, but turned out to contain a second, which in turn contained a lead coffin. A solderer was brought in to cut through the lead covering. What followed is worthy of one of Blake's Memorable Fancies: "But now there issued forth effluvia in such abundance and of such a sort that the candles went out, and all the observers were obliged to rush head over heels out of the burial vault in order not to be smothered." The investigators were, however, persistent.

> The candles [Broling continues] were relighted—the church was fumigated with vinegar—the windows opened—and once more a descent was made to continue the investigation. It was found that SWEDENBORG'S remains really still lay in the coffin, without any special ravages of time, which, deprived of the assistance of the air, had not greatly changed the features of the face. It was observed as a peculiar fact, and perhaps not without reason, that the half of the face nearest the wall of the vault preserved its almost natural roundness. But as to whether this examination, for the rest, strengthened or weakened the Doctor's faith, of that Tradition does not say a single word.

A basically similar report of these events was published by J. I. Hawkins in *The Times* for 24 April 1823. According to Hawkins, however, the instigator was a learned Swede:

> About the year 1790, a Swedish philosopher, then in London, who was a great admirer of Swedenborg's philosophical writings but had no relish for the theological, became acquainted with some of the members of the New Church, and warmly opposed Swedenborg's tenet that the soul takes a final leave of the material body at death, and enters on a new scene of superior activity in a spiritual body, more suited to obey its energies. The learned Swede endeavored to persuade them, that all great philosophers had, by virtue of their profound

wisdom, the power of taking with them, into the world of spirits, their natural bodies; and he asserted his full conviction, that Swedenborg whom he considered one of the first philosophers, had taken away his body out of the coffin.[49]

C. T. Odhner identifies the Swedish philosopher as the poet and critic Thomas Thorild, but there does not appear to be any evidence for this.[50] Thorild was indeed in London from 1788 to 1790, and in 1790 Robert Hindmarsh published Thorild's *True Heavenly Religion Restored*, with the author identified only as "a Philosopher of the North." However, Thorild's book is a pro-Swedenborgian polemic which in no way can be made to conform to Hawkins' description of the instigator as someone who did not admire Swedenborg's theological writings. On the contrary, Thorild concludes "that this true and Divine Religion is, as to the general Character, even that of EMANUEL SWEDENBORG: Who, if God, Spirits, a Religion, be at all—has certainly brought us sublime Revelations, and may be considered as a Prophet of a third rising Covenant, or that of *open Truth*" (p. 119).

Yet a third minor variant is provided by Robert Hindmarsh, who says that the instigator was not a Swedenborgian at all but "a foreign gentleman who held the absurd tenets of the sect of Rosicrucians." At a dinner at the house of a Swedenborgian, the Rosicrucian declared that Swedenborg had discovered an elixir by which he could "protract his existence as long as he pleased." Then, "desirous to put off the infirmities of age, [he] had renewed his existence and withdrawn to some other part of the world, causing a sham funeral to be performed to avoid discovery." This then led to the opening of the tomb and the discovery of Swedenborg's remains therein. Although the three sources differ as to how the opening of the tomb was instigated, they agree in presenting the investigation as a test of whether Swedenborg's body possessed some magical property that would have removed it from the coffin altogether—a test which culminated in the discovery that Swedenborg's mortal remains were like anyone else's. The experiment was then repeated a few days later by Hindmarsh and four or five associates. They found the corpse in a very good state of preservation: "The features were still perfect, the flesh firm," says Hindmarsh; but when he placed his hand on the forehead, he found that "the lower part of the nose gave indications of approaching decomposition.'' No doubt as a result of its exposure to air, the body was "afterwards found. . .speedily being reduced to ashes."[51] These two openings of the tomb, the first witnessed by perhaps a dozen people and the second by five or six new spectators, can hardly have been kept a secret.

The Marriage of Heaven and Hell is widely recognized to be a satire directed toward Swedenborg and the Swedenborgians.[52] The title unites what Swedenborg had perceived as divided; Angels and Devils are juxtaposed, but with subversive intent. Swedenborg's static "equilibrium" is displaced by Blake's dynamic interplay of contraries. In *The Marriage* Memorable Fancies parody Swedenborg's Memorable Relations: marvelous events are related matter-of-factly, sudden transitions are made from one world to another, and the narrator always has the last word. Even the *Marriage* of the title may be an ironical allusion to Swedenborg, for in *A Sketch of the Chaste Delights of Conjugal Love* Swedenborg asserts:

> That Hell is formed from Adulteries, is because Adultery is from the Marriage of Evil and False, from which Hell in its whole Complex is called Adultery; and that Heaven is formed from Marriages, is because Marriage is from the Marriage of Good and Truth, whence also Heaven in its whole complex is called a Marriage. . . .(p.20)

This arrogation of libidinal energy to "Evil" and of passive restraint to "Good" is corrected by Blake throughout *The Marriage of Heaven and Hell*. Of course *The Marriage* is much more than an anti-Swedenborgian polemic, but its full significance can only be appreciated in the light of Blake's knowledge of Swedenborg's doctrines and of the history of the New Jerusalem Church.

The first page of prose in *The Marriage* begins:

> As a new heaven is begun, and it is now thirty-three years since its advent: the Eternal Hell revives. And lo! Swedenborg is the Angel sitting at the tomb; his writings are the linen clothes folded up.[53]

The first reference is of course to Swedenborg's declaration that a new heaven was opened in 1757,[54] and the second sentence alludes to the episode in John XX where Christ's body is found to be gone from the tomb:

> So they ran both together: and the other disciple did outrun Peter, and came first to the sepulchre. And he stooping down, and looking in, saw the linen clothes lying; yet went he not in. Then cometh Simon Peter following him, and went into the sepulchre, and seeth the linen clothes lie, And the napkin, that was about his head, not lying with the linen clothes, but wrapped together in a place by itself. (4-7)

For Blake the body of Christ's teaching is absent from Swedenborg's writings; the latter are seen as a garment which can be discarded. As Damon remarks, "Swedenborg finds himself left behind in his own eschatology."[55] The reader conversant with the circumstances surrounding the openings of Swedenborg's tomb could have seen a further ironical allusion here. Unlike Christ, Swedenborg was securely in his tomb when his followers came seeking him. Such a contrast is of course unfair to Swedenborg, who never claimed any extraordinary powers for his mortal body; but Blake's purpose here is to expose what he perceives as the errors of Swedenborgianism rather than to do justice to Swedenborg as a historical figure.

Blake's fourth Memorable Fancy both attacks Swedenborg's doctrine and parodies his techniques. The author's journey through visionary worlds is of course a familiar feature of Swedenborg's writings. When Leviathan is perceived "to the east, distant about three degrees," we are meant to recall Swedenborg's precise readings of the celestial map: for example, the Sun "appears above the Earths which the Angels inhabit, in an Elevation of about forty-five Degrees. . . ."[56] The interplanetary voyage with Swedenborg's volumes in hand imitates the similar ones in *Earths in Our Solar System*, while the discussion of "my eternal lot" refers to the "enrolling" of *Divine Providence*. When Blake tells the Angel "Here. . .is your lot, in this space, if space it may be called," he reminds us of Swedenborg's statement that "the Spaces and Distances, and consequent Progressions, which occur in the natural World, are in their Origin and first Cause,

Changes of the State of Interior things. . . ."[57] Subsequently, Blake "in my hand brought forth the skeleton of a body, which in the mill was Aristotles Analytics"; in *Earths in Our Solar System* Aristotle is described sympathetically, and Swedenborg says, "Afterwards I discoursed with him, concerning the analytic science. . . ."[58] In the fifth Memorable Fancy, where the converted Angel "stretched out his arms embracing the flame of fire & he was consumed and arose as Elijah," there also appears to be a Swedenborgian source; for on Jupiter, according to Swedenborg, "the Spirits of that Earth, when they are prepared, are taken up into Heaven and become Angels: On such occasions there appear Chariots and bright Horses as of Fire, by which they are carried away in like Manner as Elias. . . ."[59] In instances such as these, Blake uses Swedenborgian material to intensify the irony of his anti-Swedenborgian satire.

Of the many other Swedenborgian allusions in *The Marriage*, several are worth particular attention. "Some will say," Blake writes, "Is not God alone the Prolific? I answer, God only Acts & Is, in existing beings or Men."[60] This seems to be aimed explicitly at Swedenborg's admonition in *Divine Love and Divine Wisdom*: "Let every one beware of falling into that execrable Heresy, that God hath infused himself into Men, and that he is in them, and no longer in himself."[61] The invidious comparison of Swedenborg to Paracelsus and Boehme takes on an added significance when we note that Swedenborg explicitly denied having read Boehme, and that this denial was published in the *New Jerusalem Magazine* early in 1790. Thus when Blake says that "Swedenborg's writings are a recapitulation of all superficial opinions, and an analysis of the more sublime," he is probably playing on Swedenborg's assertion that "I was prohibited reading dogmatic and systematic theology, before heaven was opened to me. . . ."[62] More generally, the erotic mysticism of *The Marriage* can be seen in one aspect as Blake's response to the concubinage dispute—not that it is in any way limited to that meaning. Just as Berkeley's *Siris* begins as a disquisition on tar-water and becomes a statement about the nature of the universe, so *The Marriage*, in its inception an anti-Swedenborgian satire, develops into Blake's most comprehensive statement about human existence up to the time of its composition.

IV

For about a decade following the beginning of *The Marriage*, there is little to indicate Swedenborgian interests in Blake's poetry and art. Then, from about the turn of the century and well into the nineteenth century, Blake displays a renewed interest in (though by no means a simple attitude toward) Swedenborg. Perhaps the most dramatic instance of this interest may be seen in Blake's *Descriptive Catalogue* of 1809. Among the sixteen pictures that Blake chose to show in his exhibition in that year was one, now unfortunately lost, on a Swedenborgian subject. Its title was "The spiritual Preceptor, an experiment Picture," and it was based on a Memorable Relation in *True Christian Religion*. According to Blake:

> This subject is taken from the visions of Emanuel Swedenborg. Universal Thelology, No. 623. The Learned, who strive to ascend into Heaven by means of learning, appear to Children like dead horses, when repelled by the celestial spheres. The works of this visionary are well worthy the attention of Painters and Poets; they are foundations for grand things; the reason they have not been more attended to, is, because corporeal demons have gained a predominance; who the leaders of these are, will be shewn below. Unworthy Men who gain fame among Men, continue to govern mankind after death, and in their spiritual bodies, oppose the spirits of those, who worthily are famous; and as Swedenborg observes, by entering into disease and excrement, drunkenness and concupiscence, they possess themselves of the bodies of mortal men, and shut the doors of mind and of thought, by placing Learning above Inspiration. O Artist! you may disbelieve all this, but it shall be at your own peril.[63]

The "experiment picture" may of course have been executed years before the exhibition, but these comments in Blake's *Descriptive Catalogue* reveal a strong renewal of interest in Swedenborg by 1809. Another picture which indicates such interest is "The Death of the Good Old Man," engraved after Blake by Schiavonetti for Blair's *Grave* (1808).[64] In this design, the soul of the Good Old Man, identical in appearance to his dead body, is escorted upwards by angels. As H.W.

Janson points out with respect to Flaxman, such a depiction of the "full-bodied soul" immediately after death is based on a Swedenborgian conception: "Man rises again immediately after death, and he then appears to himself in a body just as in this world, with a similar face, members, arms, hands, feet, breast, belly, and loins; so that when he sees and touches himself, he says that he is a man as in the world."[65] Janson argues that such a portrayal of the "full-bodied soul" is to be distinguished from the depiction of the soul at the Last Judgment, when all shall be resurrected. As we know, Blake and Flaxman influenced each other in many ways, and it is possible that "The Death of the Good Old Man" derives from such funerary sculptures as Flaxman's Agnes Cromwell monument in Chichester Cathedral. Nevertheless, given the wide extent of Blake's reading of Swedenborg, he would have known that in "The Death of the Good Old Man" he was using a specifically Swedenborgian idea.

One source of Blake's renewed interest in Swedenborg may have been his frienship with Charles Augustus Tulk, son of a founding member of the New Jerusalem Church and also a friend of Flaxman's and of Coleridge's.[66] (It was Tulk's copy of the *Songs* that Coleridge borrowed in February 1818, and it was probably information from Tulk that led Coleridge to write of Blake, "He is a man of Genius—and I apprehend, a Swedenborgian."[67]) In the memoir which Tulk's daughter dictated to his grand-daughter, it is said that "William Blake, the Poet & Painter, with his wife, were rescued from destitution by Mr. C.A. Tulk, & became much impressed with the Spiritual Truths in Swedenborg's Writings. He made drawings from the Memorable Relations, one of them of a female Angel instructing a number of children in the spiritual world."[68] Unfortunately, this drawing is not known to exist today; nor is a picture which is said to have had a marginal note in Blake's hand recommending Swedenborg's *Worship and Love of God*, a work first published in complete English translation in 1799-1801.[69] Despite the fact that Blake's pictures on Swedenborgian subjects either have not survived or have not been identified, it is clear from the evidence we have cited that Swedenborg had once more assumed major importance to Blake by 1809. We can find this interest reflected in Blake's poetic works as well.

One of the most striking instances of Swedenborgian conceptions in Blake's later work occurs in plate 48 of *Jerusalem*. Here the condition of man has fallen to its lowest point; on the preceding plate, Albion speaks his last words—"Hope is banish'd from me" (E 194). Then the Saviour receives Albion and in mercy reposes his limbs on the Rock of Ages.

> In silence the Divine Lord built with immortal labour,
> Of gold & jewels a sublime Ornament, a Couch of repose,
> With Sixteen pillars: canopied with emblems & written verse.
> Spiritual Verse, order'd & measur'd, from whence, time shall reveal.
> The Five books of the Decalogue, the books of Joshua & Judges,
> Samuel, a double book & Kings, a double book, the Psalms & Prophets
> The Four-fold Gospel, and the Revelations everlasting
> Eternity groan'd & was troubled, at the image of Eternal Death![70]

As Damon was the first to point out, these books of the Bible—thirty-three in all—are precisely those which Swedenborg had declared possessed the internal sense of the Word; and as Bentley has noted, the General Conference of 1789 re-affirmed that only these were the "Books of the Word."[71] It cannot be a coincidence that Blake chose these books to form that canopy that would shield the sleeping body of man while the work of redemption took place. Blake's notion of Albion the Eternal Man is itself derived from Swedenborg, who conceives of the three Heavens as composing a Grand Man, with the various human members and organs having their corresponding celestial parts. This doctrine was probably first encountered by Blake in *Heaven and Hell* (#59-67), but it does not appear in his own work until *The Four Zoas*—which is to say, no earlier than the late 1790s. This analogy of the human microcosm with a human macrocosm provided Blake, as Schorer puts it, with "the metaphorical tool that enabled him to counter the prevailing mechanical view of man and the universe with his own organic view."[72] These important debts to Swedenborg are well established, but others scarcely less important have not previously been discussed.

The central action of Blake's *Milton*, the redemptive descent of Milton to "Eternal Death" to deliver the sleeping body of man, is in part an amplification and revision of a Swedenborgian doctrine. In his great speech on plate 14, Milton says:

> I in my Selfhood am that Satan: I am that Evil One!
> He is my Spectre! in obedience to loose him from my Hells
> To claim the Hells, my Furnaces, I go to Eternal Death.[73]

In *True Christian Religion* Swedenborg says that the Last Judgment of 1757 involved "the Subduing of the Hells, restoring the Heavens to Order, and establishing a new Church" (#115); and elsewhere he asserts "That the Lord was to come into the World, to accomplish a complete or final Judgement, and thereby subjugate the then prevailing power of the Hells, which was effected by Spiritual Combats, or Temptations admitted to assault the Humanity derived from the Mother, and by continual victories then obtained. . . ."[74] Blake's Milton likewise triumphs over temptations and assaults "in conflict with those Female forms"[75] (his wives and daughters), striving with the demon Urizen and his codes of Law, tempted by the sons and daughters of Rahab and Tirzah. Milton's sublime act has as its paradigm the Incarnation, and there are parallels in Plato's fable of the Cave and in Gnostic mythology; but in Swedenborg and in Blake we also find a plurality of hells and a putting off of the Maternal Humanity. The latter feature also appears in *Jerusalem*: "by his Maternal Birth he [Christ] is that Evil-One/And his Maternal Humanity must be put off Eternally" (90:35-36, E 247). Swedenborg declares "That the Lord Successively put off the humanity which was taken from the Mother, and put on the humanity from the Divinity in himself, which is the Divine Humanity and the Son of God."[76] For Blake the Maternal Humanity was the purely material aspect of Christ's being; this must be "put off" so that he may "put on" his spiritual body.

Blake and Swedenborg also share a similar conception of history according to which "Churches" succeed one another, each reaching its "period" and then giving way to its successor. As Damon suggests, Blake's use of Biblical names to denote the Churches of history derives from Swedenborg,[77] but in addition the idea of a crisis in the modern Church leading to its "Consummation" is also common to both. In *Divine Providence*, Swedenborg describes the process by which this happens, declaring, "But the successive Vastation of the Christian Church in its final Period, is described by the Lord in Matthew Chap. xxiv, in Mark, Chap. xiii, and in Luke, Chap. xxi; and the Consummation itself in the Apocalypse."[78] This theme was sounded at the opening of the General Conference of 1789, where an extract from *True Christian Religion* was read, asserting "that the Christian Church, which is founded on the Word, and is now at its period, may again revive and derive Spirit through Heaven from the Lord."[79] In *Milton*, Blake both appropriates and subverts the Swedenborgian idea.

> Seeing the Churches at their Period in terror & despair:
> Rahab created Voltair; Tirzah created Rousseau;
> Mocking the Confessors and Martyrs, claiming Self-
>   righteousness;
> With cruel Virtue: making War upon the Lambs Redeemed[80]

For Blake the "Period" of the Churches culminates in the consolidation of the rationalistic system which he calls Deism; this necessarily precedes a Last Judgment in which history will be abolished. Swedenborg conceived the New Church to be the result of the vastation of the Christian Church, but Blake perceives Swedenborg himself as the victim of the Churches of history—as the passage in *Milton* goes on to say;

> O Swedenborg! strongest of men, the Samson shorn by the
>   Churches!
> Shewing the Transgressors in Hell, the proud Warriors in
>   Heaven:
> Heaven as a Punisher & Hell as One under Punishment:
> With Laws from Plato & his Greeks to renew the Trojan Gods,
> In Albion; & to deny the value of the Saviours blood.[81]

This is essentially the same criticism Blake made in *The Marriage*: that Swedenborg, in accepting the necessity of repressive law and in re-affirming the existence of an afterlife of rewards and punishments, committed the same errors that the Churches had. But Swedenborg is no longer demeaned as "A man [who] carried a monkey about for a shew, & because he was a little wiser than the monkey. . .conceiv'd himself as much wiser than seven men" (E 42). Instead, he is the "strongest of men," the shorn Samson whose tragic fate indicates something of Blake's profound ambivalence toward Swedenborg at this point.

Another Swedenborgian idea which finds its way into Blake's later work is the special meaning attached to Great Tartary. In *Jerusalem* when Urizen builds his "Mighty Temple," we are told that "his inmost hall is Great Tartary"; and one of the activities of those who consummate bliss and are generated on Earth is "Viewing the Winding Worm on the Desarts of the Great Tartary."[82] Commentators have generally taken "Great Tartary" to be a geopolitical symbol signifying the eastern part of the world: thus the Winding Worm on the deserts of Great Tartary has been interpreted as the advance of Napoleon's armies into Russia.[83] But *Great* Tartary—as distinguished from Crimean Tartary—was in Asia,[84] and of course Napoleon did not attack Asiatic Russia. In order to understand the symbolism of these passages, we must turn to Swedenborg, who in *True Christian Religion* maintains the existence of a Word which existed before the Word which the World now possesses. Speaking of "that ancient Word, which was in Asia before the Israelitish Word," he asserts "It is still preserved amongst the People who live in Great Tartary. . . ."[85] These people, he goes on, have the Book of Jasher (mentioned in Joshua x. 12, 13, and in II Samuel i. 17, 18) and the Wars of Jehovah and the Denunciators (the last, according to Swedenborg, being mistranslated as "Composers of Proverbs" in our Bibles). Thus we can see why Great Tartary should be the *inmost* hall of Urizen's Temple of Urizen, representing as it does the primordial Word. Again, the reference to the warrior's spear and sword reaching "from Albion to Great Tartary" indicated that even the wisdom of the ancient Word is threatened by the modern code of love and war. When those who consummate bliss regard the generated world, they see an aspect of themselves in the Winding Worm reaching to Great Tartary: the Worm of mortality, whose winding also suggests the cycle of history, is seen inhabiting the place of the world's ancient wisdom and presumably corrupting it. Blake's meaning in all three of these instances is particularized by its Swedenborgian reference.

Numerous other examples of references to Swedenborg may be found in Blake's late writings and conversation; but only a few especially interesting examples need be mentioned here. The vortices which figure prominently in *The Four Zoas* and in *Milton* are likely to have come to Blake via Swedenborg; though their ultimate source is Descartes,[86] it is unlikely that Blake read the Cartesian account directly. Swedenborg says that at the Creation Nature "Folded herself up into a kind of Vortexes," and in *The Four Zoas* Vala, who is in one aspect Nature, is personified as "The Nameless Shadowy Vortex."[87] The extended account of passing through a Vortex in *Milton* may be indebted to one of Swedenborg's Memorable Relations. When Blake told Henry Crabb Robinson that he had seen the Spiritual Sun on Primrose Hill, he was clearly alluding to Swedenborg's account of two suns, one material and one spiritual, in *Divine Love and Divine Wisdom*.[88] Not so obvious an allusion is Blake's statement to Robinson "I saw nothing but good in *Calvin's* house—In *Luther's* there were Harlots."[89] In this instance Blake's comment is precisely opposite to what Swedenborg maintains: we are told in *True Christian Religion* that after the Last Judgment of 1757, Luther became convinced of his errors and renounced them, but "Calvin betook himself to a house frequented by Harlots, and there abode for some time."[90] These and other instances[91] show that Swedenborg was much in Blake's thoughts in the nineteenth century, sometimes as a promulgator of ideas to be opposed, but in either respect as a powerful intellectual force.

Swedenborg was much in Blake's thoughts in the nineteenth century.

It is easy to see the reason for Blake's ambivalence toward Swedenborg. A seer of visions and the Messenger of a new age, Swedenborg was yet, for Blake, bound within the same limits that confined other founders of "Churches." Whitefield and Wesley were preferable not necessarily because of their doctrines, but because of the active nature of their ministry. Blake appears to have expressed his attitude rather diplomatically to Charles Augustus Tulk. According to Dr. J. J. Garth Wilkinson

> Blake informed Tulk that he had two different states; one in which he liked Swedenborg's writings, and one in which he disliked them. The second was a state of pride in himself, and then they were distasteful to him, but afterwards he knew that he had not been wise and sane. The first was a state of humility, in which he received and accepted Swedenborg.[92]

Blake's remarks to Crabb Robinson on the same subject were considerably less circumspect. "He was a divine teacher," Robinson reports Blake as saying of Swedenborg in 1825, and continues:

—he has done much and will do much good he had correct[d] many errors of Popery & also of Luther & Calvin—Yet he also said that *Swedenborg* was wrong in endeavour[g] to explain to the *rational* faculty what the reason cannot comprehend he should have left that—As B. mentioned *Swedenb*: & Dante together I wished to know whe[r] he considered their visions of the same kind As far as I co[d] collect he does—[93]

A further reflection recorded by Robinson reads: "*Swedenborg* Parts of his scheme are dangerous. His sexual religion is dangerous."[94] "Sexual" in Blake's later vocabulary has the special meaning of something's becoming materialized and in so doing betraying its essential quality, and so here again Blake is concentrating on that aspect of Swedenborgianism which he sees as resembling historical Christianity—complete with angels, devils, an afterlife with rewards and punishments, and a church. In his last known comment on Swedenborg, it is once more this aspect which Blake vehemently attacks. On the back of Dante design 7, showing Homer at the center of a diagram of the universe, Blake condemns Dante as a worshipper of Nature, adding "Swedenborg does the same in saying that this World is the Ultimate of Heaven" (E 668). Perhaps Blake might have more correctly told Tulk that in one state he regarded Swedenborg's visions metaphorically, and then they seemed consistent with his own; while in the other state he viewed them literally and as conflicting with his own. In the former state, he tended to regard his disagreements with Swedenborg merely as a matter of Swedenborg's not having gone far enough; in the latter, he condemned Swedenborg for the same reason. In this divided attitude, Blake resembles another great Romantic, Ralph Waldo Emerson. Emerson, like Blake, accuses Swedenborg of over-literalism, "Hebraism," and want of poetry; and like Blake Emerson compares Swedenborg unfavorably with Boehme, who, says Emerson, "is healthily and beautifully wise."[95] Emerson's remarks on Swedenborg's angels are consonant with Blake's in *The Marriage*: "They are all country parsons: their heaven is a *fête champêtre*, an evangelical picnic, or a French distribution of prizes to virtuous peasants."[96] Yet in the book where these remarks occur, *Representative Men*, Emerson chooses Swedenborg as his example of "The Mystic." Likewise for Blake, Swedenborg, the Angel sitting at the Tomb, the Samson shorn by the Churches, is a powerful visionary figure of pervasive interest.

Notes

1. See Alexander Gilchrist, *Life of William Blake* (1863, rev. ed. 1880), ed. Ruthven Todd (London and New York: J.M. Dent and E.P. Dutton, rev. ed., 1945), p. 13.

2. See J.G. Davies, *The Theology of William Blake* (Oxford: The Clarendon Press, 1948), pp. 31-53; David V. Erdman, "Blake's Early Swedenborgianism: a Twentieth-Century Legend," *Comparative Literature*, V (1953), 247-57; Nancy Bogen, "The Problem of William Blake's Early Religion," *Personalist*, XLIX (1968), 509-22.

3. On the dating of *The Marriage*, see David V. Erdman, "Dating Blake's Script: the *g* Hypothesis," *Blake Newsletter*, III (1969), 8-13; G.E. Bentley, Jr., *Blake Books* (Oxford: the Clarendon Press, 1977), pp. 285-88.

4. *M* 22:50, in *The Poetry and Prose of William Blake*, ed. David V. Erdman (Garden City, N.Y.: Doubleday & Co., 4th printing, 1970), p. 117. The edition will be cited hereafter as E, followed by plate, line, and page numbers.

5. *Energy and the Imagination: a Study of the Development of Blake's Thought* (Oxford: The Clarendon Press, 1970). Swedenborg is discussed on pp. 11-13, 17-18, 76-77, and 120.

6. As Blake refers to this book as "Worlds in [the] Universe," Erdman speculates on the possible existence of "a different translation, perhaps of a later date" (E 800). But *Worlds in the Universe* was evidently an alternate title for *Earths in Our Universe*, and the 1787 edition is cited under the former title in *The Apocalypse Revealed* (Manchester: C. Wheeler, 1791), II, #716.

7. On Jacob Duché, see *DAB*, s.v., and Charles Higham, "The Reverend Jacob Duché, M.A.: II. His Later Life and Ministry in England," *New Church Review*, XXII (1915), 404-20. Duché's son, Thomas Spence Duché, was a young artist who studied under Benjamin West in London and who may have visited the Prophets of Avignon in 1788; see Albert Frank Gegenheimer, "Artist in Exile: the Story of Thomas Spence Duché," *PMBR*, LXXIX (1955), 3-26.

8. *Rise and Progress of the New Jerusalem Church in England, America and Other Parts*, ed. Edward Madely (London, 1861), pp. 40-41. This account by an eyewitness to and participant in the early history of the New Jerusalem Church is our most important single source of information about the development of Swedenborgianism in England. However, it must be remembered that Robert Hindmarsh was not a disinterested party as concerns the schisms within the New Jerusalem Church, and his accounts must be balanced by other, independent ones such as those of Manoah Sibley and, most notably, Thomas Robinson (see below).

9. Annotations to *Divine Love and Divine Wisdom*, E 598.

10. Reprinted in *Rise and Progress*, pp. 98-99.

11. See R. Sundelin, *Svedenborgianismens Historia i Sverige* (Uppsala: W. Schultz, 1886), p. 259.

12. *Rise and Progress*, p. 107.

13. Blake's copy (published 1784) is in the Harvard College Library. Bentley (*Blake Books*, p. 696) makes a "plausible guess" that the marginalia were written in 1788.

14. London: W. Chalken, 1788. Blake's copy is in the British Library. Bentley (*Blake Books*, p. 696) asserts that the reference by Blake to "what was asserted in the society" suggests a date of annotation after the General Conference of 1789; however, as mentioned above, the reference could be to the earlier Theosophical Society. Bentley's conjectural ?1789 remains a plausible date for the annotations nevertheless.

15. *There is No Natural Religion* (2 sets) and *All Religions are One*, E 1-2. On Poetic Genius, see *Energy and the Imagination*, pp. 24-27.

16. On the general subject of Swedenborg's influence on Blake, see Mark Schorer, *William Blake: the Politics of Vision* (New York: Vintage, 1959 [Henry Holt, 1946], pp. 93-106; and S. Foster Damon, *A Blake Dictionary* (Providence: Brown University Press, 1965), pp. 392-94. The longest published study of Blake and Swedenborg, *The 'Heaven' and 'Hell' of William Blake* by G.R. Sabri-Tabrizi (London: Lawrence and Wishart, 1973), is unfortunately so simplistic as to be virtually useless. Ray H. Deck's unpublished dissertation, *Blake and Swedenborg* (Brandeis University, 1978), which I had the opportunity of reading after completing my own study, includes an informative and detailed comparison of the two figures. Also of interest is Jacques Roos, *Aspects Littéraires du Mysticisme Philosophique et l'Influence de Boehme et de Swedenborg au début du Romanticisme: William Blake. Novalis. Ballanche.* (Strasbourg, 1951).

17. See John Howard, "Swedenborg's *Heaven and Hell* and Blake's *Songs of Innocence*," *Papers on Language and Literature*, IV (1968), 390-99; Kathleen Raine, *Blake and Tradition* (Princeton: Princeton University Press, 1968) I, 3-33; Morton D. Paley, Introduction to *Twentieth Century Interpretations of Blake's "Songs of Innocence and of Experience"* (Englewood Cliffs, N.J.: Prentice-Hall, 1969), pp. 2-5.

18. Note to Clowes' translation of Swedenborg's *True Christian Religion* (London, 1781), #189.

19. *Concerning the Earths in Our Solar System* (London: R. Hindmarsh, 1787), #174.

20. Swedenborg's notion that "The Africans . . . worship the Lord under a human form" reappears in *America*, where the Shadowy Female calls Orc "the Image of God who dwells in darkness of Africa" (2:8-9, E 51); cf. the extract headed "That the Lord Now establishes a Church in Africa," *New Jerusalem Magazine*, I (1790), p. 183.

21. *William Blake*, p. 106

22. *True Christian Religion*, #78.

23. E 20-22. Raine mistakenly views these poems as a Neo-Platonic allegory, resulting in a confused interpretation according to which "why Blake chose to substitute a lion for Pluto will be made clear by a further quotation from Macrobius"; when the interpretation breaks down, Blake is seen to be at fault—"In Lýca's cave it seems as though Blake, in attempting to keep all his multiple meanings in mind simultaneously, has failed at this point." (*Blake and Tradition*, I, 128-49).

24. London: R. Hindmarsh, 1790. Blake's copy is in the collection of Sir Geoffrey Keynes. This translation is attributed to N. Tucker.

25. Harold Bloom writes, "Swedenborg's own later writings affirm predestination and eternal punishment, doctrines abhorrent to Blake" (E 801). Sabri-Tabrizi interprets Swedenborg's supposed predestinarianism as a projection of his supposed class bias: "According to Swedenborg the social positions of those in 'Heaven' and 'Hell' are predestined and thus the social relationship is established and fixed." (*The 'Heaven' and 'Hell' of William Blake*, p. 83). *Blake*, p. 83). However, #185 (annotated by Blake) is about *rich* men who bring hell on themselves.

26. *Letters to the Members of the New Jerusalem Church, formed by Baron Swedenborg* (J. Thompson: Birmingham, 1791; sold in London by Joseph Johnson). Priestley's view that God's form is "infinite space" (p. 51) would of course have conflicted with Blake's, while Blake continued to retain the Swedenborgian notion of God's human form; and in general it can be said that Blake retained numerous Swedenborgian ideas even during the period in which he repudiated Swedenborgianism.

27. *Milton* 22:55-23:2, E 117. See also *Jerusalem*, 52, E 199, and 72:51, E 225.

28. See David V. Erdman, *Blake: Prophet Against Empire* (Princeton: Princeton University Press, 3rd ed., 1977 [1954]).

29. *Rise and Progress*, p. 142.

30. Ibid., p. 131n.

31. Ibid., pp. 111, 118.

32. Ibid., p. 126.

33. See Thomas Robinson, *Remembrances of a Recorder* (Manchester and Boston, 1864), p. 94.

34. *An address to the Society of the New Church meeting in Friar Street, near Ludgate Hill, London*, pp. 3-4.

35. The English equivalent would be "The Form of Organization of the New Jerusalem," The book was published in Copenhagen because at this time the Lutheran Church exercised the right of censorship in Sweden and effectively prevented the publication of Swedenborgian literature there. A German translation was published in the *Magazin für kirchengesichte und kirchenrecht des Nordens*, Altona, 1792, II (3), 102 ff. See Sundelin, *Svedenborgianismens Historia i Sveriege*, pp. 261-62.

36. Letter of 11 September 1820, quoted by C. T. Odhner, "The Early History of the New Church in Sweden," *New Church Life*, XXXI (1911), 171, from *The Medium*, III (1851) 309.

37. *Minutes of the First Seven Sessions of the New Jerusalem Church Reprinted from the Original Editions* (London: James Speirs, 1885), n.p. The "Frederic" referred to is undoubtedly Charles Frederick Nordenskjöld, younger brother of Augustus. Charles Frederick was in England in 1791, while Augustus left England in that year to take part in the Sierra Leone colony originally projected by Wadström. See Appendix A for further information about A. Nordenskjöld and Wadström.

38. As suggested by Sundelin, p. 261.

39. #54, translated by C. T. Odhner and published in his *Robert Hindmarsh: A Biography* (Philadelphia: Academy Book Room, 1895, pp. 29-30. The rest of *Församlings Formen* has never been published in English. It is a very rare book; a copy is in the Royal Library, Stockholm.

40. *Conjugial Love (De Amore)* is not to be confused with the extract from *Apocalypsis Explicata* (#981-1010) published in English as *A Sketch of the Chaste Delights of Conjugial Love* (London: J. Denew, 1789). Part of *De Amore* was published in 1790 as a serial in the *New Jerusalem Magazine*, then as a separate volume; but this edition comprises only #1-55 and thus does not include the section on concubinage. However, the anonymous Preface does contain what may be an allusion to the concubinage dispute, stating: "In the following work the author likewise proves, in the most satisfactory and clear manner, that true Conjugal Love can only subsist between one husband and one wife, and thus cautions

the mind against that dangerous and Antichristian doctrine of a plurality of wives, which has lately been propagated and confirmed from certain passages of the Old Testament falsely understood" (p. iii). This is particularly interesting because the edition is likely to have been the responsibility of either or both the editors of the *New Jerusalem Magazine*, Henry Servanté and Charles Bernhard Wadström, and both were among those expelled in 1790.

41. Nevertheless, concubinage never attains the status of marriage in Swedenborg's view. Concubinage is only "a cloathing, compassing it [conjugal love] round about," and "this cloathing is taken away from them after death" (#475). Neither does Swedenborg seem to have envisioned the possibility of a women's taking a male concubine.

42. See Sundelin, p. 262.

43. Hindmarsh, though expelled, continued to participate regularly in the meetings for worship of the Great Eastcheap Society until 1792, when he precipitated a new schism on the issue of church hierarchy. Hindmarsh and his few adherents advocated an episcopal system of organization; this was rejected by the majority, but Hindmarsh obtained the lease of their place of worship, and the majority moved to a site in Store Street (near Tottenham Court Road).

44. *Emanuel Swedenborg's New-Years Gift to His Readers for MDCCXCI*, p. 21. The work is written throughout in the persona of Swedenborg. Elsewhere Chastanier writes, "There is no other true religion for rational beings to follow but love, namely, love of the sex, and brotherly love..."—*A Word of Advice To a Benighted World* (London, 1795), p. 16.

45. See R. L. Tafel, *Documents Concerning the Life and Character of Emanuel Swedenborg* (London: Swedenborg Society, 1877), I, 639-44. Another account to this effect was published in the *Appendix to the New Jerusalem Magazine* (1791), p. 263. According to General Tuxen of Denmark, Swedenborg had proposed marriage early in life to the daughter of his superior, the engineer Polhem, but she had refused him. "I then enquired,

whether in his youth he could keep free from temptations with regard to the sex? He replied, not altogether; In my youth I had a mistress in Italy."

46. *The Life of William Blake*, ed. Geoffrey Keynes (London: Oxford University Press, 1971), p. 72.

47. *Antechningar under en resa i England* (Stockholm, 1811), I, 47. The passage on Swedenborg's tomb is included in English translation in J.V. Hultkrantz, "The Mortal Remains of Emanuel Swedenborg," *Nova Acta Regiae Societas Scientarum Upsaliensis*, ser. IV, II (1910), 6-7. Although Dr. Hultkrantz's conclusions concerning Swedenborg's skull were subsequently refuted (see Folke Henschen, "Emanuel Swedenborg's Cranium: a Critical Analysis," *Nova Acta Regiae Societas Scientarum Upsaliensis*, ser. IV, SVII, No. 9, 1960), this does not affect our discussion of the first two openings of the tomb, the skull having been removed at a later date.

48. This person is identified by Hultkrantz, without any indication as to evidence, as probably either Wadström or Augustus Nordenskjöld.

49. Reprinted, with other material concerning the openings of the tomb, by David George Goyder, *The Autobiography of a Phrenologist* (London: Simkin, Marshall, 1857), p. 136. Goyder also prints (p. 137) a similar account from *The Times* signed "Tertius Interveniens" and attributed to J.P. Wahlin account was reprinted in Swedish in 1846, along with those of Hawkins and of S. Noble (*Dägslandor* [Norrköping: Östlund, Berling], pp. 219-225).

50. *Annals of the New Church* (Bryn Athyn, Pa.: Academy of the New Church, 1904), p. 150. Odhner cites Hindmarsh, *Rise and Progress*, and Goyder (see below), but neither of these mentions Thorild.

51. *Rise and Progress*, p. 399.

52. See Martin K. Nurmi, *Blake's "Marriage of Heaven and Hell": a Critical Study*, Kent State University Bulletin, Research Series III (1957), pp. 25-30, 45-57; and John Howard, "An Audience for *The Marriage of Heaven and Hell*," *Blake Studies*, III, (1970), 19-52.

53. E. 34. In copy F (originally the Butts copy, not in the Pierpont Morgan Library), the date "1790" is written over the first line.

54. *A Treatise Concerning the Last Judgment* (London: R. Hindmarsh, 1788), #45.

55. *William Blake: His Philosophy and Symbols* (Boston: Houghton Mifflin, 1924), p. 316.

56. E. 40; *Divine Love and Divine Wisdom*, #104.

57. E. 41; *Earths in Our Solar System*, #125.

58. Ibid., #38.

59. E. 42; Ibid., #82.

60. E. 39.

61. #125.

62. E. 42; *New Jerusalem Magazine*, p. 73.

63. E. 537. *Universal Theology* is the alternative title for *True Christian Religion*. An almost identical anecdote is related in *Apocalypse Revealed*, #311.

64. For a detailed discussion of this design, see Robert N. Essick and Morton D. Paley, *Robert Blair's "The Grave" with the Illustrations of William Blake* (London: the Scolar Press, forthcoming).

65. H.W. Janson, "Thorvaldsen and England," in *Bertil Thorvaldsen: Unterschungen zu zeinem Werk und zur Kunst seiner Zeit* (Museen der Stadt Köln, 1977), p. 111. The quotation is from *Arcana Coelestia* #5078, but the idea is encountered frequently in Swedenborg's writings. I am indebted to Dr. David Bindman for calling Janson's article to my attention.

66. On Tulk, see *DNB, s.v.*; Geoffrey Keynes, "Blake, Tulk, and Garth Wilkinson," *The Library*, 4th ser., XXVI (1945), 190-92; and Raymond A. Deck, Jr., "New Light on C.A. Tulk, Blake's Nineteenth Century Patron," *Studies in Romanticism*, XVI (1977), 217-36.

67. Letter to H.F. Cary, 6 February 1818, *Blake Records* p. 251. If Blake could be called a Swedenborgian, however, it was not because of any affiliation with the New Jerusalem Church. According to Crabb Robinson, "He was invited to join the Swedenborgians under Proud, but declined, notwithstanding his high opinion of Swedenborg. . . ." *Blake Records*, p. 452, from "William Blake," *Vaterländisches Museum*, I (January 1811), 107-31. Bentley suggests that this undated reference probably refers to the period 1797-99, when Proud was attracting large numbers of people to his services in Hatton Garden. Glaxman was a member of Proud's congregation at this time. —*Blake Records*, p. 440, n.6.

68. *Blake Records*, p. 250. The memoir does not give the dates of these activities. Bentley places the entry in 1818.

69. See H.N. Morris, "Blake and Swedenborg," *The Quest*, XI (1919), 80. However, the Catalogue of the British Fine Arts Club Exhibition of 1876 (in which exhibition Morris claims the picture was shown) indicates no such detail.

70. *Jerusalem* 48:5-12, E 194.

71. Damon, *William Blake: His Philosophy and Symbols*, p. 454, citing *Arcana Coelestia*, X, #325; Bentley "Blake and Swedenborg, *Notes and Queries*, CXCIX (N.S. I, 1954), 264-65.

72. *William Blake: The Politics of Vision*, p. 96.

73. *Milton* 14:30-32, E 107.

74. *The Doctrine of the New Jerusalem Concerning the Lord* (London: R. Hindmarsh, 3rd ed., 1791), #3.

75. 17:7, E 109.

76. *New Jerusalem*, #35.

77. *William Blake: His Philosophy and Symbols*, p. 427. Briefly Swedenborg postulates five Churches in history, beginning with Adam and Eve. Second comes "the Ancient Church," described by Noah, his three sons and their posterity. Heber, eponymous founder of the Hebrew Church, instituted sacrificial worship. The Word was written under the Israelitish and Jewish Church. (Heber and the Israelitish Church are at times combined into one by Swedenborg). These four Old Testament Churches are represented by Nebuchadnezzar's dream in Dan. ii. 32, 33. The fifth Church is the Christian Church. "And it may be seen from the Word, that all these Churches in Process of Time declined, till there was an End of them, which is called the Consummation." *Divine Providence*, #328.

78. *Divine Providence*, #328.

79. *Minutes*, ed., Speiers, p. 9.

80. 22:40-44, E 116.

81. 22:50-54, E 117.

82. 58:36, E 206; 86:46, E 243. In a third, less important reference, the warrior who beholds the beauty of the daughter of Albion is smitten, and "his spear/And sword faint in his hand, from Albion to Great Tartary" (68:51-52, E 220).

83. Erdman, *Blake: Prophet*, pp. 464, 466. Blake's three other references to Tartary (unmodified) may have this meaning.

84. See Inge Jonsson, *Emanuel Swedenborg* (Twayne: New York, 1971), p. 175.

85. #265, #278.

86. See Damon, *Blake Dictionary*, p. 440. On a related Swedenborgian source, see Nelson Hilton, "The Sweet Science of Atmospheres in *The Four Zoas*," *Blake/An Illustrated Quarterly*, 46(xii,2), p. 80.

87. *True Christian Religion*, #79; *Four Zoas*, VIIb, E 395.

88. # 163-66; for Blake's annotations, see E 594.

89. *Blake Records*, p. 541.

90. # 796-98.

91. It is likely that Blake's description of the regenerate Albion "Speaking the Words of Eternity in Human Forms" (*Jerusalem* 95:9, E 252) may be indebted to Swedenborg's idea that the speech of spirits "is the universal of all languages, by means of ideas, the primitive of words" (*Arcana Coelestia*, # 1641; see D.J. Sloss and J.P.R. Wallis, *The Prophetic Writings of William Blake* (Oxford: The Clarendon Press, 1926), I, n. 631. As John Howard points out, "The Writing/Is the Divine Revelation in the Litteral Expression" (*Milton* 42:13-14, E 142) "is a Swedenborgian concept involving what Swedenborg calls 'simultaneous order which is a spiritual order arranged from center to circumference,' inner to outer" (*Blake's "Milton": a Study in the Selfhood* (Rutherford, N.J.: Fairleigh Dickinson University Press, 1976), p. 283 n. 42.

92. James Spilling, "Blake the Visionary," *New Church Magazine*, VI (1887), 210.

93. *Blake Records*, p. 312.

94. *Blake Records*, p. 313.

95. *Representative Men: Seven Lectures* (Boston: Phillips, Sampson, 1850), p. 142.

96. Pp. 141-142.

"Opposition Is True Friendship"
Emanuel Swedenborg and His Influences on William Blake

HARVEY F. BELLIN

A GRADUATE of Yale College with High Honors in the History of Art, and of the Yale School of Drama with an M.F.A. in Directing, Harvey F. Bellin is a motion picture and television writer/director/producer. In partnership with Tom Kieffer, he has produced documentaries about culture and religion around the world and a television series about Shakespeare. Their award-winning television programs for the Swedenborg Foundation include: *Blake: The Marriage of Heaven and Hell*, a docu-drama starring Anne Baxter and George Rose; *Swedenborg: The Man Who Had To Know*, a docu-drama featuring Lillian Gish; *Johnny Appleseed and the Frontier Within*, about the Swedenborgian frontier-missionary, Johnny "Appleseed" Chapman; and *Images of Knowing*, narrated by Anne Baxter.

In the following, Mr. Bellin examines Blake's connections to Swedenborg in the context of an overview of Swedenborg's life and writings, and traces Swedenborgian roots of the mythology Blake created in his illuminated poems.   . –Ed.

I. "THE END OF A GOLDEN STRING"

Father O Father what do we here
In this Land of unbelief & fear
The Land of Dreams is better far
Above the light of the Morning Star

  Blake, *The Land of Dreams* (17-20; E. 486-7)[1]

LONDON, 1772

In a sterile abattoir of bone-white, plaster-cast, dismembered bodies, William Blake spent the last years of his childhood. For five years he had copied copies of life—ossified heads, hands and feet from classical sculptures; eyes, ears and noses from Renaissance engravings. His white-wigged instructors, wielding sharp compasses and dividers, dissected and trisected the fragments, reducing them to the circles, squares, triangles and solid geometrical forms of which logical art was made. Thus, the fiery-haired boy of fourteen, his Imagination pulsing with vivid pictures and poems, had been taught "art" at the Pars School of Drawing

Blake was coming of age in the Age of Reason, an era enamored of its new goddess, Science, and her handmaiden, Mathematics. It was an age which built its churches and synagogues in the mathematical form and likeness of classical temples, and built its philosophies upon the mathematical formulations of its patron saint, Sir Issac Newton. In the irrefutable logic-language of numbers, Newton had revealed universal laws governing everything from the orbit of planets to the fall of apples. Henceforth, all matters, cosmic and pedestrian, sacred and secular, were expected to yield their dark secrets to the Enlightenment and her vanguard of scientists.

Blake's psyche, however, had not evolved the appropriate wheels and gears to mesh with this new mathematical logic. He was a creature of another time, an anachronism, like a rough-hewn gothic gargoyle in an age of polished steam engines. His eyes were not adapted to the clear light of Reason; they perceived more in the tinted, stained-glass light of "The Land of Dreams." They saw visions—a spectre of God peered into his window, and sent him screaming; a tree on the fields of Peckham Rye blossomed with angels, "bright angelic wings bespangling every bough like stars."[2]

Upon completing his training at the Pars School, as he and his father searched London for a master-engraver with whom young William could apprentice, Blake was perhaps seeking a mentor of another sort—one who had mastered the hidden knowledge of the "Land of Dreams."

Around the same time, in the same city, in rented rooms above a wig-maker's shop, an octogenarian Swedish scientist, Emanuel Swedenborg, informed his English maid that several matters required his immediate attention, since he would be dying in three weeks time at five o'clock in the afternoon. The maid, Elizabeth Reynolds, later recalled: "He was as pleased as if he were going to have a holiday, and go to some merrymaking."[3]

Swedenborg was not a man who despised his life or his times; on the contrary, he had partaken of the fruits of the Age of Reason with great delight. He was an accomplished scientist and inventor, and author of many thick volumes of refined Latin prose on science, philosophy, psychology, and theology. Despite a recent stroke, he remained actively involved in the theological writings to which he had devoted the past twenty-eight years. He simply had no fear of death, of which he had written: "Death is not an extinction, but a continuation of life . . . merely a transition from one state to another."[4]

Three weeks later, on March 29, 1772, at 5:00 p.m.,

Swedenborg asked Elizabeth Reynolds the time. Upon hearing her answer, he replied: "That is good, I thank you. God bless you." He then died peacefully.[5]

Two days before his death, he was visited by a resident pastor of the Swedish Church, the Reverend Arvid Ferelius, who advised him to recant the new theological ideas set forth in Swedenborg's books—writings some clergy had branded as heretical. Swedenborg rose up from his sickbed, smiled at the pastor, and replied: "As truly as you see me before your eyes, so true is everything I have written . . . When you enter eternity, you will see everything; and then you and I shall have much to talk about."[6]

Swedenborg's writings did give others in London "much to talk about." Shortly after his death, his books, such as *Heaven and Hell*, *Divine Love and Wisdom*, *Divine Providence* and *Universal Theology* (*True Christian Religion*) were widely known and discussed, and were in the personal libraries of many progressive thinkers, including a young engraver, William Blake.

LONDON, APRIL 13, 1789

Although Swedenborg had never initiated the formation of a new religious denomination, a number of his English and Continental followers gathered in a chapel in Great East Cheap, London, on April 13, 1789, to convene a General Conference for establishing a sectarian church founded upon "the truths contained in the Theological Writings of the honorable Emanuel Swedenborg."[7] Among those signing the register of the General Conference were William Blake and his young wife, Catherine.

The church was to be called The New Jerusalem, an image cited in *Revelation*, which Swedenborg saw as his emblem for a new age of spiritual liberation. When William and Catherine Blake entered the New Jerusalem chapel, they passed through a portal with a sign proclaiming the motto of the new church: "NOW IT IS ALLOWABLE." Swedenborg had seen this phrase in a vision, inscribed over the door of a crystal-walled church; and he interpreted it to mean: "Now it is allowable to enter intelligently into the mysteries of faith" (*TCR*, 508).

Blake's Imagination would pass through a portal proclaiming "NOW IT IS ALLOWABLE" time and again in future years. In the frontispiece of his most ambitious illuminated poem, aptly titled *Jerusalem*, Blake portrays himself as the mythic poet, Los, entering such a portal with a bright lantern.

Where does this gateway lead? To the New Jerusalem? To the "mysteries of faith"? To the subconscious realm, the "Land of Dreams"? To the wellsprings of art? To the worlds beyond the grave? Or to a world very much like our own?

For both Blake and his spiritual predecessor, Swedenborg, all these are synonymous. The essence of spiritual liberation, the substrata of visions and dreams, the imagery of deeply moving works of art, the shapes of the afterlife, and the living forms of nature are all intertwined—are each threads of a "golden string" leading back to a single source:

> *I give you the end of a golden string,*
> *Only wind it into a ball,*
> *It will lead you in at Heaven's Gate,*
> *Built in Jerusalem's Wall.*
> *Jerusalem* (77:1-4; E.231)

Blake would not find "Heaven's Gate" immured within the formal doctrines and prescribed rituals of the New Jerusalem Church; for he felt that "The whole of the New Church is in the Active Life and not in Ceremonies at all."[8] He quickly broke with the fledgling church and never returned.[9] He had, however, found the "end of a golden string" in Swedenborg's writings, which addressed many of Blake's own inner conflicts and doubts.

Blake's early engraved books of pictures and designs, *Songs of Innocence* and *The Book of Thel*, both created around the time of the 1789 General Conference, brim with Swedenborgian metaphor and message.[10] Despite his leaving the New Jerusalem Church, Blake maintained close friendships with prominent Swedenborgians, such as the sculptor, John Flaxman, and the legislator, C. A. Tulk,[11] till the end of his life.

Presumably, Blake never met Swedenborg;[12] it was the legacy of Swedenborg's writings, their articulate affirmation of much of what Blake had himself intuited, which created the "golden string" linking Blake to the Swedish scientist-theologian. But even a golden string can break; and it did so, resoundingly, in a book Blake created in the early 1790s, which contained this warning:

> *The man who never alters his opinion is like*
> *standing water, & breeds reptiles of the mind.*
> (MHH 19; E.42)

LONDON, 1793

By 1793 Blake had completed an anonymous book, which he wrote, illustrated, engraved, and printed in his home workshop. He titled it *The Marriage of Heaven and Hell*—a clear satire of Swedenborg's *Heaven and its Wonders, and Hell.*

Blake; *Jerusalem* frontispiece

In this social-political-religious allegorical romp through the fires of Hell, Blake exalts Energy and Poetic Genius, and seems to permanently damn Swedenborg into the "Satanic" pantheon of intellectual malfeasants into which Blake had cast Newton, Locke and other shapers of the Age of Reason. Swedenborg's influences, however, would re-emerge as a dominant force throughout Blake's career.[13]

Blake left an intriguing clue to his own "reptilian" change of opinion about Swedenborg in a paradoxical line he engraved beneath a scaly Leviathan on plate 20 of *The Marriage of Heaven and Hell*. In this chapter, Blake challenges an angel-follower of Swedenborg to: "shew me my eternal lot . . . and see whether your lot or mine is most desirable." They fight a conjurer's duel, materializing the bestiaries lurking within each other's psyches. The angel casts Blake's lot between rows of vast black and white spiders who prey upon "the most terrific shapes of animals sprung from corruption." Blake counters, casting the angel into a deep pit beneath a church on Saturn, where they enter a charnel house of cannibalistic simians, and exit carrying the "skeleton of a corpse"—Swedenborg's books, transformed into Aristotle's dry *Analytics*.

In the midst of this duel, from out of a "cataract of blood mixed with fire," the giant Leviathan emerges. Engraved beneath this "reptile of the mind," partially obscured by Blake's thick patina of watercolor pigments in several copies of this hand-painted book, is Blake's final comment on his battle with Swedenborg's angelic alter ego:

Opposition is true Friendship

Blake; *Marriage of Heaven and Hell*, 20 (detail)

Opposition is true Friendship. . . . Blake declared his artistic independence . . . but the imprint [of Swedenborg] remained.

When is opposition true friendship? It is when a young man discovers his own unique mission, declares his independence, and leaves his father's house without ever losing the legacy of his roots. In a similar way Blake declared his artistic independence in the early 1790's. Shouting loud "opposition" to his former "true friendship" with Swedenborg's theological writings, he departed; but the imprint remained—so deeply ingrained, that Blake assimilated much of Swedenborg's vision and made it his own.

Others influenced Blake's thoughts—Jacob Boehme, in particular; and Blake never resolved his differences with some of the theological propositions he had read in the pious, transliterated, early editions of Swedenborg's books. Nonetheless, in large measure, the essence that Swedenborg articulated in measured Latin prose formed a golden string which Blake would continue to weave in handmade books of pictures and poems. Both men had been shaped by profound visionary experiences, and each dedicated his energy, wealth, and talents to promulgating the inner realities he had come to know.

Much of their shared vision is represented in Blake's engraving of a caterpillar and sleeping human-faced chrysalis, titled "What is Man!"

What is human existence—nothing more than the course of a mouth-first caterpillar, a "mortal worm," eating its path along a darkened leaf of vegetable nature? Or is there more—a promise of metamorphosis, a flight on radiant wings, in the dreams of the sleeping chrysalis? Will the chrysalis waken from his occluded cocoon, forgetting his dreams, and simply procreate another round of mortal worms?

Blake left the answer to the viewer, as he indicated in a couplet engraved beneath the emblematic insects:

What is Man!
The Suns Light when he unfolds it
Depends on the Organ that beholds it.
(*GP* frontispiece; E.260)

The Gates of Paradise: For the Sexes frontispiece

In a later work, Blake again considered the "organ that beholds," and concluded:

Mental things are alone real.
(VLJ p. 84; E.565)

Over half a century earlier, Swedenborg had reached similar conclusions, but he had arrived there along a very different route. He began as a most reasonable product of a most reasonable age, who beheld "the organ that beholds" in the clear light of the Enlightenment.

II. EMANUEL SWEDENBORG
(1688-1772)
The Man Who Had to Know

If the mind is truly connected with the organs of the senses, in other words, if man is truly rational, he is perpetually aspiring after wisdom. . . . The means which are especially conductive to a truly philosophical knowledge are three in number—EXPERIENCE, GEOMETRY, and the FACULTY OF REASONING.

— Swedenborg (PRIN I, 1:1, p.1)[14]

Thus began Swedenborg's theoretical scientific tome, *The PRINCIPIA, Or the First Principles of Natural Things, Being New Attempts Toward a Philosophical Explanation of the Elementary World*, which he published in 1734.

Had Blake read the PRINCIPIA, he would have railed loudly at Swedenborg's evocation of the terrific trinity: Experience (experimental facts), Geometry (measurement), and the Faculty of Reasoning. Blake had little faith in these three Muses of the scientific age: "He who sees the Infinite in all things, sees God. He who sees the Ratio only, see himself only. If it were not for the Poetic or Prophetic character the Philosophic & Experimental would soon be at the ratio of all things & stand still, unable to do other than repeat the same dull round over again" (NNR; E.3).

Blake was yet to be born, however, when the PRINCIPIA was written; and Swedenborg was in the midst of a brilliant scientific career, which seems to have earned him the distinction of having been the last man on earth to master all the knowledge of his times. He was a consumate intellectual in an intellectual age.

The son of a Bishop of the Swedish Church, later ennobled by royal decree, Swedenborg was born in 1688, one year after the birth of modern scientific theory in Sir Isaac Newton's *PRINCIPIA (Mathematical Principles of Natural Philosophy)*. The pivotal role of this book in sparking the Age of Reason was summarized in a couplet by another man born in 1688, Samuel Pope:

Nature and Nature's laws lay hid in night:
God said, Let Newton be, and all was light.

"All was light"—the Enlightenment was born, and young Emanuel Swedenborg jumped in, headfirst. He began with a classical education, entering Sweden's Upsala University at the age of eleven, and graduating with honors. He then undertook independent "Grand Tours" of European intellectual and scientific centers, where he conferred with such notables as the astronomers Flamstead and Halley (godfather of Halley's Comet). He mastered classical Greek, Latin and Hebrew, and six modern languages. He learned lens-grinding, watchmaking, and engraving. He studied fossils, and dissected a cadaver or two.

He put his experiences to use, applying the new ideas of the Enlightenment in his native Sweden, where he served as a progressive legislator in the House of Nobles, and as Royal Assessor of the all-important mining industry. A prolific inventor, his designs included advanced machinery for Swedish mining and smelting operations. He co-founded Sweden's first scientific journal, *Daedalus Hyperboreus*, in which he published his design for a revolutionary new machine.

Swedenborg's "Design of a Machine To Fly in the Air"

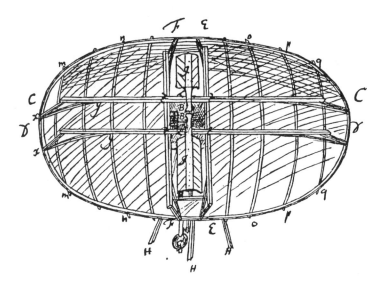

"A machine might be invented which could carry us through the air . . . we are not to be excluded from the overhead element." (*Daedalus Hyperboreus* IV, 1716)

Perhaps on the advice of older, less daring men, perhaps because his omnivorous intellect had already turned to other pursuits, the twenty-eight year old Swedenborg never built or tested this design for an egg-shaped, manned glider.[15] He might not have been dissuaded so easily, had he been privy to the following assessment of his design in a twentieth-century aviation journal:

> It is surprising to learn that the great Swedish philosopher, Emanuel Swedenborg, anticipated modern features of airplane design in his little known invention of a flying machine. . . . In England, the Royal Aeronautical Society published a description of the invention and called it "the first rational design for a flying machine of the airplane type."
> — *Popular Aviation*, Jan. 1938

One can only speculate on the consequences of Swedenborg's having followed through with his glider-design, but he did demonstrate his genius elsewhere—in the theoretical sciences. He published over seventy treatises, running the gamut from astronomy to zoology. His discoveries laid the foundations for the sciences of metallurgy and crystallography. Contradicting the theories of his leading contemporaries, he anticipated many later findings, such as the wave-motion of light, the molecular basis of magnetism, the nebular origin of planetary systems, and the nature of the atom.

In an era when science and philosophy had become trendy salon amusements of the idle rich, Swedenborg, himself a well-heeled aristocrat, was a true scientist in every respect. In books such as *Motion and Position of the Earths and Planets* (1719), *Principles of Chemistry* (1720), and *Philosophical and Mineralogical Studies* (3 vols., 1734), all of which he published at his own expense, Swedenborg articulated his theories and discoveries in exquisite mathematical minutiae, honoring the three muses: Experience, Geometry, and the Faculty of Reasoning.

In these books of meticulous Latin prose and mathematical formulations, Swedenborg was addressing a pan-European intelligentsia which deified science and reason, and relegated the biblical Deity to the role of "cosmic mechanic" or vestige of an unenlightened, superstitious past. To these "enlightened" persons, Swedenborg boldly proclaimed that his science was predicated on very different assumptions:

Possibly there may be innumerable other spheres, and innumerable other heavens similar to those we behold . . . yet being but finite, and consequently having their bounds, (they) do not amount to a point in comparison with the infinite. Consequently, if all the heavenly hosts are not even a point in respect to the infinite; if the whole visible expanse, which to our eye appears so immense, is only a point in relation to the finite universe; if our solar vortex forms only a part of this expanse, and our own world only a small part of the solar vortex; truly we may ask, *What is man!*

. . . Behold and see how small a speck thou art in the system of heaven and earth; and in thy contemplations remember this, that if thou wouldst be great, thy greatness must consist in this—in learning to adore Him who is Himself the Greatest and the Infinite.

[Emphasis mine] (*PRIN* II, 3:1, pp. 238-9)

Swedenborg's metaphor has a familiar ring, strangely similar to the imagery of scientific and sci-fi literature and motion pictures of our own times. His underlying religious message, however, might seem out of place for a scientist-philosopher, and possibly seemed old fashioned to his own contemporaries, especially when he stated:

True philosophy and contempt of the Deity are two opposites. Veneration for the Infinite Being can never be separated from philosophy; for he who fancies himself wise, while his wisdom does not teach him to acknowledge a Divine and Infinite Being . . . he has not a particle of wisdom. (Ibid., I, 1:1, p. 35)

In his refutation of the learned advocates of a mechanistic, Newtonian universe, Swedenborg is strikingly similar to a later scientist who shattered the Newtonian model of nature:

You will hardly find one among the profounder sort of scientific minds without a religious feeling of his own . . . His religious feeling takes the form of a rapturous amazement at the harmony of natural law, which reveals an intelligence of such superiority that, compared with it, all systemic thinking of human beings is utterly insignificant reflection. . . .

The ancients knew something we seem to have forgotten. All means prove but a blunt instrument, if they have not behind them a living spirit . . . science without religion is lame, religion without science is blind.

— Albert Einstein[16]

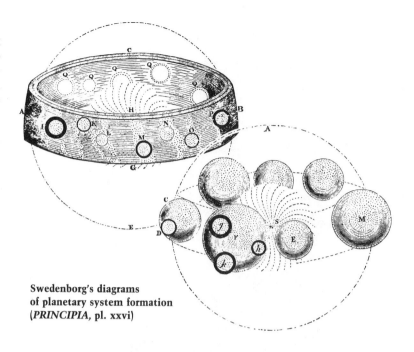

Swedenborg's diagrams
of planetary system formation
(*PRINCIPIA*, pl. xxvi)

Swedenborg, as he approached his fiftieth year, continued to envision a literal link between physical science and the "living spirit" of religion; and sought to apply his science to extricating the reality of that living spirit. He narrowed the focus of his research, concentrating on anatomy and physiology, with but one intention:

I have pursued this anatomy with the single purpose of searching out the soul. (*RS* intro.)
[For] she is represented in the body, as in a mirror. (*AK* intro.)

While pursuing this spiritual intention, Swedenborg made several significant physical discoveries, including the function of the endrocrine glands. He drafted extensive research on the blood, respiratory system, gastro-intestinal tract, the skin, senses, and procreative organs, and published many of his findings. He continued on relentlessly: "I am resolved to allow myself no respite . . . I shall open all the doors that lead to her, and at length, contemplate the soul herself" (*AK* intro.).

He then narrowed in even further, concentrating his search for the seat of the soul on a single organ:

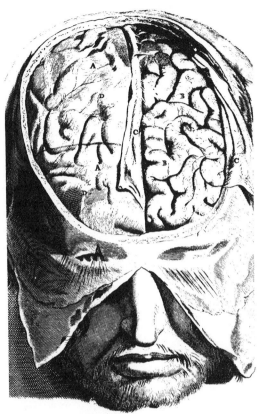

Anatomical reference from Swedenborg's *The Cerebrum*

I am determined . . . for the sake of a closer approach to examine her very brain, where the soul has disposed her first organs. (Ibid.)

In 1743-44, Swedenborg compiled a staggering four-volume treatise, *The Brain*. In it, he was the first to discover the functions of the cerebellum, pituitary gland and spinal fluid, the localization of thinking and memory in the cerebral cortex, and the integrative action of the nervous system.

But he did not find the soul lurking between the synapses of the cerebral cortex. He had pushed objective science to the limits, and failed. His three muses—Experience, Geometry and the Faculty of Reasoning—had gone mute. He would not meet the soul *in vitro*, in the flayed tissues or corpses or in cold calculations; if she was to be discovered, she must be seen *in vivo*.

As he continued his anatomical studies, a new muse began to emerge, sending seismic shock waves to the very core of this objective man of the Age of Reason. The process started with a series of disturbing dreams, which he carefully recorded in a private journal:

> . . . Stood beside a machine, that was set in motion by a wheel. The spokes entangled me more and more and carried me up so that it was impossible to escape. . . . Wakened.

> Freely and boldly I descended a great staircase. Below there was a hole leading down into a great abyss. It was difficult to reach the other side without falling in. On the other side were people to whom I reached out my hand, to help me over. . . . Wakened. . . . Signifies my danger of falling into the abyss, if I do not get help.

> — *Journal of Dreams*, n. 18, 20 (March 24-25, 1744)[17]

Where could he "get help" to understand the process unfolding within himself? Alone, in temporary rooms rented during his frequent overseas travels, in the mid-eighteenth century, Swedenborg tried to decipher the hidden meanings of dreams. He need no longer pursue the soul from the outside in; she was beginning to speak to him, in her own language, from the inside out. Her message, however, was not clear, was not phrased in logical terms. Her language consisted of bizarre, disjointed images; her tone was disconcerting. She remained distant, appearing only in the night, in the darkened mirror of dreams.

Then, with horrific power, she began to manifest herself in waking visions:

> I was in London and dined rather late one night. . . . Towards the end of the meal I noticed a dimness before my eyes; this became denser, and then I saw the floor covered with horrid crawling reptiles. . . .

> I was amazed; for I was perfectly conscious, and my thoughts were clear. (*Docs.* I, p. 35)

As Blake would later warn: "The man who never alters his opinion is like standing water, & breeds reptiles of the mind" (*MHH* 19; E. 42).

Swedenborg's opinions began to alter. He realized that he could no longer rely on his intellect alone; he would need other, more intuitive ways of knowing. He was now at great risk, his sanity was at stake; but his long quest seemed to be nearing fruition.

His life was rushing toward a crucial turning point. The man who had invented an egg-shaped glider was about to experience the meaning of an egg-hatched cherub, one of Blake's *Gates of Paradise* engravings, titled:

> At length for hatching ripe
> he breaks the shell.
> (*GP* 6; E.262)

Gates of Paradise: For the Sexes 6

III. "A THEATRE REPRESENTATIVE OF THE LORD'S KINGDOM" Swedenborg's Theology

Divine Providence has ruled the acts of my life since my youth . . . so that by means of the knowledge of natural things [through science] I might be able to understand the things which lie deeply concealed in the Word of God, and thus serve as an instrument for laying them bare.

— Swedenborg (*WE* 2532)

Whatever force had been emerging within the fifty-six year old Swedenborg, became "for hatching ripe" on the night after Easter, April 6-7, 1744.

He had been reading about the miracles Moses performed, and was questioning the logic of the mechanisms involved. He smiled to himself and noted in his journal that "angels and God reveal themselves to shepherds, but never to the philosopher,"[18] such as himself, who is so easily ensnared in his own intellectual minutiae. He then went to sleep. . . .

> . . . At about 12:00, 1:00 or 2:00 in the night a strong shuddering came over me from head to foot, with a thundering noise as if many winds beat together, and shook me. . . . I found that something holy was upon me. . . . (*JD* 51,52)

He found himself prostrate, his hands clasped in prayer. He experienced a vision of Jesus, instructing him to redirect the course of his life. It was a compelling event:

> From that day I gave up the study of all worldly science, and laboured in spiritual things. . . . The Lord opened my eyes . . . so that in the middle of the day I could see into the other world, and in a state of perfect wakefulness converse with angels and spirits. (*Docs.* I, p. 35-36)

Swedenborg devoted the rest of his life, over a quarter century, to "spiritual things," writing volume upon volume of visionary theology. He published in Latin, at his own expense, signing most of the books simply, "A Servant of the Lord." Throughout, he maintained the methodical, analytical approach which had been the hallmark of his "worldly science."

What is to be made, however, of Swedenborg's tranformation experience? Had this disciplined scientist simply gone too far, and fallen victim to his own delusions?

Swedenborg recognized the magnitude of his claims:

> I am well aware that many will say that no one can talk to spirits and angels ... that it is a fantasy, that I invent it to gain credence for my writings. ... But by all this I am not deterred; for I have seen, I have heard, and I have felt. (AC 68)

An important insight into what Swedenborg "saw," "heard" and "felt" occurs in the writings of the late psychologist, Dr. Carl G. Jung, who was quite familiar with Swedenborg's career:

> I admire Swedenborg as a great scientist and a great mystic at the same time. His life and work has always been of great interest to me, and I read seven fat volumes of his writings when I was a medical student.[19]

In another context, Jung proposed that visionary experiences (such as those of Swedenborg and Blake) are not to be automatically dismissed as symptoms of insanity, for they can be remarkable breakthroughs to the deepest strata of human awareness:

> Too few people have experienced the divine image as the innermost possession of their own souls. Christ only meets them from without, never from within the soul ... (for) they cannot see to what extent the equivalent images are lying dormant in their own unconscious.
>
> The believer should not boggle at the fact that there are *somnia a Deo missa* (dreams sent by God) and illuminations of the soul which cannot be traced back to external causes. ... The soul must contain in itself the faculty of relationship to God, i.e., a <u>correspondence</u>, otherwise a connection could never come about. *This* <u>correspondence</u> *is, in psychological terms, the archetype of the God-image.*
>
> [Extra emphases mine] *Psychology and Alchemy*, pp. 10-13[20]

It was precisely this concept of "correspondence," the powerful links inherent in the "images lying dormant in the unconscious," that gave Swedenborg his key to the soul and formed the core of his theological writings. What he had not found by peeling back the tissues of cadavers, he would now discover, wonderously alive, by peeling back the layers of his own psyche.

In seeking the meanings of his dreams, Swedenborg had noticed that literal, physical images seemed to have deeper, psychological meanings. For example, when he was approaching a crisis, and dreamt of being in danger of falling into a deep abyss, it was his mental balance, not his physical agility, which was being represented. He began to recognize that his inner awareness, his soul, was writing these dramas to tell him something of importance. She was communicating in her own powerful image-language, with a vocabulary so bizarre that it defied rational analysis, yet seemed to convey its meanings at a deeper, more direct level of awareness.

Swedenborg set out to understand this image-language and how it worked.

He gained direct access to this image-language of "correspondences," this "stuff as dreams are made on," in the visions he continued to experience until the end of his life. Most occurred while he was fully awake, others in a hypnogogic state midway between sleep and wakefulness. Some were out-of-body experiences, in which his perceptions were "more acutely sensitive than ever in physical wakefulness."[21] He had discovered an inner arena, where transient external thoughts are stilled, and the deepest levels of the psyche can unfold themselves; and where, as Swedenborg noted: "angels and spirits can be seen ... heard, and remarkably, touched."[22]

Drawing open the curtain of the psyche, he set free her *dramatis personae*. He saw, heard and felt their living presence; and discovered that "all the world's a stage" in this mental proscenium—that the realities of the physical world are re-cast by the psyche into their corresponding spiritual roles:

> *The visible universe is nothing else than a theatre representative of the Lord's Kingdom.* (AC 3483)

To which Blake would later add:

> *There Exist in that Eternal World the Permanent Realities of Every Thing we see reflected in this Vegetable Glass of Nature.* (VLJ, p. 69; E.555)

Swedenborg spent years compiling lexicons of the image-

Blake, *Songs of Innocence* 25 (detail)

language of the "Eternal World," tracing the correspondences between the "Permanent Realities" of the soul and their reflections in "this Vegetable Glass of Nature." His former zeal for studying natural phenomena Swedenborg would now apply to spiritual phenomena by deciphering "correspondences"—"representations of spiritual and heavenly things in natural things" (*TCR*, 204).

Swedenborg proposed that correspondences operate through built-in channels within the psyche, which react to our perceptions of the physical world. Every aspect of creation—sun and stars, earth and air, fire and water, minerals and plants, birds, beasts, creeping things, and other people—each of these triggers a specific resonance somewhere deep within us, beneath the surface of ordinary awareness. Through these "correspondences" the natural world strikes specific keys, which pluck specific strings, that play emotionally-charged notes within the chambers of the mind.

The music plays on, usually at a volume below perception, but affecting the tempo and rhythm of our actions. It reveals itself when the noisy chatter of the intellect is stilled—in dreams and visions, and in seemingly inexplicable responses to nature: a rapturous sensation when we witness the flight of a butterfly or a richly-hued sunset; a sense of loathing triggered by a crawling spider or winter darkness. We respond to each of these quite differently, almost out of reflex, as if they corresponded to different parts of ourselves.

The composer and conductor of this inner symphony is the human Imagination (i.e., the image-making faculty), which links each individual to all of creation through correspondences. Swedenborg's writings translated the scores of these symphonies of the Imagination into more accessible formats; and as such they have been magnets to artists and writers such as Blake. The 1980 Nobel Laureate Poet, Czeslaw Milosz, heralded Swedenborg's unique contribution to artists:

In effect, his system constitutes a kind of "meta-aesthetics"....If Swedenborg did not glorify art, he nonetheless effected a shift from object to subject, whereby the role of the artist became exalted, something readily seized upon by Blake.

[For Swedenborg] the visible world is merely a reflection of the spiritual world, everything perceived on Earth by the five senses is a "correspondence," an equivalent of a given state in the spiritual realm....That some flowers, beasts, trees, landscapes, human faces are beautiful and others ugly derives from the fact that they are spiritual values....Here Swedenborg is heir to the medieval, Platonic-inspired axiom, "as above, so below," which held that *the whole of creation was one of the two languages in which God spoke to man—the other was Holy Writ.* [Emphasis mine][23]

"Holy Writ," the Bible—that was the arena for Swedenborg's theological triumph. He had studied the Bible since childhood; and, as he noted on the night of his transformative vision, the literal text of the Bible often seemed illogical, unrealistic, only acceptable by an act of faith. For example, how could God separate light from dark before he created the sun and other sources of illumination? If this compendium of Judeo-Christian beliefs is truly the Word of God, ought it not to make sense? His intellect could never resolve this puzzle.

After he "gave up the study of all wordly science," Swedenborg began to re-read the Bible in his visionary state. He then recognized that many passages are written in an image-language similar to that of dreams and visions—that the Bible contains a spiritual subtext, written in "correspondences":

The spiritual sense of the Word is not that meaning which shines forth from the literal text when one is studying and explaining the Word to confirm some dogma of the church... The Spiritual sense does not appear in the literal text; it is within it, as the soul is within the body, as thought is in the eyes, and as love is in the face. (*SS* 5)

Since the Word interiorly is spiritual and celestial, therefore it is written in pure correspondences.... It is holy in every sentence, in every word, sometimes in the very letters. Therefore the Word conjoins man to the Lord and opens heaven. (*SS* 8,3)

Swedenborg is making a subtle, but important distinction:

For Swedenborg . . . The holiness of the Bible . . . is in its very imagery.

The holiness of the Bible—which he devoutly believed to be the Word of God—is in neither its literal narrative nor its moral lessons, but in the very nature of its imagery. Like the soul-revealing imagery of dreams, the words and images of the Bible are correspondences—representations of inner development which trigger direct channels into the subconscious. As such, the Bible is truly a transcultural, spiritual guide, which "conjoins man to the Lord and opens" the heavens within each individual psyche.

Swedenborg was not alone in this belief. For centuries Jewish Kabbalism has viewed the Torah (Five Books of Moses) as an outward vessel of history and law housing an inner flame which illuminates the bridge between human consciousness and its divine origins. The Torah, therefore, is sacred down to the very shape and number of its flame-crowned, Hebrew letters. There is a similar sense of exegesis in the *Epistle to the Hebrews*, and, as Milosz noted, in the Neoplatonic tradition.

One must turn to the writings of Blake, however, to find the clearest reflection of Swedenborg's thoughts:

> Why is the Bible more Entertaining & Instructive than any other book. Is it not because (it is) addressed to the Imagination, which is the Spiritual Sensation. . . .[24]
> The Hebrew Bible & the Gospel of Jesus are not Allegory but Eternal Vision or Imagination of All that Exists. . . . Fable or Allegory are a totally distinct & inferior kind of Poetry. Vision or Imagination is a representation of what Eternally Exists. Really & Unchangeably. (*VLJ*, p. 68; E.554)

Blake was convinced that "The Old and New Testaments are the Great Code of Art,"[25] and strove to incorporate a biblical style of correspondences in his own "prophetic books." For Swedenborg, the Bible was the great code of the art of living. In seeking its hidden meanings, he created his own monumental legacy of writings, including *Arcana Coelestia* (1749-56), his eight-volume study of correspondences in Genesis and Exodus, and his detailed exegesis of the Book of Revelation, *Apocalypse Explained* (1757-59) and *Apocalypse Revealed* (1766).

As he continued to explore "the things which lie deeply concealed in the Word of God,"[26] Swedenborg began to realize that the channels of correspondences can operate as two-way streets: Just as particular images from the physical world can trigger specific responses deep within the psyche, so too, deeply felt images within the psyche can trigger our responses to, and perceptions of, the physical world. In Blake's terms: "The Suns Light when he unfolds it/Depends on the Organ that beholds it" (*GP* frontis.; E.260).

Swedenborg recognized to what a large extent we each live in a mind-made universe of our own; how our deeply-felt needs and beliefs color and fill in the details of the world we each experience:

> Everything that happens or emerges in the outer, or natural, person, happens or emerges from the inner, or spiritual. . . . For whatever a person earnestly gives his mental attention becomes, so to speak, present to him. (*HH* 92, 196)

This recognition of how inner needs can create perceived outer realities helped Swedenborg address the question of an afterlife. He could not accept the mechanistic model of eternity advocated by his Christian contemporaries: a Day of Judgment, when the deceased are assembled like scientific specimens, their moral balance-sheets weighed and measured, and their souls dispatched to either devilish tormentors or angelic choirs.

Through his understanding of correspondences, Swedenborg saw how people will often create their own living heaven or hell by projecting into their environment their own personal angels or demons. In Swedenborg's holistic vision of existence, these psychological realities persist after death:

> When a person dies, he simply crosses from one world to another. . . . All of his intentions and loves remain with him after death. . . . He leaves nothing behind except his physical body. (*HH* 445,547,461)

Swedenborg envisioned the afterlife not as an end product, but as a process—a process of psychological clarification and self-discovery. The external circumstances and social masks worn on earth disappear, and each person is freed to create new circumstances which can best fulfill his or her deepest inner needs. Inner and outer realities continue to correspond, but in much more precise ways:

> Once a spirit is in the state proper to his inward concerns . . . he is acting on the basis of what really belongs to

him. If he was inwardly involved in something good in the world, he then behaves wisely—more wisely, in fact, than he did in the world, because he is released from his ties with a body and therefore from those things that darken and, so to speak, cloud things over.

On the other hand, if he was involved in something wicked in the world, he then behaves crazily—more crazily, in fact, than he did in the world, because he is in freedom and is not repressed. (HH 505)

Swedenborg described these resulting conditions—the state of heightened wisdom, and that of profound insanity—in the traditional terms, "heaven" and "hell." These are not physical places, however, they are *states*, outer circumstances which are the crystallizations of corresponding inner needs.

For example, someone who has been driven by a lifelong need for ego-satisfaction will "behave crazily," like a starved cur in a butcher shop, once freed of all social and legal restraints. In the totally psychological medium of the afterlife, these inner needs continue to project outward, creating a mental environment in which to enact their ends. This is the state Swedenborg called "hell." It is a mind-made hell, born of oneself, rather than of Divine judgment:

> The evil within a person is hell within him. . . . And after death, his greatest desire is to be where his own evil is. . . . Consequently, the person himself, not the Lord, casts himself into hell. (HH 547)

The hell Swedenborg visualized is somewhat akin to a prison for the criminally insane without guards or supervisors. Each of the inmates is free to act upon his or her prevailing drives. In the economy of this state, no devils are needed, since the perpetrators are each other's victims. This hell is not simply a Dante's *Inferno* minus its cloven-hoofed demons; it is a mind-made reality, the collective projection of like-minded people.

This hell corresponds to the psycho-logics of daily realities: It is a hell because it is a state of endless striving after meaningless, selfish goals, and never attaining them. It is a hell of mutually thwarting, unchecked egos. It is a hell, the worst hell, because it is the state of ultimate aloneness, of being cut off, wanting no one and being unwanted.

Swedenborg envisioned heaven as an opposite, but comparable correspondence to mind-made realities. He did not share his contemporaries' image of a dull and pious heaven, populated with android Christian angels forever recycling top hits from the hymnals of their favorite earthly churches. Swedenborg saw heaven as an active state of affirmation, a magnifying mirror of the earthly joys of exchanging love, sharing wisdom, and exercising one's most cherished talents through useful deeds.

"There is no happiness in life apart from activity," Swedenborg wrote; "praising and honoring God is not the right kind of active life, for God has no need of praise and honor. He rather wants people to perform useful deeds" (HH 403-04).

This focus on "useful deeds" over formal worship is central to Swedenborg's theology. The need to perform useful acts for others, rather than the need to perform prescribed church rituals, is the truest correspondence to the state of heaven:

> Heaven is in man, and people who have heaven in themselves come into heaven. . . . It includes all people who live in the good of charity in accord with their own religious persuasion. (HH 319,328)

This "heaven," this state experienced by "all who live in the good of charity in accord with their own religious persuasion," is predicated on transcultural psychological realities rather than on religious doctrine, and is decidedly pluralistic. It is a conceptual cousin of another, "self-evident Truth" born of the Age of Reason—"that all men are created equal, that they are endowed by their Creator with certain inalienable Rights . . . Life, Liberty, and the Pursuit of Happiness." Swedenborg's vision of heaven is a similar celebration of individual freedom, of the inalienable right of each individual to shape his or her own destiny; and, since all outward forms in this mind-made heaven correspond to their inward meanings, Swedenborg visualized a composite representation of heaven in the form of a "Grand Man," an emblem of his conviction that:

> God is very man. (DLW 11)

"God became as we are that we may be as he is," Blake echoed in the pages of the first "illuminated" books he created with his own hands.[27] This refrain continued throughout his works, and into the verses of his late, unfinished *Everlasting Gospel*:

Thou art a Man   God is no more
Thy own humanity learn to adore.
                    (EG k:71-72; E.520)

Or, in Swedenborg's words:

Love is the life of Man. . . . and the Lord, because
he is Life itself, is Love itself. *(DLW 1,4)*

In 1825, the critic, Henry Crabb Robinson, to whom Blake
had acknowledged his debt to Swedenborg as a "divine
teacher," asked Blake to define the divinity of Jesus. "He is
the only God," Blake replied, then added: "And so am I, and
so are you."[28]

"God is very man." Perhaps that is Swedenborg's and
Blake's shared answer to the question "What is Man!" which
Blake had posed beneath his engraving of a sleeping, human-
faced chrysalis.

Swedenborg's recorded answers to this question reflect his
transformation from the days when he was a young scientist,
and wrote:

What is man?. . . . Behold and see how small a speck
thou art in the system of heaven and earth.
                    (PRIN II, 3:1,p.239)

After his many years of visionary experiences, Swedenborg
reversed this cosmology:

Man is both a heaven and an earth in microcosm. *(HH 90)*

Experience can bring wisdom, but it has its price. . . .

IV. "THE PRICE OF EXPERIENCE"
Swedenborg's Final Years

What is the price of Experience
do men buy it for a song
Or Wisdom for a dance in the street!
No it is bought with the price
Of all that a man hath. . .
        Blake *(FZ II:11-13; E.325)*[29]

The last years of Swedenborg's life had a curious twist.
After reaching the age of seventy, Swedenborg would
have been content to continue his established practice of
publishing his theological writings anonymously through
printing houses in Holland and England (where he enjoyed
a freedom of the press lacking in his native Sweden). He had
little need of personal fame; but, in 1759, he was thrust into
public attention because of several demonstrations of his
clairvoyant talents.

On one such occasion, in July 1759, while dining at the
home of the Gothenburg merchant, William Castel, Swedenborg suddenly saw a detailed vision of a fire which had broken
out in Stockholm—a city three hundred miles away. After
a few troubled hours, Swedenborg reported that the conflagra-
tion had been safely extinguished just before it had ignited
his own house in Stockholm. Two days later, a messenger
arrived in Gothenburg and described the fire exactly as
Swedenborg had seen it in his vision.[30] Because of this and
other similar episodes—one of which involved the Swedish
royal family—Swedenborg's fame spread through Europe: He
was even interviewed by an envoy sent by Emanuel Kant.[31]

As a result of this attention, people began to identify this
clairvoyant Swede as the author of certain anonymous books
of visionary theology; and fame brought its price.

When Swedenborg's books became better known in Sweden, a group of conservative local clergymen condemned his
ideas as heresy, and demanded a trial. They made him an
object of public ridicule, and conspired to confine him to a
mental asylum. Upon their insistance, the Swedish Royal
Council issued a decree on April 26, 1770, in which it "totally
condemned, rejected, and forbade the theological doctrines
in the writings of Swedenborg," and prohibited the import
of his books.[32]

So much for the Age of Reason in Sweden.

Swedenborg left his homeland, but continued writing and
publishing abroad. In September, 1772, he arrived in London,
where young William Blake was copying plaster-cast fragments of classical sculptures at the Pars School. Six months
later Swedenborg saw a vision of his own death, and the
vision came true.

Blake probably was unaware of this precognitive vision
until several years later. His own link with Swedenborg,
however, was to be reinforced by another of Swedenborg's
visions—one which was not of death, but, instead, concerning the year of Blake's own birth.

V. WILLIAM BLAKE (1757-1827)
A "Blake-smith" Who Would Forge a New Jerusalem

The Eternal Female groaned! it was heard over all the
*   Earth. . . .*
In her trembling hands she took the new born terror
*   howling. . . .*
The fire, the fire, is falling!
Look up! look up! O citizens of London.

Blake, *A Song of Liberty* (MHH 25; E.44)

Blake's "self-portrait"; *Milton, a Poem 29*

"The new born terror," William Blake, entered the mortal world as the son of a London hosier, James Blake, on November 28, 1757.

In that same year, a "New Jerusalem" was born in the visions of Emanuel Swedenborg. Several times in 1757, he experienced powerful visions of cosmic events—a re-ordering of the heavens, and a dawning of a new age of spiritual liberty—happenings which mirrored the visions of John in Revelations XXI:

> And I saw a new heaven and a new earth. . .
> And I, John, saw the holy city, the New Jerusalem, descending from God out of heaven, prepared as a bride adorned for her husband. . . .
> And he that sat on the throne said: Behold, I make all things new.

Swedenborg adopted the image of a "New Jerusalem" as emblematic of a new age of spiritual liberation from the mind-limiting dogmas of the past:

> The state of the world will be precisely what it was before . . . as to outward form. . . . but men of the church will be in a freer state of thinking on matters of faith. . . . Because spiritual liberty has been restored. . . . He can better perceive inner truth, if he so desires. (*LJ* 73-4)
> Now it is allowable to enter intelligently into the mysteries of faith. (*TCR* 508)

Blake, who was well acquainted with Swedenborg's writings concerning 1757,[33] and who was endowed with a singular affinity for the miraculous, no doubt felt a strong identification with this new age of spiritual/psychological awakening, which, like himself, was born in 1757. Blake possibly saw in Swedenborg's 1757 visions something quite real, which is not readily apparent at first glance.

It would be logical to dismiss Swedenborg's 1757 New Jerusalem visions as his own deeply-felt personal experience, which he projected out of all proportion, and claimed to signify the advent of a new age. Historical evidence points to few cosmic changes occurring in 1757, other than the Vatican's lifting its ban on books about the rotation of the earth. If anything, history would indicate a source of Swedenborg's apocalyptic visions in the famed 1755 earthquake which destroyed Lisbon and claimed upwards of 40,000 lives in the ensuing tidal wave, week-long fires and panic. Because the earthquake occurred on All Saints Day while most of the population was attending church, and because its rumblings were felt from Scotland to Asia Minor, it was seen by many as the beginning of a Last Judgment. Even that most reasonable man, Voltaire, wrote his pessimistic satire, *Candide*, in response to the Lisbon cataclysm.

Swedenborg's 1757 visions, however, dealt with something far more subtle and far-reaching. In his own words: "The state of the world will be precisely what it was before . . . as to outward form" (*LJ* 73). According to his paradigm of correspondences, the outward manifestations will result from their germination in human thoughts and desires. The new age he saw unfolding was a psychological process: In 1757, percolating within the minds of intellectual giants and commonfolk, were the seeds of the great political, social, industrial, commercial, scientific, and artistic revolutions of the late eighteenth century. When these thoughts later became physical realities, such as the American and French Revolutions, they did, in fact, initiate a new age of liberty by dramatically changing the institutions of the past. These apocalyptic changes had existed in the preceding decades as antecedent thoughts in the minds of those bold enough to "enter intelligently into the mysteries of faith." It was almost as if Swedenborg had tapped into the collective psychology of 1757, and had seen its essence represented, through the psychological image-language of correspondences, in the form of apocalyptic events re-ordering the heavens.

Blake seized the meaning of Swedenborg's New Jerusalem visions at a critical point in his own life.

Blake, in the late 1780s, saw many of these revolutionary outward manifestations taking place before his eyes. He seized upon the meaning of Swedenborg's New Jerusalem visions at a critical point in his own life; and during this period of his most intense direct ties with Swedenborg's writings and Swedenborgian circles, Blake formulated his own life-mission—to become a champion of this new age as a spiritual artist. He determined his own "great task": "to

open the Eternal Worlds, to open the immortal Eyes / of Man inwards" (J 5:17-19; E.147); and, as he later explained, he felt himself to be properly qualified for fulfilling this "great task":

> The Thing I have most at Heart! more than life or all That seems to make life comfortable without, Is the Interest of True Religion and Science. . . .[34]

> I am not ashamed afraid or adverse to tell you what Ought to be Told. That I am under the direction of Messengers from Heaven Daily & Nightly. . . .

> If we fear to do the dictates of our Angels & tremble at the Tasks set before us. If we refuse to do Spiritual Acts because of Natural Fears and Natural Desires! Who can describe the dismal torments of such a state!—I too well remember the threats I have heard!—If you who are organized by Divine Providence for Spiritual communion Refuse & Bury your Talent in Earth even tho you should want Natural Bread, Sorrow & Desperation pursues you thro life! & after death shame and confusion of face to Eternity.

> (Letter to T. Butts, Jan. 10, 1803; E.723-24)[35]

Such threats of "Sorrow & Desperation," "shame and confusion," delivered by his messengers from heaven, would, no doubt, spur Blake on to the great task assigned him by Divine Providence. His mission, however, might have been a response to a more gentle prodding from Swedenborg's writings. The New Jerusalem of Swedenborg's visions was a potential energy existing in a spiritual/psychological dimension; to further her manifestations as kinetic energy in the world of men would require the active intervention by:

> . . . A man, who is not only able to receive these teachings in his understanding, but is also able to publish them by the press. (*TCR* 779)

Swedenborg met this task, writing and publishing many thick volumes of these new age teachings, at his own expense. Blake would have followed this pattern gladly, but he faced a significant obstacle. Like Swedenborg, Blake would find no help from the established publishers, and would have to become his own publisher; but unlike the independently wealthy Swedenborg, Blake was rarely in possession of discretionary funds. He and his wife were often at the brink of absolute poverty, and survived through the benevolence of a few patrons, such as the middle-level civil servant, Thomas Butts, to whom the preceding letter was written.

It was clear to Blake that: "I must create a System, or be enslav'd by another Man's" (*J* 10:20; E.153). Around 1788 he devised an ingenious appropriate technology which freed him from the publishers' monopoly of letterpress equipment. Using acid-resistant varnish, he painted the words and designs of his illuminated poems directly onto copper printing plates, in mirror-image. He poured acid onto the plates, etching away the unpainted areas. The result was a relief-plate with raised-up areas where he had painted the words and designs. Unlike intaglio engraved plates, which require the pressure of a heavy press to lift ink out of the incised lines and onto printing paper, Blake's relief-plates could be printed on the simple, wooden proofing-press in his home workshop. He had created a medium for combining poetry and visual art which would last him a lifetime.[36]

Perhaps Blake's new system had been born of necessity; Blake, himself, attributed the discovery to the spirit of his departed brother, Robert, who "in a vision of the night ... stood before him, and revealed the wished-for secret."[37] It is significant, nonetheless, that Blake devised this system during his formative period of greatest involvement with Swedenborg's writings, and that the early works he created with this system are deeply Swedenborgian in both intent and imagery.[38] In many ways Blake's discovery of both the mission and method of his life's work seem to answer the call for a man who could receive the teachings of a New Jerusalem and "publish them by the press."

In the early 1790s, after Blake broke with the New Jerusalem Church, his printing method assumed a new metaphor. In *The Marriage of Heaven and Hell*, he proclaimed ironically: "I was in a Printing House in Hell & saw the method in which knowledge is transmitted from generation to generation ... (by) fire raging around & melting the metals into living fluids" (*MHH* 15; E.40). He deemed his fiery, acid-etching process "the infernal method," and mythologized it as a kind of alchemy—a physical transformation by purifying fires, which yields a spiritual transformation:

... This I shall do, by printing in the infernal method, with corrosives, which in Hell are salutary and medicinal, melting apparent surfaces away, and revealing the infinite which was hid.

If the doors of perception were cleansed everything would appear to man as it is: infinite. For man has closed himself up, till he sees all things thro' narrow chinks in his cavern.
(*MHH* 14; E.39)

Even in this context, Blake seems to echo Swedenborg, who wrote of "realities that exist in the spiritual world that ... can be seen by man when his internal sight is opened" (*AC* 1966); but, because of external concerns and dogmatic thinking, "there is no opening, for they obstruct and close the door, which cannot be opened by the Lord, but only by the man himself. ... The Lord continually entreats man to open the door to Him, as is plain from the Lord's words in Apocalypse (III:20): 'Behold I stand as the door and knock; if any hear my voice and open the door, I will come in to him' " (*DP* 119).

After *The Marriage of Heaven and Hell*, Blake's references to Swedenborg are few, and are generally quite positive.[39] The self-appointed mission Blake has assumed before declaring "opposition" to Swedenborg's writings continued as a strong undercurrent in his prophetic books of the 1790s,[40] and resurfaced in his nineteenth-century works. In the Preface to his 1804-08, *Milton, a Poem in 2 Books*, Blake states: "When the new age is at leisure to Pronounce, all will be set right." He then re-affirms his own role in bringing about this new age:

I will not cease from Mental Fight,
Nor shall my Sword sleep in my hand:
Till we have built Jerusalem,
In Englands green & pleasant Land
(*M* Preface; E.95-96)

The mental fight to build Jerusalem in England's green and pleasant Land is told in the greatest work created by Blake's infernal method, titled *Jerusalem The Emanation of the Giant Albion* (1804-20).

Jerusalem is depicted on the bottom of the title page of this book in the form of a butterfly-winged woman, a prophetic fulfillment of the sleeping human-faced chrysalis of Blake's earlier "What is Man!" engraving (*GP* frontispiece). She too is asleep, since, like the New Jerusalem of Swedenborg's visions, she remains a dormant, radiant-winged essence not yet "for hatching ripe" into the mortal realm without active intervention. Her direct kinship with Swedenborg's New Jerusalem, the age in which "spiritual liberty has been restored" (*LJ* 74), is clearly indicated in Blake's definitions of his butterfly-winged Jerusalem:

Blake, *Jerusalem* title page

JERUSALEM IS NAMED LIBERTY
AMONG THE SONS OF ALBION
(*J* 26; E.171)

The form is the Divine Vision. . .
This is Jerusalem in every Man. . .
And Jerusalem is called Liberty among
   the Children of Albion
                (*J* 54:2,3,5; E.203)[41]

In Blake's mythos, Jerusalem, the not so distant avatar of Swedenborg's new Jerusalem, becomes the "Emanation" (anima) of Albion,[42] a primordial Giant whose name was synonymous with England, the island he conquered. Blake gives Albion an additional meaning, that of the Universal Man. Albion is like Adam Kadmon, the "Universal Man" of the Kabbalah, as Blake noted in a chapter of the poem addressed "To The Jews": "You have a tradition, that Man contained anciently in his mighty limbs all things in Heaven & Earth." (*J* 27; E.171) Blake does not acknowledge the more direct source of his Universal Man—Swedenborg's image of the "Grand Man," "the microcosm of heaven and earth" (*HH* 90).

These Swedenborgian connections unfold in the central drama of the poem—the struggle to awaken Jerusalem and unite her with Albion: in other words, to bring about the era of the New Jerusalem in "England's green & pleasant Land." Albion, however, has himself fallen into a "sleep of death":

England! awake! awake! awake!
   Jerusalem thy Sister calls!
Why wilt thou sleep the sleep of death?
   And close her from thy ancient walls. (*J* 77 b:1-4; E.233)

Awake! Awake Jerusalem! O lovely Emanation of Albion
Awake and overspread all Nations as in Ancient Time
For lo! the Night of Death is past and the Eternal Day
Appears upon our Hills: Awake Jerusalem, and come away.
                (*J* 97:1-4; E.256)

Despite these calls, Albion cannot awaken to receive his Emanation, his spiritual liberation, because his "doors of perception" have been locked by Locke, Newton, and Bacon, the materialistic propagators of the Age of Reason:

Albion & Jerusalem; *Jerusalem* **14 (detail)**

. . . O Divine Spirit sustain me on thy wings!
That I may awaken Albion from his long & cold repose.
For Bacon & Newton sheathd in dismal steel their terrors
*   hang*
Like iron scourges over Albion. . . .

I turn my eyes to the Schools and Universities of Europe
And there behold the Loom of Locke whose Woof rages dire
Washd by the Water-wheels of Newton, black the cloth
In heavy wreaths folds over every Nation; cruel Works
Of many Wheels I view, wheel without wheel, with cogs
*   tyrannic*
Moving by compulsion each other:. . . .

(J 15:9-12,14-19; E.159)

"Cruel Works of many Wheels . . . with cogs tyrannic /
Moving by compulsion each other"—the hardware of the
Industrial Revolution and its birth in the software of the Age
of Reason, enfolding Europe in deadly sleep under heavy
wreaths of black cloth. The image is reminiscent of Swedenborg's dream about a "machine set in motion by a wheel,"
with spokes that entangled him and carried him up until "it
was impossible to escape" (*JD* 18;p.5). As Swedenborg warned
at the height of his scientific career: "the intelligence of the
soul is not mechanical . . . he who thinks he can possess any
wisdom without a knowledge and veneration of the deity
has not even a particle of wisdom" (*PRIN* I, 1:1; pp. 28,35).

Both Swedenborg and Blake know that the places to gain
this wisdom, the sources of spiritual/psychological awakening, are not to be found in either material progress or in
church dogma, but within the recesses of one's own psyche
(within Albion, the Universal Man), for here is contained a
reflection of the Eternal World.

Who is to be the champion, the standard-bearer of the New
Jerusalem, able to enter this Eternal World to rescue the
dormant Jerusalem and restore her to Albion? Who can kindle
a light bright enough to awaken Albion from his own deadly
sleep—a light bright enough to re-enlighten the men of the
Enlightenment?

In the frontispiece of *Jerusalem*, Blake depicts this hero
carrying a bright lantern into a Gothic portal. [see illustration
on page 37]. He is "Los," the blacksmith, the archetypal
poet-artist, and Blake's personification of the Imagination.
This light-bearing champion's name seems to be an anagram
of "sol" (the sun); and since he is portrayed wearing Blake's
own hat and coat, one might detect an autobiographical pun
in that Los, the blacksmith, is very much a "Blake-smith."[43]

Blake's self-portrait as Los represents the poet-blacksmith
entering a dark portal into the "interiors of Albion's Bosom"
(the universal subconscious) to restore Albion's Emanation,
Jerusalem (spiritual liberty); for as was proclaimed over the
portal of the New Jerusalem church which Blake himself
entered in 1789; "Now it is allowable to enter intelligently
into the mysteries of faith" (*TCR* 509) Thus, Los began his
quest:

> *Fearing that Albion should turn his back against the Divine*
> *   Vision*
> *Los took his globe of fire to search the interiors of Albion's*
> *   Bosom. . . .*
> *The articulations of a mans soul.* (*J* 45:2-3,10; E.194)

Los' "globe of fire" can illuminate "the articulations of a
mans soul" because Los is the Imagination, the image-making faculty; and as such, Los is the master of correspondences.
He is the intuitive center of consciousness, conversant in
the psyche's own language—the image-language of correspondences. He is the poet-artist, guided by this same image-
language in "the Great Code of Art," the Old and New Testaments (*Laoc*; E.274). He is the blacksmith-alchemist,
smelting the crude ore of perceived realities, and reworking
the purified essence on his anvil into Eternal Realities
through the medium of correspondences. As he searches "the
interiors of Albion's Bosom" (the universal subconscious)

Los & his Spectre; *Jerusalem* 6 (detail)

Los forges pathways of correspondences to the angels of the brightest heavens, and to the most terrifying creature of the mind-made hells—the Spectre, each person's own black and opaque inner demon.

As master of correspondences, Los, the Imagination, is the human faculty most qualified to awaken Albion and to forge the new age of Albion's dormant Emanation, Jerusalem. Los can find the way through the "articulations of a mans soul" because within the chambers of Los' own halls, in the "Eternal World of Imagination," are the "Permanent Realities (correspondences) of Every Thing we see reflected in This Vegetable Glass of Nature":[44]

> *All things acted on Earth are seen in the bright Sculptures of*
> *Los's Halls & every Age renews its powers from these Works*
> *With every pathetic story possible to happen from Hate or*
> *Wayward Love & every sorrow & distress is carved here*
> *Every Affinity of Parents Marriages & Friendships are here*
> *In all their various combinations wrought with wondrous Art*
> *All that can happen to Man in his pilgrimage of seventy years*
> *Such is the Divine Written Law of Horeb & Sinai:*
> *And such the Holy Gospel of Mount Olivet & Calvary.*
>
> (*J* 16:61-69; E.161)

Blake's "bright Sculptures of Los' Halls" are a poetic reincarnation of Swedenborg's paradigm of correspondences.

Such is the redeeming power of Imagination, custodian of the archetypal images from which art is made.

The "bright Sculptures of Los's Halls" are the poetic reincarnation of Swedenborg's paradigm of correspondences—particularly since both the authors define the content of these psychological repositories as both "all things acted on Earth" and all things of "Divine Written Law (&) The Holy Gospel" (Old and New Testaments). Los' Halls are the seat of the soul, which Swedenborg had sought for so many years; and they are the *sanctum sanctorium*, the "awful cave," in which Blake learned the "wond'rous art of writing."

VI. "BRIGHT SCULPTURES OF LOS' HALLS"
Blake's Visionary Arts

> *Reader! lover of books! lover of heaven,*
> *And of that God from who all books are given,*
> *Who in mysterious Sinais awful cave*
> *To Man the wond'rous art of writing gave,*
> *Again he speaks in thunder and fire!*
> *Thunder of Thought, & flames of fierce desire:*
> *Even from the depths of Hell his voice I hear,*
> *Within the unfathomed caverns of my Ear.*
> *Therefore I print; nor vain my types shall be:*
> *Heaven, Earth & Hell, henceforth shall live in harmony.*
>
> — Blake, *Jerusalem* (3:1-10; E.145)

William Blake's poetic and visual imagery has an uncanny impact; it "speaks in thunder and fire," even when its meanings elude rational understanding. It resonates "within the unfathomed caverns of [the] Ear," because it is patterned on the "bright Sculptures of Los's Halls"—the archetypal imagery of correspondences. Blake's unique gift was his ability to think, write and draw in correspondences, the medium of the Imagination—a spiritual medium for conveying spiritual truths directly into the spiritual receptors of the reader or viewer.

Like Swedenborg, Blake gained direct access to this imagery through vision; and many of Blake's works seem very much like visions or dreams. It is often difficult to follow his story-lines, precisely because his stories are not linear; nor is his time sequential, nor his space geometrical. Cosmic phenomena, political events, and Blake's personal concerns shift abruptly from one to another. Characters change form, molt, merge, split, evolve and devolve. Everything seems to exist in a universe of liquid time, space, and event; however, as Blake asserted in the introduction to his poem, *Jerusalem*, there is nothing random or arbitrary in his art:

> *Every word and every letter is studied and put into its fit place: the terrific numbers are reserved for the terrific parts— the mild & gentle, for the mild and gentle parts . . . all are necessary to each other. (J 3; E.146)*

"Every word and letter . . . in its fit place," as a vehicle for its inner meanings—this is precisely how Swedenborg described correspondences in the Bible:

> Such is the style of the Word that it is holy in every sentence, in every word, and sometimes in the very letters. Therefore the Word conjoins man to the Lord and opens heaven. (SS 3)

Creating an art form which could mirror the Bible's power to "conjoin man to the Lord and open heaven," was the consuming passion of William Blake, a man who subtitled his poem *Milton*: "To Justify the Ways of God to Men" (E.95). Blake saw himself as the artist-missionary of a new age, and was audacious enough to attempt the creation of its new illuminated bible, beginning with his "prophetic books" of the 1790s. His *The (First) Book of Urizen*, *The Book of Los*, and *The Book of Ahania* not only echo the narratives of The Book of Genesis and Book of Exodus, but even explicitly copy the two-column format of printed bibles from Blake's era.

Swedenborg's influences on the evolution of these prophetic books has been overlooked to a large extent by scholars who have focused on the Swedenborgian roots of Blake's works from earlier and later periods. Just as Blake had found a new poetic metaphor for his early engraved poems in Swedenborg's lexicons of correspondences, so too would he draw upon Swedenborg in creating a new poetic medium for his prophetic books.

Blake seems to have recognized a core achievement in Swedenborg's visions of heaven and hell which could serve as a model for a mythic new testament. To see this core, one must subject Swedenborg's heaven and hell to Blake's alchemical "infernal method," "to reveal the infinite which was hid." . . . Dissolve Swedenborg's theology in fiery

Satan; Blake's *Job* 6 (detail)

acid . . . Melt away all conventional terms, such as heaven and hell, good and evil . . . Etch down even further, melting away all references to the Lord and his holy Word . . . What precipitates out in adamant crystals is Swedenborg's finely detailed, kinetic sculptures of the human psyche, set in a high-relief landscape of a totally psychological universe.

Swedenborg himself was quite clear in defining his angels, heaven and hell as representations of the psyche, the spirit within man:

> The inside of a man, his spirit, is essentially an angel. . . . An angel is a perfect human form. (HH 314,73)
> In common with angels, man's inward elements are patterned after heaven. . . . Heaven, take as single whole, reflects a single person . . . In Revelation 21:17, this is described: "he measured the wall of holy Jerusalem, 144 cubits, the measure of a man—that is, of an angel." (HH 57,73)

Swedenborg's multi-hundred page descriptions of the daily life of heaven and hell are descriptions of the daily workings of mind. They form a vital almanac of the time, space, seasons, cosmology and geology, flora and fauna, and human inhabitants of a totally psychological universe. If man is heaven in microcosm—in fine print—then heaven and hell are the mind of man spelled out in upper-case bold type.

Blake easily adapted Swedenborg's almanac of the afterlife into a medium for his prophetic books—a totally psycho-logical art, based on the logic of the psyche. Within this new medium, Blake made his own unique achievement: the creation of a mythology for a new age. He peopled his psychological universe with mythic personifications of the functions of mind, archetypal beings called "Giant Forms." As Blake later explained about the figures of Moses and Abraham in one of his paintings: "The Persons Moses and Abraham are not meant here but the states signified by those names[;] the individuals being but representatives or Visions of those States" (VLJ p. 76; E.556).

Blake easily adapted Swedenborg's almanac of the afterlife into a new medium for his prophetic books—a totally psycho-logical art, based on the logic of the psyche.

Blake's "Giant Forms"—Tharmas, Urizen, Luvah, Los (Urthona); their Emanations: Enion, Ahania, Vala, and Enitharmon; and all their myriad offspring and hybrid mutations—these creatures do not exist in any lexicon of mythology, rather they are themselves the mythic lexicons of human existence. They are the "bright Sculptures of Los's Halls," and the distillates of biblical figures and inhabitants of

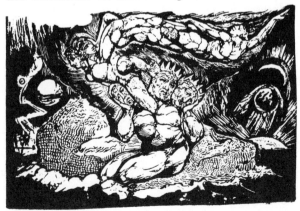

Hybrid mental being; *Jerusalem* 50 (detail)

Swedenborg's heaven and hell, filtered through the permeable membranes of Blake's Imagination.

In fashioning his epics of the Mental Wars of liberation waged by his Giant Forms, Blake drew upon Swedenborg as a textbook of the non-physical physics in a dimension created by and for psychological beings. The angels of Swedenborg's heaven exist in a universe where "Mental Things are alone Real,"[45] where psychological states are the building blocks of external environments:

> [Angels'] outward elements correspond to their inward ones. . . . The states of different things visible to their sight change . . . and choose a form that accords with the things within them. (*HH* 173,156)
> [For example,] when angels are at the peak of love, they are in light and warmth . . . surrounded by radiance. When they are at the bottom of the scale, they are in shade and cold. (*HH* 155)

It is this quality of mind-made light which illuminates Blake's illuminated poems. Like Swedenborg's angels, Blake's characters transform according to their inner states—they brighten into their lovely Emanations, or darken into their terrific Spectres. Their dramas unfold in the tinted gothic light of the "Land of Dreams"; in fact, some of Blake's figures are delineated with such thick lines around their musculature, that they, themselves, appear to be made of leaded elements from a stained glass window. Here again, "outward elements correspond to their inward ones."

The master of these correspondences, and hero of Blake's prophetic books is Los, the poet-blacksmith. In Blake's mythology, Los is one of the Four Zoas,[46] eternal beings who correspond to the fundamental aspects of man: Tharmas (Body), Urizen (Reason), Luvah (Emotions), and Los or Urthona (Imagination). The Zoas represent the cardinal points of the universe within Albion (the Universal Man) and Los sits in the northern, ruling position. Mental War erupts within Albion when the other Zoas try to usurp the rightful throne of Los (Imagination).

Blake usually portrays Los as a flame-enshrouded, red-haired,[47] naked youth, often armed with blacksmith's tools. On first impression, Blake seems to have cast Los in the outward form of a devil, yet Los is just the opposite: He represents the redeeming, spiritual faculty, Imagination.

This apparent paradox is resolved by viewing Los from the perspective of correspondences. His flames are not hell fire, they are an external manifestation of the "light and radiance" of his inner nature—like the auras depicted around Jesus, the Buddha, and other "enlightened" beings. And, as such, Los' attributes are patterned on Swedenborg's descriptions of the photo-dynamics and thermodynamics of a mind-made heaven:

> Heaven's light is not a natural light . . . it is a spiritual one. (*HH* 127) Heaven's Light is the Divine-True . . . This light varies according to [an angel's] acceptance of the Divine Truth from the Lord. . . . Light among angels corresponds to their intelligence and wisdom." (Ibid. 128,131)

Los, the Imagination, is the human faculty singularly adapted to perceiving "Divine Truth," and is therefore engulfed in light. Because he is the inner (spiritual) core of the psyche, Los is the embodiment of the innermost core of Swedenborg's heaven, the "celestial kingdom," and he is enshrouded with its special kind of "fiery" light:

> The light in the celestial kingdom [highest or innermost heaven] looks fiery, since the angels there accept light directly from the Lord as the sun. (*HH* 128)

Similarly, Los' flames and blacksmith's forge embody the psycho-logics of Swedenborg's heavenly thermodynamics— they correspond to the fiery intensity of Los' mission:

> A person is kindled and warmed in proportion to the extent and quality of his love. . . . That is why love and warmth in heaven correspond to each other. (*HH* 134,135)
> Heaven's warmth constitutes the life of an angel's intending, since heaven's warmth is the . . . Divine love. (Ibid. 136)

"Heaven's warmth constitutes . . . intending." Throughout Blake's poems, the artist-poet (in the form of Blake, or the blacksmith, Los) invokes the fiery implements of his spiritual "intention":

> *Bring me my Bow of burning gold:*
> *Bring me my Arrows of desire:*
> *Bring me my Spear: O clouds unfold!*
> *Bring me my Chariot of fire!* (M 1:9-12: E.95)

Los; Blake's *Book of Urizen* 18 (detail)

And, in the next stanza, Blake clearly states the goal of his fiery intention:

> *I will not cease from Mental Fight,*
> *Nor shall my Sword sleep in my hand:*
> *Till we have built Jerusalem,*
> *In Englands green & pleasant Land.* (Ibid.,1:13-16)

Since Los, the Imagination, is the most appropriate "mental warrior" to champion the New Jerusalem, he is clad in the armour of this crusade—he is light-enveloped and totally naked, as are the angels of Swedenborg's inmost heaven:

> The clothes angels wear correspond to their intelligence . . . The most intelligent have clothes that gleam as if aflame. The angels of the inmost heaven, though, are naked. (*HH* 178)

"The angels of the inmost heaven," the living powers at the core of the psyche, are naked truths. Blake concurred: "Art can never exist without Naked Beauty displayed. . . . The Eternal Body of Man is The Imagination [Los]" (*Laoc*; E.273-74).

Jerusalem attended & Vala; *Jerusalem* **46 (detail)**

Similarly, Blake depicted Jerusalem, that innermost of the inmost aspects of the psyche, as a lovely naked figure (sometimes with butterfly wings), and defined her in terms strikingly parallel to Swedenborg's vision of the gleaming light which clothes the angels in enlightenment:

> *In Great Eternity, every particular Form gives forth or*
> *Emanates*
> *Its own peculiar Light, & the Form is the Divine Vision*
> *And the Light is his Garment This is Jerusalem in every Man.*
> (*J* 54:1-3; E.203)

In contrast, Blake's earth goddess, Vala, is depicted veiled, since she is emblematic of those natural realities which can be an occluding veil over spiritual truths—a shell which is shattered on Los' forge, so that the inner light of correspondences can be revealed.

Jerusalem's champion, Los, plays a unique role in this cosmic scheme. He is Imagination, the ultimate power in a mind-made universe. As such, he can boast:

> *Both time and space obey my will.* (*M* 22:17; E.117)

Time and space obey Los' will in Blake's poems according to the principle governing heaven and hell in Swedenborg's Vision: "Outward elements correspond to their inward ones" (*HH* 173).

Both Blake and Swedenborg had confirmed this principle through their visionary experiences. The spaces they entered did not conform to any present Cartesian grids; for in a psychological universe, space is organic:

> *The Microscope knows not of this nor the Telescope. they*
> *alter*
> *The ratio of the Spectators organs but leave objects*
> *untouched*
> *For every Space larger than a red Globule of Mans blood*
> *Is visionary: and is created by the Hammer of Los*
> *And every Space smaller than a globule of Mans blood opens*
> *Into Eternity of which this vegetable Earth is but a shadow.*
> Blake (*M* 29:17-22; E.127)

Psychological space is fluid; it warps to correspond to its mental prototypes:

> This can be understood more clearly by considering a man's thoughts, in that spaces do not exist for them. For whatever a person earnestly gives his mental attention to becomes, so to speak, present to him. (*HH* 196)

This is the space which Swedenborg experienced in his visions of heaven: "Angels have no concept of place or space. . . . There are no spaces in heaven except states that correspond to inner ones" (*HH* 191, 193). Under these circumstances, the paranormal becomes the normal, and psychokinesis or mental teleportation are common occurrences:

> All journies in the spiritual world are simply changes of state . . . nearnesses are similarities, and distances, dissimilarities. . . . Consequently, people who are in dissimilar states are far apart. (*HH* 192-93)

With devastating poetic flair, Blake applied Swedenborg's model to the spaces of his own narrative of Eternal happenings: When Blake's Giant Forms argue, their "dissim-ilarities" of opinion cause a corresponding rending apart in the mountains of Eternity—a great hemorrhage in the vision-ary "Globule of Mans blood":

> Rage, fury, intense indignation
> In cataracts of fire blood and gall
> In whirlwinds of sulphurous smoke. . . .
> Sund'ring, dark'ning, thund'ring!
> Rent away with a terrible crash
> Eternity roll'd wide apart
> Wide asunder rolling
> Mountains all around
> Departing; departing; departing:
> Leaving ruinous fragments of life
> Hanging frowning cliffs & all between
> An ocean of voidness unfathomable.
> (Ur 4:45–5:11; E. 72-73)[48]

In the mind-shaped spaces of Blake's prophetic books and Swedenborg's heaven, thoughts can and do move mountains; "for whatever a person earnestly gives his mental attention to, becomes . . . present to him" (HH 196).

Psychological time is also a function of internal states; as Los declared: "Both Time and Space obey my Will."

Swedenborg showed that common sense demonstrates the mechanisms of mind-made time: "People are aware that time originates in states, because times . . . seem short when people are engaged in happy or pleasant affections, long when they are engaged in unpleasant or disagreeable ones" (HH 168). The same principle applies in the afterlife, but in a more pervasive manner: "Angels do not know what time is. . . . there are no years or days in heaven, but changes of state" (HH 163). In the eternal, timeless realm of heaven, the ticking of the clock corresponds to the tempo of the heart—time slows or quickens as feelings drop or rise.

Blake's alter ego, Los, is an extension of Swedenborg's paradigm of the heavenly pendulum: When Los is exercising his true talents, performing useful deeds as a spiritual poet-artist, time corresponds to his inner state of heaven, and his great task is accomplished in a densely packed instant—the creative flash:

> Every Time less than a pulsation of the artery
> Is equal in its period & value to Six Thousand Years.

> For in this Period the Poets Work is Done: and all Great
> Events of Time start forth & are conceivd in such a Period
> Within a Moment: a Pulsation of the Artery.
> (M 28:62–29:3; E.127)

When Los' arteries pulse to a different beat, time will as-sume a correspondingly altered tempo. In The Book of Uri-zen, when Los has captured his enemy, Urizen (Reason), and bound him in chains, Los is suddenly overcome with pity: "He saw Urizen deadly black/ In his chains bound, & Pity began" (13:50-51). As the space about them freezes into an image of Los' inner state, Los stands transfixed in time:

> Ages on ages rolld over them
> Cut off from life & light frozen
> Into horrible forms of deformity
> (Ur 13:41-43; E.77)

Los is no longer master of time and space. His inner state, "cut off from life & light," no longer corresponds to heaven. His inward realities externalize, "frozen into horrible forms of deformity," indicative of a state Swedenborg called "hell"—the psychological domain of Los' arch-foe, Urizen.

Urizen, whose name seems to be a pun on "Your Reason,"[49] haunted Blake's life. He was probably that terrify-ing face of God which set the four-year-old Blake screaming after his first visionary experience.[50] He was among the most pervasive images in Blake's art, from his sketchy prototype in Blake's first relief-engraved book[51] till his apotheosis in the last painting Blake completed before his death.[52] The myth of Urizen and his mental wars with Los was the focus of Blake's 1784 Book of Urizen,[53] and remained a dominant theme in subsequent narrative poems.

On first impression, Urizen, unlike the fiery Los, seems a goodly, if not godly, sort. Venerable, white-bearded, and white-robed, he looks like a Sunday School picture of God—and it was precisely that mistaken image of God which Blake was refuting with this figure. Urizen is Reason; unfeeling, law-bound Reason. He is the deity of the materialistic philosophers of the Age of Reason, and is the impotent, aging icon of those churches Swedenborg condemned for teaching people that they "are sanctified if only they fold their hands and look upwards, and utter some customary form of prayer" (AR 263).

Urizen writing his laws; *Book of Urizen* **title page**

Urizen is not a philosophical metaphor, he is a living psychological reality. He is that aspect of mind which sets limits and draws boundaries. His razor-edged mental matrices slice life into tiny fragments, to be weighed, measured, and evaluated according to a ledger of his own design, while the living essence escapes his notice. He formulates the doctrines, codes, and laws which impose a thick, occluding veil over naked truths. He darkens what is bright, chills what is warm.

Urizen is not inherently evil, however: Reason is an indispensable function of mind, one of the fundamental Four Zoas.[54] Urizen becomes dangerous and destructive when individuals or societies elevate him to the throne of the one true god, as was done in the Age of Reason (and, to a large extent, in our own century).

As supreme deity, as ruler of consciousness, Urizen creates those "-isms" which close the doors of perception, and enslave people into myopic "-ists." Then Urizen (Reason) will trample creativity and Imagination (Los), ban his books, censor his thoughts, and bind his aspirations "In chains of the mind locked up/ Like fetters of ice shrinking together" (*Ur* 10:25-26; E.75).

This is dramatized in Blake's myth when Urizen appears before Los, and "Thus Urizen spoke collected in himself in awful pride":

> *Obey my voice young Demon*
> *I am God from Eternity to Eternity*
> (*FZ* I, 12:22-23; E.307)[55]

Urizen (Reason) deified will invert the positions of heaven and hell, casting the Spiritual Faculty (Los) into the role of a rebellious "Demon." In trying to reshape reality to his matrix, Urizen's own demonic "awful pride" creates a living hell, as he was warned by the Daughters of Albion:

> *O Urizen! Creator of Men! Mistaken demon of Heaven:*
> *Thy joys are tears! thy labour vain, to form men in thine*
> *image.* (*VDA* 5:3-4; E.48)

Their cries seem an echo of Swedenborg's similar cautioning about the dangers of losing sight of inner (spiritual) realities, and vainly attempting to "form men in [the] image" of a religion predicated on Reason alone:

> Intellectual faith . . . is to see falsities for truths and evils for goods. The fire that kindles that light is the love of self and the conceit therefrom of one's own intelligence.
> So far as one excels in ingenuity, he is able to rationalize anything he wants. . . . This is especially so when any given dogma is assumed as the very truth . . . and confirmed to be so only by *reasonings.* . . . A man who looks at all the dogmas of his religion this way may assume whatever principle he wants, and by the light of confirmation make it appear to be a truth from heaven, although it is *a falsity from hell.* [Emphases mine.] (*AE* 846)

The deified Urizen is also the high priest of his own religion founded on the "falsities of hell" (i.e., on dogmas which do not correspond to psychological realities). He is that demonic holyman who sets the impetus for holy wars and Inquisitions; that Satanic architect of vast prisons for those who do not conform to the religious, racial, or political norms of his codes. Blake's *Book of Urizen* is "the dark vision of torment . . . of the primeval Priests assum'd power" (*Ur* 2:7,1; E.70).

Blake's "dark vision" seems to parallel another of Swedenborg's cautionings: "Priests ought not to claim for themselves any power over the souls of men. Still less ought they to claim the powers of opening and shutting heaven."[56]

It is the state of hell, rather than that of heaven, which opens in Blake's depiction of Urizen's empire. It is a seemingly paradoxical hell, however: Rather than a glowing scorching landscape of fire and brimstone, hotter than the hinges of hell, Urizen's realm is a "ninefold darkness" (*Ur* 3:9). . . . "where winter beats incessant" (*BA* 2:23-24). Here, Urizen assembles his icy intellectual powers:

> *His cold horrors silent, dark Urizen / Prepar'd. . . .*
> *In his hills of stor'd snow, in his mountains*
> *Of hail & ice; voices of terror / Are heard. . . .*
> (*Ur* 3:27-33; E.71)

Such are the seasons of Urizen, which could be a page from Swedenborg's almanac of the mind-made seasons of Eternity, where. . .

> . . . Anything temporal in phenomenon on a man's level are changed into a concept of state . . . Spring and morning are changed into a concept of love and wisdom as in the first state of angels . . . *night and winter* to a concept of *conditions prevailing in hell.* [Emphases mine] (*HH* 166).

"Night and winter," the "conditions prevailing in hell," become the "ninefold darkness". . . "where winter beats incessant" in the mind-made hell of Urizen. Just as Blake seems to have patterned the bright and fiery state of his hero, Los, on the psycho-logics of Swedenborg's vision of heaven, so too he seems to have derived the dark and wintery state of his mythic villain, Urizen, from Swedenborg's vision of hell.

From the top of his snowy-white mane to the hem of the quasi-biblical white robe which almost invariably covers his nakedness, Urizen seems to correspond to Swedenborg's vision of hell who "run away from heaven's light and plunge

---

Just as Blake seems to have patterned the bright and fiery state of his hero, Los, on Swedenborg's vision of heaven, so too he seems to have derived the dark and wintery state of his mythic villain, Urizen, from Swedenborg's vision of hell.

---

into their own light" (*HH* 553). Urizen is cut off from heaven's light (psychological truths). In his cavern of wintery darkness, he tries to discover truths through his own light—through his own "infernal method," the scientific method of Experience, Geometry, and (his own) Faculty of Reasoning:

> *He form'd a line & a plummet*
> *To divide the Abyss beneath.*
> *He form'd a dividing rule:*
> *He formed scales to weight;*
> *He formed massy weights;*
> *He formed a brazen quadrant;*
> *He formed golden compasses*
> *And began to explore the Abyss.*
> (*Ur* 20:33-40; E.80-81)

Urizen measuring the heavens; Blake's *Europe, a Prophecy* frontispiece

Despite his many cleverly fashioned probes, Urizen (Reason) cannot pierce the ninefold darkness of his Abyss, for his wintery hall lacks the fiery light of the "celestial kingdom" which illuminates the realm of Los (Imagination). Filtered through the cold metallic glow of Reason, the fiery light of Divine Truths (spiritual-psychological realities) becomes distorted or invisible. Reason can only discern those literal, quantifiable facts (natural realities) which are visible to the silicon eyes of binary logic in the cold glow of a computer screen. As Swedenborg explained:

> True things outside heaven are not radiant the way things within the heavens are. True things outside the heavens have *a cold radiance*, like something *snow-white* without warmth. This is because they do not draw their essential substance from what is good [loving] the way true elements within heaven do. [Emphases mine] (*HH* 132)

Blake's snow-white Urizen embodies, corresponds to, this loveless knowledge of "true things outside heaven"; yet he will not be dissuaded from his myopic quest to impose himself as "God from Eternity to Eternity." The fire which burns within Urizen's icy bosom, unlike the divinely inspired flames which warm Los' forge, rages from a demonic need to elevate himself at the expense of others. Urizen's fire corresponds to what Swedenborg deemed "hellfire":

> There is warmth in the hells, too. . . .Warmth in heaven is what is meant by "holy and heavenly fire," while warmth of hell is what is meant by "hellfire." Each one refers to love—heavenly fire to love for the Lord and love towards's one neighbor. . . while *hellfire refers to love of self* and love of the world. [Emphasis mine.] (*HH* 134)

The "hellfire" within Urizen leads to that "vision of dark torment" which is his myth. "The Lord does not cast anyone into hell, each individual casts himself in," Swedenborg explains (*HH* 548). Swedenborg's hell corresponds to a torment that is born of love of self—that torment of an ego which never can be satisfied, which becomes a self-enclosed horror, cut off from others, alone, un-nurtured. It is precisely this sort of self-made "Demon" which Urizen has become at the beginning of Blake's *Book of Urizen*:

> Lo, a shadow of horror is risen
> In Eternity! Unknown, unprolific!
> Self-closd, all-repelling: what Demon
> Hath form'd this abominable void
> This soul-shudd'ring vacuum!—Some said
> "It is Urizen", But unknown, abstracted
> Brooding secret, the dark power hid. (Ur 3:1-7; E.70)

Blake's Urizen, a dark "shadow of horror," is also a very clear mirror of Swedenborg's vision of the self-made demons of hell, a state in which. . .

> . . .all of them are reflections of their own hell. . . . Each is a model of his own evil quality. . . they are forms of contempt for other people and menace for people who do not pay them homage . . . their faces are frightful . . . their bodies grotesque . . . All of them [correspond to] forms of self-love and love of the world. (*HH* 553-54)

The psychological monsters born of Urizen's self-love take form, and he codifies them into a book of laws written in metal—the new bible of his self-made hell. With consummate pride, he announces to all Eternity:

> Here alone I in books formd of metals
> Have written the secrets of wisdom
> The secrets of dark contemplation
> By fightings and conflicts dire,
> With terrible monsters Sin-bred:
> Which the bosoms of all inhabit;
> Seven deadly Sins of the soul.
>
> Lo! I unfold my darkness: and on
> This rock, place with strong hand the Book
> Of eternal brass, written in my solitude. (Ur 4:24-33; E.72)

Urizen's bible, that "dark contemplation" written in "eternal brass," and placed on rock (Mt. Sinai) by the "strong hand" of Urizen, is what Swedenborg had termed "a picture written in dark colors on a black stone" (*TCR* 441)—a beknighted religious creed without any basis in spiritual (psychological) realities.

All Eternity recoils when Urizen reveals his metal laws, with their artificial hell of "monsters Sin-bred," and their absurd litany of egocentricity guised as monotheism: "One command, one joy, one desire,/ One curse, one weight, one measure/ One King, one God, one Law" (*Ur* 4:38-40). As the mountains of Eternity are rent asunder, whirlwinds of Eternal Truths pour down upon Urizen in "cataracts of fire blood & gall (*Ur* 4:46); and Urizen reacts exactly like those self-condemned to a state of hell in Swedenborg's visions—he flees "in howlings & pangs & fierce madness" (*Ur* 5:24).

Urizen crumbles, "hoary, age-broke, and aged," (*Ur* 5:26) and his inward realities materialize about him in corresponding outward form:

> *And a roof, vast petrific around*
> *On all sides He fram'd: like a womb;*
> *. . . . & like a black globe*
> *View'd by sons of Eternity, standing*
> *On the shore of the infinite ocean*
> *Like a human heart struggling & beating*
> *The vast world of Urizen appear'd* (Ur 5:28-9, 33-7; E.73)

This image of the "vast world of Urizen," "a black globe" . . . "like a womb," seems to echo Swedenborg's

Urizen in his black globe; *Book of Urizen* **10 (detail)**

image of "A faith that is like a sterile seed. . . like an egg without a prolific principle" (*TCR* 441)—a characterization of the sterile moral code of Urizen, which materalized "like a black globe" about this "age-broke" body.

In a grotesque re-writing of Genesis, Los helps the gestating Urizen evolve within his "black globe," until, at length for hatching ripe, Urizen breaks the shell. Urizen awakes and explores his dens. He finds a world teeming with "Portions of life; similitudes/ Of a foot, or a hand, or a head/ Or a heart, or an eye" (*Ur* 23:4-6)—like the fragmentary similitudes of life young William Blake had copied at the Urizenic Pars School of Drawing. And like Blake's subsequent art, these fragments coalesced into living forms—the children of Urizen. But Urizen "curs'd/ Both sons & daughters; for he saw/ That no flesh nor spirit could keep/ His iron laws one moment" (*Ur* 23:23-26).

Urizen departed, wandering the heavens "in weeping & pain & woe"; but he left his offspring a dark legacy, born from "the sorrows of Urizens soul":

> *A cold shadow follow'd behind him*
> *Like a spider's web, moist, cold & dim*
> *Drawing out from his sorrowing soul*
> *The dungeon-like heaven dividing. . . .*
>
> *Till a Web dark & cold, throughout all*
> *The tormented element stretch'd*
> *From the sorrows of Urizen's soul*
> *And the Web is a Female in embrio*
> *None could break the Web, no wings of fire.*
>
> *So twisted the cords, & so knotted*
> *The meshes: twisted like to the human brain.*
>
> *And all call'd it, The Net of Religion.*
>
> (Ur 25:9-10, 15-22; E.82)

Curiously, Urizen's attempts to create a theology ended where Swedenborg's had begun—at the threshold of the knotted, twisted cords of the human brain. Unlike the threshold of Swedenborg's visionary New Jerusalem, which beckons all with a sign proclaiming: "Now It Is Allowable,"[57] Urizen's Net of Religion closes the threshold of the brain with a "Web dark & cold," which signifies: "Thou Shalt Not!—Do Not Enter!"[58]

Swedenborg's legacy, as reworked by Blake on Los' forge, was intended to "conjoin man to the Lord and open heaven." Urizen's legacy—which remains a reality, and not simply a metaphor—is intended to fetter man to the earth with "mind-forged manacles," by obscuring and closing the channels of correspondences and hiding away the ever-present Jerusalem from the children of Urizen:

> No more could they rise at will
> In the infinite void, but bound down
> To earth by their narrowing perceptions
>
> They lived a period of years
> Then left a noisom body
> To the jaws of devouring darkness (Ur 25:45-28:3, E.83)

The legacy of Reason-made beliefs is that of a dark and hopeless, mind-made hell.

Urizen in his Net of Religion Book of Urizen **27 (detail)**

VII. "THE DARK RELIGIONS ARE DEPARTED"

Awake! awake O sleeper of the land of shadows, wake!
* expand!*
I am in you and you in me, mutual in love divine:
—Blake, *Jerusalem* (4:6-7; E.146)

Blake's myth did not end with the children of Urizen permanently ensnared in his Net of Religion until each died into the "jaws of devouring darkness." Blake reworked the myth for many years, and late in his life he was able to portray a resolution to the struggle between Reason and Imagination within the Universal Man, who awakens in psychological wholeness to restore his Divine Vision, Jerusalem.

Perhaps somewhere within Blake there was a similar Jerusalem, a hidden bright Emanation he had found in his youth, when he had needed her most. Despite the occasional "opposition" he voiced against her, the richly hued patterns of her wings seem to have cast their colors brightly across the pages of his books throughout his adult life.

Ultimately, the degree to which Swedenborg had influenced Blake is less important than the degree to which their individual visions and missions had corresponded. Each, without support or affirmation from any secular or religious power, without any expectation of reward, chose to devote his life, talents and wealth to a revolutionary and revelatory "great task." Perhaps in our own Age of Reason there remains something to be learned from a Swedish scientist who saw angels, and a British poet-artist who saw every species of visionary creature. Perhaps in our own, all too infrequent, moments of inward attention, after the noise is temporarily stilled, we too can sense dim reflections of something which they had seen glowing bright with promise.

At the height of his scientific career, Swedenborg wrote:

> If the principles I have advocated have more truth in them than those which are advocated by others. . . I shall gain the assent of those who are able to distinguish what is true from what is untrue, if not in the present, then in some future age. (*PRIN* II, Appendix; pp. 365-66)

It is therefore fitting that Swedenborg made one of the most eloquent summaries of his life's work to a representative of a future age—a child. After he became famous for his visionary experiences of heaven and hell, a neighbor's daughter repeatedly asked Swedenborg to teach her how to see angels. He finally consented. Swedenborg brought her to a small cottage in his garden which housed his library, and requested that she stand before a curtain drawn across a wall. "Now you shall see an angel," Swedenborg proclaimed, as he drew aside the curtain. Behind the curtain was a mirror in which the girl saw herself reflected.[59]

Blake too knew the redeeming powers of Imagination in drawing aside curtains. At the end of an immense epic poem written in his private notebook, Blake evoked Urthone (the "earth-owner"),[60] the ultimate creative power of Imagination, of whom Los is but a spectre, to arise in "the golden armour of science[61] for intellectual War", as a new age dawns:

Jerusalem 97 (detail)

> *The Sun has left his blackness and found a fresher morning*
> *And the mild moon rejoices in a clear & cloudless night*
> *And Man walks forth from midst of the fires the evil is all*
> * consumd*
> *   . . . . & one Sun*
> *Each morning like a New born Man issues with songs & Joy*
>
> *   . . . . & Urthona rises from the ruinous walls*
> *In all his ancient strength to form the golden armour of*
> * science*
> *For intellectual War The War of swords departed now*
> *The dark Religions are departed & sweet Science reigns.*
>
> *End of the Dream*
> *(FZ 138:20-28, 139: 7-10; E.406-07)[62]*

Perhaps Swedenborg was evoking that same "sweet Science" at the conclusion of his own book on heaven and hell:

> Anything which is loved brings light with it into the mind's concepts—especially when what is what is true is loved, for everything true is in the light. (*HH* 603)

"If not in the present, then in some future time . . ."

Notes

THE END OF A GOLDEN STRING

1. Quotations from Blake's writings are taken from *The Complete Poetry and Prose of William Blake*, ed. David V. Erdman (Garden City, N.Y.: Anchor Books, 1982 revised edition), which was first published in 1965 under the title, *Poetry and Prose of William Blake*. References are cited by plate number and line (for engraved poems) or page number (for manuscripts and letterpress books), and the letter "E," followed by Erdman's page number. Titles of Blake's works are abbreviated: see the Abbreviations list in this anthology.

2. As described by Blake's Victorian biographer, Alexander Gilchrist, in *The Life of William Blake* 2 vols. (London & Cambridge: Macmillan and Co., 1863), I, p. 7.

3. R. L. Tafel, *Documents concerning the Life and Character of Emanuel Swedenborg*, 2 vols. (London, 1875,1877), II, p. 546. Hereafter, Tafel's *Documents* is abbreviated as "*Docs.*"

4. Swedenborg, *True Christian Religion* (Amsterdam, 1771), n. 792.

5. *Docs.* II, p. 546.

6. Ibid., pp. 557-8.

7. For an account of the 1789 General Conference and the theological propositions adopted by its participants, please see the excerpt from Hindmarsh's *Rise and Progress of the New Jerusalem Church* reprinted in the "Historical Contexts" section of this anthology.

8. From Blake's annotations to Swedenborg's *Divine Love and Wisdom*, n. 220 (E.605).

9. For a complete discussion of Blake's changing relationship to Swedenborg's writings and to the early New Jerusalem Church, please see Paley's "A New Heaven Is Begun: Blake and Swedenborgianism" in this anthology.

10. For a detailed analysis of Swedenborg's influences on Blake's early works, please see Raine's "The Swedenborgian Songs" in this anthology.

11. Please see Deck's "C. A. Tulk, Blake's 19th Century Patron" in this anthology.

12. Please see Gilchrist's excerpt in the "Historical Contexts" section of this anthology for an amusing speculation about Blake and Swedenborg having "met unwittingly in London streets."

13. Please see Raine's "The Human Face of God" in this anthology for a discussion of the Swedenborgian basis of Blake's late, mature works.

SWEDENBORG: THE MAN WHO HAD TO KNOW

14. *Principia* is Volume One of Swedenborg's three-volume *Opera Philosophica et Mineralia*, a wide-ranging philosophical/scientific study of solar and stellar vortices, mechanisms of magnetism, origins of planetary systems, fire, and so forth, which he published in Dresden and Leipzig in 1734.

Quotations from *Principia* are taken from Rev. Augustus Clissold's translation (London, 1846), as reprinted by the Swedenborg Scientific Association (Bryn Athyn, Penn., 1976). Quotations are cited as "*PRIN*" followed by volume number (I or II), part: chapter, and page number.

15. Mr. Henry Söderberg, a retired vice president of Scandinavian Airlines Systems, has been undertaking extensive research on Swedenborg's glider design for a book he is writing on Swedish aviation. In a letter of December 11, 1984 to the author, he wrote: "Swedenborg himself was so far ahead of his time that he hardly believed himself in the realization of his own suggestion. It is, however, a recorded fact that he was the first one in history to suggest a fixed-wing concept. Unfortunately at that time, 1714, he and nobody else knew where to get the effective power from. . . . During the course of my own research I have found Swedenborg's place in history very much underrated and minimized, especially in his own country, Sweden, probably because of his later refuge to more spiritual matters. Swedes do not like that." (Mr. Söderberg's dating the glider-design as 1714, is in reference to Swedenborg's original manuscript, currently in the cathedral library of Lincoeping, Sweden. Swedenborg's 1716 article in *Daedalus Hyperboreus* was his summary of that manuscript.)

16. Reprinted from Albert Einstein's *Ideas and Opinions*, Carl Seelig ed. (New York: Dell, 1973), pp. 49-50, 53, 55, by permission of The Crown Publishing Group; copyright © 1954, Crown Publishing, Inc.

17. Swedenborg, *Journal of Dreams*, translated by J. J. G. Wilkinson (1860), edited by William Ross Woofenden (New York, Swedenborg Foundation, 1977), p. 5,6. This private journal of 104 pages, which Swedenborg wrote in Swedish during his critical transitional period of 1743-4, was never intended for the public, and had remained unknown until the Royal Library in Stockholm purchased the original manuscript in October 1858. Woofenden's 1977 edition is the most complete English translation available to date.

A THEATRE REPRESENTATIVE OF THE LORD'S KINGDOM

18. *JD*, n. 49; p. 15

19. Dr. C. G. Jung, as quoted in *Tributes to Emanuel Swedenborg*, Howard Miller, ed., 2nd edition (Boston: Massachusetts New Church Union, 1980) p. 6

20. Reprinted by permission of the publisher from *THE COLLECTED WORKS OF C. G. JUNG*, trans. R. F. C. Hull; Bollingen Series 20, Vol. 12: *Psychology and Alchemy* (Princeton: Princeton University Press, 1968). Copyright © 1953 by Princeton University Press.

21. *HH*, n. 440.

22. Ibid.

23. Reprinted by permission of the publisher from Czeslaw Milosz's *The Land of Ulro*, trans. Louis Iribarne (New York: Farrar, Straus & Giroux, Inc.)

24. From Blake's letter of August 23, 1799 to Rev. Dr. Trusler (E.702).

25. From Blake's Laöcoon engraving (E.274)

26. *WE* 2532

27. From Blake's *There is No Natural Religion ii*, "Application" (E.3); printed c.1788.

28. From the diaries of Henry Crabb Robinson, reprinted in G. E. Bentley Jr., *Blake Records*(Oxford: Clarendon, 1969); also cited in Michael Davis, *William Blake, A New Kind of Man* (Berkeley and Los Angeles: University of California Press, 1977), pp. 158-59, and elsewhere.

THE PRICE OF EXPERIENCE

29. Citing specific quotations from Blake's unpublished, much reworked manuscript, *The Four Zoas (Vala)*, is, as always, a complex Urizenic tangle. As is the case in the other Blake quotation cited herein, this is taken from Erdman's 1982 edition of *Complete Poetry and Prose of William Blake*, in which these lines represent "Night the Second" (II), page 35, lines 11-13, as reprinted on page 325 of Erdman (E.325). These same lines in the *Blake Concordance* of 1968, and in the various editions of Keynes (K.) represent "Night the Third," lines 397-99 (III 397-99) in the pagination scheme used by Keynes.

30. As reported in Tafel's *Documents*, and retold in Cyriel Odhner Sigstedt's classic biography, *The Swedenborg Epic* (London: The Swedenborg Society, 1981) pp. 269-79

31. Ibid., pp. 278,303-04.

32. Ibid., pp. 387-409.

A "BLAKE-SMITH" WHO WOULD FORGE A NEW JERUSALEM

33. As evidenced in *MHH* 3: "As a new heaven is begun, and it is not thirty-three years since its advent." Please see Paley, "A New Heaven Is

Begun: Blake and Swedenborgianism," in this anthology.

34. "Science" in this context is not that materialistic pursuit of the Newtonian Age, which Blake so frequently condemned; rather it is that "sweet Science" (*FZ* IX,139:10; E.407) of essential wisdom, as derived from the Latin root *scientia*, "to know". Please see S. Foster Damon, *A Blake Dictionary* (Boulder: Shambala, 1979), pp. 359-60, for an exposition of Blake's two contrary meanings of the word "science."

35. Although Blake has himself dated this letter "Jan. 10, 1802," Erdman's *Complete Poetry and Prose of William Blake* dates the letter as Jan. 10, 1803, based on evidence in E. B. Murray's "A Suggested Redating of a Blake Letter to Thomas Butts", in *Blake: An Illustrated Quarterly* 13 (1979-80), pp. 148-51.

36. For an excellent study of Blake's graphic arts techniques, please see Robert N. Essick's *William Blake, Printmaker* (Princeton: Princeton University Press, 1980).

37. As described by Gilchrist, *The Life of William Blake*, 1863 ed., p. 69.

38. Please see Raine, "The Swedenborgian Songs," in this anthology.

39. Please see Raine, "The Human Face of God," and Paley, "A New Heaven is Begun," in this anthology.

40. Please see the following section, "Bright Sculptures of Los' Halls."

41. Quotations from *Jerusalem* are taken from Erdman's *Complete Poetry and Prose of William Blake* (1982 edition), and follow the pagination of Chapter 2 in copies A, C, and F of *Jerusalem*, which differs from the arrangement in the text of Geoffrey Keynes (based on copies D and E).

42. Jerusalem's relationship to Albion in Blake's mythos is fairly complex. Generally, in the poem which bears her name she is seen as Albion's Emanation (his bright female portion; or in Jungian terms, his anima). However when Albion fell into self-division, his wife Brittannia "divided into Jerusalem and Vala" (the earth goddess). (*J* 36:26) In Blake's unpublished poem *The Four Zoas*, she is the daughter of Albion and Brittannia. She is also the chosen wife of Jesus, as foretold in Revelation XXI; and in this context, Albion takes Vala as his wife (*J* 20:40, 63:7, 64:19, 65:71; K.) When Albion falls into his deadly sleep, he

hides Jerusalem away from Jesus, and loses his own Divine Vision (*J* 4:33). The drama of the poem, *Jerusalem*, is the struggle to restore her.

For a more complete discussion of these complex relationships, please see Damon, *A Blake Dictionary*, pp. 9-13, 206-13.

43. Ibid., pp. 246-53, for a detailed definition of Los, the hero of Blake's mythos.

44. *VLJ* p. 69; E.555

BRIGHT SCULPTURES OF LOS' HALLS

45. Blake, *VLJ*, p. 94; E.565

46. Blake's term "Zoa" seems to derive from a Greek plural word used to describe the four beings seen in John's apocalyptic vision (*Revelation* IV:6), and in Ezekiel's vision by the river Chebar (*Ezekiel* I:5 ff.). Zoas is often translated as "beasts," but a more appropriate choice would be "living creatures." In this context Blake uses the term to describe the four essential aspects of man, in a manner foreshadowing the writings of Jung. For a full discussion of the Four Zoas and their meanings, please see Damon, *A Blake Dictionary*, pp. 458-60.

47. Los, Albion and Los' son, Orc (the fiery spirit of Revolution) all tend to resemble each other, and to resemble their red-haired creator, William Blake, in idealized form. Perhaps they each represent Blake's self-image at various stages in his career, as he was creating many books in which these figures are depicted.

48. *Ur* will be used as an abbreviation for Blake's 1794 *The (First) Book of Urizen*, which he re-published under the title *The Book of Urizen*, after he had found alternate titles for the books which continued the Urizen myth.

49. For definitions of Urizen's name and details of his myth, please see Damon, *A Blake Dictionary*, pp. 419-26.

50. According to a Feb. 2, 1852 entry in Henry Crabb Robinson's *Reminiscences* (London, 1869), Blake's wife, Catherine, said to Blake: "You know dear, the first time you saw God was when you were four years old, and he put his head to the window and set you a'screaming."

51. A compass-wielding, crawling, proto-Urizenic figure appears on the "Application" page of Blake's *There is No Natural Religion*, which to-

gether with his *All Religions are One*, constituted Blake's first use of his relief-printing process (c.1788).

52. Shortly before his death, the bed-ridden Blake painted one last print of the frontispiece of his book, *Europe, a Prophecy*, which depicts Urizen measuring the heavens with a giant metal compass. As reported by Gilchrist, this image was "a singular favorite with Blake and one it was always a happiness to him to copy." (Gilchrist, *The Life of William Blake*, 1863 ed.; vol. I, pp. 359-60)

53. Please see note 48, above.

54. Please see note 46, above.

55. This quotation is i:319-20 in Keynes.

56. Compressed from Swedenborg's *AC* 10,189-89, as reprinted in *A Compendium of Swedenborg's Theological Writings*, Samuel M. Warren, ed. (New York: Swedenborg Foundation, 1974 reprinting of 1875 edition), p. 443

57. In *TCR* 508, Swedenborg relates a vision of a crystal-walled chapel, which had an inscription over the door, "Nunc Licet," which is variously translated as "Now it is permitted," "Now it is allowable," etc. This became the motto of the New Jerusalem Church, as stated earlier.

58. In his *Song of Experience*, "The Garden of Love," Blake writes of a chapel built in his garden where he used to "play on the green. / And the gates of this Chapel were shut, / And Thou Shalt not. writ over the door" (*SE* 44:4-6; E.26).

THE DARK RELIGIONS ARE DEPARTED

59. Tafel, *Swedenborg Documents* II, 724-25; an anecdote about Swedenborg's young neighbor, Greta Askbom, as related by the historian, Anders Fryxell.

60. For definition of Urthona, please see Damon, *A Blake Dictionary*, pp. 426-27

61. Please see note 34, concerning Blake's definitions of "science"

62. These lines are equivalent to *FZ* ix:25-33 and 52-55 in Keynes

The Swedenborgian Songs

KATHLEEN RAINE

BEGUN early in Blake's career, *Songs of Innocence and of Experience* are among his most familiar works. In the following analysis of Blake's *Songs*, Kathleen Raine asks: "How came Blake in the late eighteenth century to emerge as a symbolist poet?" She finds much of the answer in the influences of Swedenborg, whose "doctrines of influx and correspondence present a world symbolic in its whole and in its parts, not by some literary choice but in its very nature, a world informed throughout with imagination and beauty."

Dr. Raine has a long and distinguished career in Blake scholarship, with an emphasis on establishing Blake's position within the lineage of Platonic, Hermetic and mystical thinkers. She has modestly defined her task thusly: "To learn Blake's symbolic language . . . is a difficult but rewarding labour. My only qualification to write this commentary is that I have over many years been living with that language." Among her many publications are the two-volume *Blake and Tradition* (1968), her popular book about Blake as an artist, *William Blake* (1970), and her study of Blake's Book of Job engravings, *The Human Face of God* (1982). —Ed.

How came Blake, in the late eighteenth century, to emerge, from his earliest writings, as a symbolist poet? Something, certainly, must be allowed to his innate gifts: he was a natural visionary, who as a child saw angels walking among the harvesters and screamed in terror when God put his head in at the window. But how was such a gift preserved when the young poet began to experience the literary and philosophic influences of his time? The influence of Collins and Gray, Rowley and Ossian, Thomson and Spenser and Shakespeare, whose literary traces are easy to discover in the early *Poetical Sketches*, could not, singly or collectively, have given Blake the necessary training in the use of symbols. But his sudden emergence as a symbolist need not be explained by literary influences at all; Blake with his young wife, and Flaxman and his wife, were early members of the newly founded Swedenborgian Society in London. If we suppose that Blake was from his early years saturated in the atmosphere of Swedenborgian symbolism, the picture will begin to clarify. Blake was a symbolist before he was a poet, just as any man of pagan antiquity or the Christian Middle Ages inherited a symbolic way of thought as part of his environment.

We know from the best authority—his own—that Blake used Swedenborgian themes in both his paintings and his poems. In his *Descriptive Catalogue*, Number VIII, *The Spiritual Preceptor* (now lost) is described: "The subject is taken from the Visions of Emanuel Swedenborg, Universal Theology,[1] No. 623. . . . The works of this visionary are well worthy the attention of Painters and Poets; they are foundations for grand things."[2] This was written many years after *The Marriage of Heaven and Hell*, with its robust satirizing of the founder of the New Church. That satire was neither the beginning nor the end of Blake's deep interest in Swedenborgian thought. No lapsed Catholic thinks like a Protestant, still less like a positivist, and in the same way, while Blake's attitude to Swedenborg may have changed—perhaps more than once—the mark of Swedenborgian doctrine and symbolism went deep.

While Blake's attitude to Swedenborg may have changed—perhaps more than once—the mark of Swedenborgian doctrine and symbolism went deep.

There is no literary value in Swedenborg's symbolism, and nothing could be less poetic than the "visions" of that sage. It is merely raw material. But to a mind naturally gifted, the Swedenborgian doctrines of influx and correspondence present a world symbolic in its whole and in it parts, not by some literary choice but in its very nature, a world informed throughout with imaginative meaning and beauty.

In common with the Platonic schools and the Hermetic, Gnostic, cabalistic, and alchemical traditions (and indeed with Christian doctrine) Swedenborg taught that "natural cause only seems." The world of nature and of man himself are but the lowest terms in a series of dependent spiritual causes. Natural forms and appearances of all kinds are the outward manifestation of a spiritual life and energy whose effects we see as the phenomena of nature. This Swedenborg calls "influx." The divine influx alone upholds the universe; and man, as Blake says, is only "a form and organ of life" that flows into him from a divine fountain.

Together with the influx we have the related idea of correspondence: that is, everything in the physical world is symbolic in its very nature; it is the sensible representative of a spiritual essence. Correspondence is related to the older alchemical doctrine of signature and goes back to the Platonic view of the temporal world as an image of the eternal. Boehme—whom Blake held to be far greater than Swedenborg—speaks of the "vegetable glass" of nature—that is, as it were, a mirror in which spiritual realities are reflected; and again, the image of the glass goes far back into antiquity to the glass of Isis, the mirroring pool that drowned Narcissus and the dangerous toy of the child Dionysus—dangerous because in the mirror shadows take on the appearance of substance. In Swedenborg's words, then, "the whole natural world corresponds to the spiritual world, both in the whole, and likewise in its several parts; and what exists and subsists in the natural from the spiritual, is called correspondence; now the whole natural world exists and subsists from the spiritual, as an effect from its efficient cause."[3]

Place a young poet in such a world and he has no need to learn his symbolism from literary sources. Indeed, the decision to be a symbolist cannot be a literary one; symbolism, given any of the variants of the Platonic philosophy (of which Swedenborg's teaching must be accounted a descendant), becomes inevitable, for no image can be separated from its intelligible or spiritual meaning and content. Given, on the other hand, a philosophy that denies such a dependence of physical nature upon spiritual cause, symbolism is impossible. There can be no symbolist poetry produced by a materialist culture, since "divine analogy" is precluded.

The symbol is far from abstract: it is most concrete;[4] and no naturalism in poetry can be more concrete than the symbolism of a poet who sees the whole of manifested nature as a language that, as Coleridge says, "enunciates the whole" of an inseparable union of spiritual essence and physical existence.

Had this been all, the influence of Swedenborg would have been wholly good. But the symbolic language has at all times been more precise and more arbitrary than this universal and undifferentiated sacramentalism—which is, nevertheless, an underlying basis of all Blake's thought and of all symbolist systems. The most enduring and universal symbols have been evolved and have survived by reason of their natural fitness; and Swedenborg himself was often consciously or unconsciously using such traditional symbols, whose validity is intrinsic. His solar symbolism, his orientation to the four points of space, and many other elements of his symbolic vocabulary are of this kind. But in the Swedenborgian commentaries on the Scriptures we also find much that is arbitrary and, so far as one can see, personal. Every natural image, every town, country, and person named in the Bible, is taken to signify some spiritual state; and Blake at his worst follows Swedenborg into this profitless and unimaginative misuse of the Bible. When Blake lists "Moab & Ammon & Amalek & Canaan & Egypt & Aram" as spiritual states, he is incomprehensible without the key: "by Ægypt is signified what is scientific, by Ashur what is Rational, by Edom what is Natural, by Moab the Adulteration of Good, and by the Children of Ammon the adulteration of Truth, by the Philistines Faith without Charity."[5] This kind of pseudo-symbolism—for it cannot be said to correspond to Coleridge's requirement that the symbolic term form "a living part in that unity of which it is the representative"—is as disastrous in Blake as it is in Swedenborg. Fortunately, it is much less frequent.

As a rule the Swedenborgian correspondences—at least those that Blake selects—are somewhere between the two extremes of the total sacramental vision implied by the doctrine of influx and the arbitrary. Vine and oak, rose and myrtle, thorns, thistles, brambles, and nettles—all the vegetation of Blake's contrasting worlds of Innocence and Experience—belong to this language, half fitting, half arbitrary; and we often find more illumination of Blake's meaning in Swedenborg's commentaries than in the Bible itself. Thistles and thorns, for example, are constantly mentioned together in both the Old and the New Testaments—as, for example, "Ye shall know them by their fruits. Do men gather grapes of thorns, or figs of thistles?" But Swedenborg is more specific: "*Thorns and thistles* signify a curse and vastation."[6] Thorn, thistle, briar, bramble, and nettle all have a similar significance; and thorns, in particular, "denote the falsities of concupiscences." So that when Blake went

> To the thistles & thorns of the waste
> And they told how they were beguil'd,
> Driven out, & compel'd to be chaste[7]

the plants told him precisely what, within the Swedenborgian convention, they ought to say: they have been "driven out" of Paradise by God's curse and vastation; and they sym-

bolize unsatisfied desires—"concupiscences," as Swedenborg less charitably says.

In all the spiritual vegetation of Innocence and Experience we nowhere find a plant named that does not prove to be derived from some already established symbolic tradition. Not one is an observed image, elaborated into a poem. Blake might have used his rushes, sunflowers, thistles, and vines without having ever seen a living specimen of any of them. This was certainly not the case; we know that he had a real vine in his Lambeth garden that he loved too much to allow it to be pruned. For the real vine, to the symbolist, is informed by that divine life of which it is the symbol. Wordsworth found his symbols in nature—the image came first, a lesser celadine, a violet, a tree in a field—but Blake saw nature through symbol, not symbol through nature.

The Swedenborgian idiom has left its mark on the designs as well as on the poems.

The Swedenborgian idiom has left is mark on the designs as well as on the poems. The colors red, blue, and golden-white signify, respectively, love, wisdom, and the celestial state that is above both. When these colors are clear and radiant, the states of the soul to which they belong are likewise of a high order. The colors of hell are murky and dark. Yeats thought that Blake's colors were taken from Boehme, and he may be right. In any case Swedenborg's color equivalents are similar to Boehme's. The rainbow, says Boehme, is the type, in its three colors, of the three principles of the Divine Being. These colors of hell, heaven, and earth do, in general, correspond to Blake's usage—above all his murky reds and browns, as these are to be found in the *Marriage* or *The Book of Urizen*, and that exquisite light-filled yellowish white that seems to emanate, as Blake uses it, from the very essence of heaven.[8] Blake preferred love to wisdom (since "thought alone can make monsters, but the affections cannot")[9] and in nearly all copies of the *Songs*, in *Experience*, the blue of reason and the murky colors of hell tend to predominate. It is not possible to generalize absolutely about Blake's use of symbolic color, for every copy of his illuminated books is different; but the Piper of *Innocence* is rosy-clad in many copies; and the similar figure of the *Experience* wears blue. Wicksteed makes much of the ad-

Songs of Innocence frontispiece

Songs of Experience frontispiece

vancing of the right or left foot of the figures of the Job illustrations and other works; but this, also, almost certainly derives from Swedenborg, for whom whatever is on the right pertains to wisdom, on the left to love. So we find the rose-clad Piper of *Innocence* advancing his left foot and the blue-clad figure of *Experience* his right, for the first is guided by affection, the second by reason.[10] Too much may be made of this symbolism if it is taken too far; in the processions of tiny dancing figures the posture is obviously determined only by the demands of composition.

.   .   .

The very first poem of *Songs of Innocence* introduces, in the image of the child on a cloud, a Swedenborgian commonplace transmuted by Blake into an image so perfect that to suggest that it has behind it a convention may seem little better than to cast doubt upon miracle. The encounter with the child-spirit who tells the poet first to "Pipe a song about a lamb" and then to write "In a book, that all may read" has its prosaic counterpart in a dozen of those Swedenborgian "Memorable Relations" that form dry oases in the still drier deserts of his theology. Some spirit descends from heaven or ascends from hell, enters into conversation with the Seer, often instructs him to report this or write that in the world of men, and at the end of the interview vanishes. Visionary though Blake was, interviews with angels and devils (especially when so named) in his writings have less to do with vision than with this borrowed convention. This is more obvious in his failures than in his successes. The first draft of "The Human Abstract" has a Swedenborgian framework:

> I heard an Angel singing
> When the day was springing,
> "Mercy, Pity, Peace
> Is the world's release."
>
> . . .
>
> I heard a Devil curse
> Over the heath & the furze,
> "Mercy could be no more,
> If there was nobody poor."[11]

The typical Swedenborgian angel also appears in "I Asked a Thief to Steal Me a Peach" and "The Angel"; but only in the last does the Angel find his way into the published version. The Swedenborgian structure was removed from the finished version of "The Human Abstract"; and the fragment "I Asked a Thief" was not included. No doubt Blake felt that these angels and devils were lacking precisely in visionary immediacy.

It is impossible, however, to doubt that the child on a cloud was perceived by Blake's imaginative eye. Certainly he was not perceived in nature; for from the "valleys wild" to the hollow reed which Blake made his pen, as Prometheus stole fire from heaven in the same plant, all is symbolic. The "valley" is a symbol of the natural world or the body—or, in Swedenborg's world, "The Divine Natural and Sensual principle." The wild valley is the free and joyful world of nature and the senses of the bodily life of childhood, or perhaps of the young poet himself. In the later Prophetic Books the phrase "dark valley" is used, following, perhaps, Boehme rather than Swedenborg, for whom, nevertheless, the meaning is the same: "the whole *Body* of Man . . . is a dark Valley, as the Body of the Deep of this World is."[12] The "vale of Leutha," similarly, signifies sexuality. There is a consistency of meaning between the happy "valleys wild" of innocence and the "valleys dark" of the fallen man, which confirms the view that the basic meaning of valley was already intended in the early poem.

There are innumerable spirits in clouds in the writings of Swedenborg. Angelic societies, good or evil, appear in clouds more or less radiant according to the nature of the spirits they comprise; and the Lord himself is described as appearing in a cloud of multitudes of spirits. Every spirit has its "ambient Sphere"—"in Heaven sometimes under the Appearance of attenuated Flame, in Hell under the Appearance of crass Fire; and sometimes in Heaven under the Appearance of a thin and white Cloud, and in Hell under the Appearance of a thick and black Shower."[14] Blake makes frequent use of both these forms of ambient sphere, and spirits in or on clouds are no less frequent in his designs than in the text. Spirits surrounded by flames and clouds meet and embrace on the pages of the *Marriage*; in *Urizen* Orc is characteristically enveloped in his own fires; Oothoon is cloud-born. In the *Marriage* there is the deliberate satire of "Once I saw a Devil in a flame of fire, who arose before an Angel that sat on a cloud." Blake here is laughing at the "ambient sphere" imagery that he uses elsewhere with much beauty.

Swedenborg thinks habitually in pairs of opposites, angels and devils, dark clouds and bright clouds. So in Blake the laughing child on the cloud is opposed to the child of *Experience*:

> Into the dangerous world I leapt:
> Helpless, naked, piping loud:
> Like a fiend hid in a cloud.[15]

Blake's most completely—and most successfully—Swedenborgian poem [was] "The Little Black Boy."

In Blake's most completely—and most successfully—Swedenborgian poem, "The Little Black Boy" (the poem that Coleridge loved most of all the Songs), we discover something more about the meaning of the cloud symbol. Swedenborg's "ambient spheres" are probably the aura or etheric body, but Blake's black and white clouds are the physical bodies of the children:

> "And these black bodies and this sunburnt face
> Is but a cloud . . ."[16]

In Blake's symbolic language a cloud is always the body, which will "vanish" when the soul has learned to look upon the face of God unveiled. Perhaps we have here the first indication of Blake's reading of Paracelsus, and it may be that the latter's remarkable comparison of the body to smoke helped to form Blake's symbol:

> Briefly, whatsoever hath a body is nothing but curdled smoke, wherein a particular predestination lyeth hid . . . For all bodies shall passe away and vanish into nothing but smoke, they shall all end in a fume. This is the end of things corporeall both living and dead . . . Man is a coagulated fume. . . . We see nothing in our own selves but thickend smoke made up into a man by humane predestination.[17]

Only the spirit that animates the "cloud" or "smoke" can be said to possess human lineaments; for "a Spirit and a Vision are not, as the modern philosophy supposes, a cloudy vapour, or a nothing: . . . Spirits are organized men."[18] In other words, soul is form. It is the body that is a cloudy vapor possessing, as Plotinus says of matter, no inherent entity or form. The child in his cloud is the living soul that animates the body: in the world of Innocence, riding *on* his cloud, in Experience, densely enveloped and hidden *in* it.

The black boy and the white boy are evidently related to Swedenborg's good and evil angels, each in his ambient sphere; but already Blake is calling in question Swedenborg's moral dualism, for it is the black child who teaches the white, a foreshadowing of his later full-scale defense of the "devils" in the *Marriage*, where again the black spirits are wiser than the white, and devils preach to angels the wisdom of hell. But from Swedenborg comes the African, who is wiser than his European brother in spiritual matters. The Africans are represented by Swedenborg as having a natural understanding of the central doctrine of the New Church— one that Blake not only accepted but so far made his own that the very name of the Divine Humanity is now more strongly associated with Blake than with Swedenborg, from whom it originates. In the New Age, so Swedenborg taught, the worship of God as man will supersede the worship of an invisible God; and only those who can understand the nature of this Divine Humanity will partake in the new revelation. In 1757—the year of Blake's birth—the New Age was declared in the heavens, and a church began on earth that was

to be "the Crown of all Churches that have heretofore existed on this earthly Globe, because it will worship one Visible God, in whom is the invisible God, as the Soul is in the Body; and the . . . Conjunction of God with Man is thus, and in no other Way possible."[19]

It is for their natural understanding of this doctrine that the Africans are praised:

> The Gentiles, particularly the Africans, who acknowledge and worship one God the Creator of the Universe, entertain an Idea of God as of a Man, and say that no one can have any other Idea of God: when they hear that many form an Idea of God as existing in the Midst of a Cloud, they ask where such are; and when it is said that there are such among Christians, they deny that it is possible; but in Reply it is shewn,

that some Christians conceive such an Idea from this Circumstance, that God in the Word is called a Spirit, and of a Spirit they think no otherwise than of a thin Cloud, not knowing that every Spirit and every Angel is a Man.[20]

We know that Blake was struck by this passage, for he wrote in the margin of his copy of *Divine Love and Wisdom*: "Think of a white cloud as being holy, you cannot love it; but think of a holy man within the cloud, love springs up in your thoughts, for to think of holiness distinct from man is impossible to the affections."[21]

In the natural state, however (so Swedenborg affirms), God is seen, but "afar off," as a sun shedding his "beams of love." "The Worship of the Sun is the lowest of all Kinds of Worship

of a God";[22] and it is this form of worship that is taught to the black boy by his *mother* (that is, nature) "underneath a tree"—the tree of life, the natural world. In this world of innocent nature the teaching of the "mother" earth is the right and true worship:

> Look on the rising Sun: there God does live
> And gives his light, and gives his heat away.

These two lines are packed with Swedenborgian allusion. The *rising* sun is by no means a naturalistic image; for to angelic spirits the sun is always rising. The angels "constantly turn their Faces to the Lord as the Sun,"[23] and the sun "constantly appears in it's Place, and where it appears is the East."[24] Thus the blessed spirits are constantly oriented toward the *rising* sun. Let them turn as they will, the sunrise is always before their faces. This is "eternity's sun rise,"[25] in which the angels always dwell. *Light* and *heat* are also specified with clear symbolic intention; for they are correspondences of the two attributes of God: "[He] appears before the angels in Heaven as a Sun, and . . . from the Sun proceedeth Heat and Light, and . . . the Heat thence proceeding, in it's Essence, is Love, and the Light thence proceeding in it's Essence is Wisdom."[26] What God "gives away" in Blake's poem is therefore, in terms of divine analogy, love and wisdom.

The higher knowledge of God as "uncreated man" is only possible for souls at a high stage of development; only when freed from their "clouds" do the boys, who learned their first lessons from their mother, nature, "lean in joy upon our *father's* knee." This teaching Blake summed up in the lines

> God Appears & God is Light
> To those poor Souls who dwell in Night,
> But does a Human Form Display
> To those who Dwell in Realms of day.[27]

To the two children under the earthly tree of life, God is the sun; but when both come to spiritual maturity, they will know their spiritual father in his divine-human form.

·　　·　　·

Perhaps our understanding of "The Little Black Boy" is not essentially changed by the knowledge that its symbolic structure is Swedenborgian. But with "The Little Boy Lost"[28] and "Found"[29] the case is different.

In these two poems, and their accompanying designs, we can see Blake's imagination at work, transforming story to myth and illustration to vision. The story of "The Little Boy Lost" Blake owed, it seems, to Mary Wollstonecraft, whose part as the inspirer of *Songs of Innocence* was perhaps very great. Mary, a true daughter of Rousseau, was much concerned with the education of children, with guiding their natures rather than forming them, with allowing what in them is innately good to unfold. This was a way of thought altogether in keeping with Blake's own. He himself designed and engraved the plates for Mary Wollstonecraft's own book, *Original Stories from Real Life*, and we may be sure that in writing *Songs of Innocence* he must have felt that he was working with Mary in a cause dear to a woman he admired and loved.

In 1790 and 1791 Johnson the publisher, Mary's employer and Blake's friend, published a little book, translated by Mary herself from the German of the Rev. C.G. Salzmann, *Elements of Morality, for the Use of Children*, a moral narrative, showing real imaginative sympathy with the joys and fears of childhood—a much better work than Mary's own *Original Stories*. Blake engraved many of the plates, and in doing so must have given much thought to the problems of literature for children, to Mary's cause, and to the stories themselves. The best of these tells of a Little Boy Lost. In Chapter III, little Charles wanders away into a strange wood.

> Then it came into his head that he had lost himself, and was wandering still further out of his way. At his thought he felt a cold shivering run over his body, and he could hardly draw his breath, his heart was so dull. *What will become of me, thought he,* if I am obliged to remain in the wood with nothing to eat or drink! Must I—oh, must I lie in the dark; perhaps, a serpent or some bad man, may come and kill me while I slumber.[29a]

Night falls, the moon rises, the child thinks he sees phantom shapes, and he "wanted his father's advice to teach him how to think, as much as his strong arm to support a poor tired boy, whose legs tottered under him." The poor lost child "at last . . . recollected his father's advice, and fell on his knees and prayed to God to have pity on him." Almost

immediately he "saw a tall black figure approach him, with a white cap on its head, and a milk white pigeon flew before it." The figure is a kind clergyman in a white wig, carrying a white handkerchief, which the boy mistook for a pigeon. This detail is described with a vividness suggesting that Salzmann is recollecting an adventure of his own childhood, for it is, in its way, strikingly true to life. The episode is illustrated by two charming plates, one of the little boy lost, the other of Charles found by the clergyman; and here, surely, is the raw material of Blake's poems and of his two designs, and of God who appears like his father "in white"—a most curious detail in the poems which can easily be understood if we suppose that he is thinking of Charles's adventure with the tall figure with the wig and handkerchief. It is not certain that Blake was the engraver of the two plates in question, though it is very possible that he was. Keynes is doubtful; but Ruthven Todd, on grounds of style and technique, supports my own inclination to think that he was. In any case this is not the crucial point, for as one of the engravers employed on the book, and as a friend of the translator, he would have read the story, and no doubt have seen the other plates.

But Blake's two poems are much more than narrative; his little boy is "lost" in quite another sense than little Charles in the wood; and every image in the poem is symbolic. There is, in Salzmann's story, no "vapour," or "mire," or "dew"; the child was not pursuing a will-o'-the-wisp. It is true that his prayer to God was answered by the appearance of a man to save him; and in this detail Blake found the symbolic starting-point of a story which, as the poet has told it, may be seen as an illustration of the central doctrine of the Swedenborgian New Church, that God can only be known in human form.

Wicksteed[30] long ago observed that the adventures of boys in the *Songs* are religious or philosophical, those of little girls romantic; and the story of the little boy lost is a philosophical adventure. If we turn back to the passage from *Divine Love and Wisdom* about those who think of God as "a little cloud in the midst of the universe," we have the key. The two poems describe the spiritual state of those who think of God as a Spirit, and "of a Spirit they think no otherwise than of a thin Cloud, not knowing that every Spirit and every Angel is a Man." Blake's phrase about a spirit not being "a cloudy vapour" leads us back again to Swedenborg, who used the word "vapour" for this false conception of the nature of a spiritual being. It is an error, he says, to suppose that after death "Man will then be like a Vapour, or like Wind, or like Æther, or like Something floating in the Air." "Lay aside," he says, "the Idea concerning the Soul as being a Vapour or Breath."[31] As for Blake, so for Swedenborg, "spirits are organized men."[32]

The Little Boy Lost is in just this condition of error. For him God is "a cloudy vapour." Attempting to follow this will-o'-the-wisp, he loses God and strays in a dark night, far from the sun of the spiritual world. He falls into the deep "mire" of materialism:

> The night was dark, no father was there;
> The child was wet with dew;
> The mire was deep, & the child did weep,
> And away the vapour flew.

It is clear that when Blake wrote these poems, he was already familiar with the Neoplatonic symbolism of matter as mire, clay, and water, and materialist thought as immersion in mire. "The Little Boy Lost" appears first in *An Island in the Moon*, dated approximately 1787.[33] If Foster Damon is right in his identification of Sipsop the Pythagorean as Thomas Taylor the Platonist, we may conclude that Blake already knew Taylor, and is likely to have read his translation of Plotinus' *Concerning the Beautiful*, which appeared in that year. In this essay it is said that the soul becomes impure through its preoccupation with sensible forms: "it is covered with corporeal stains, and wholly given to matter, contracts deeply its nature, loses all its original splendor"[34] through its "total immersion in mire and clay." This is the darkness, the mire, and the "lonely fen" (a landscape of mire and water) that the lost child finds on every side when he follows the "vapour," the will-o'-the-wisp of an abstract god. The "dew"[35] with which the child is wet is another symbol of immersion in matter, whose symbol is water—again taken from Plotinus. When man loses his spiritual vision and becomes immersed in materialist thought, spirit (the father) is exchanged for a cloudy vapor; but he also loses the "mother," nature. According to Swedenborg everything in nature is upheld in being by the divine "influx," a doctrine that gives it substance and meaning, by its insistence that it exists

"from the Divine Humanity of the Lord."[36] Without this influx, matter is "mire" and not a loving "mother." Blake is preaching the doctrine of the New Church, "the true god is the Divine Humanity." "Finite things are the Recipients of Infinite,"[37] Swedenborg wrote, and "A Man is an organ of life, and God alone is life: God infuses his life into the organ and all its parts; and God grants man a sense that the life in himself is as it were his own"; and "Man is a Recipient of life from God."[38] Blake uses Swedenborg's very words, when he writes:

> . . . thou art but a form & organ of life & of thyself
> Art nothing, being Created continually by Mercy & Love
> divine.[39]

"God only Acts and is in created beings and men," he also writes; God's fatherhood is expressed toward earthly children in human fatherhood and not otherwise:

> Man liveth not by Self alone, but in his brother's face
> Each shall behold the Eternal Father . . .[40]

and again,

> . . . General Forms have their vitality in Particulars, & every
> Particular is a Man, a Divine Member of the Divine Jesus.[41]

It is possible that the pursuit of the will-o'-the-wisp into a miry fen came to Blake from a finely imagined passage of Plotinus, the more so as this theme gave him the symbolism of a later myth. The pursuit of matter, he says, is the pursuit of "non-entity," "avoiding the desire of him who wishes to perceive its nature. . . . So that it is a phantom, neither abiding, nor yet able to fly away. . . . Hence, too, in each of its vanishing appellations, it eludes our search . . . as it were a flying mockery."[42] Plotinus refers to the myth of Narcissus, whose legend was interpreted in the Neoplatonic schools as a myth of the death by drowning of the soul that falls in love with the "watery image" or material form, mistaking the shadow for the substance:

> For he who rushes to these lower beauties, as if grasping
> realities, when they are only like beautiful images appearing
> in water, will, doubtless, like him in the fable, by stretching
> after the shadow, sink into the lake, and disappear. For, by
> thus embracing and adhering to corporeal forms, he is precipi-
> tated, not so much in his body, as in his soul, into profound

and horrid darkness; and thus blind, like those in the infernal regions, converses only with phantoms, deprived of the perception of what is real and true. It is here, then, we may more truly exclaim, "Let us depart from hence, and fly to our father's delightful land."[43]

In Plotinus also, it is the "father" (spirit) who is able to save the lost soul from the mire. It is tempting to imagine that behind Blake's "Little Boy Lost," symbol of the intellect of man pursuing the phantom of matter, is the shadow of that less fortunate boy, Narcissus.

.   .   .

To this group of Swedenborgian poems we must add "The Divine Image" .... There could be no more simple and orthodox statement of the central doctrine of the New Church.

To this group of Swedenborgian poems we must add "The Divine Image,"[44] whose meaning is so clear as to require no exegesis. The poem illustrates the doctrine "that Esse and Existence in God-Man are Distinctly one." The qualities have their divine essence and their human existence:

> For Mercy, Pity, Peace, and Love
> Is God, our father dear,
> And Mercy, Pity, Peace, and Love
> Is Man, his child and care.
>
> . . .
>
> Then every man, of every clime,
> That prays in his distress,
> Prays to the human form divine,
> Love, Mercy, Pity, Peace.

There could be no more simple and orthodox statement of the central doctrine of the New Church.

Blake's "Religion of Jesus" was never at any time confined by the frontiers of Christendom. Swedenborg was not narrow in this matter; for he praises the Africans for their understanding of God, and cites several other instances, from the world of spirits, of those who know "the Lord" although not by the name of Jesus. Mohammedans and heathens, he says,

are "soon brought to the knowledge of and belief in the Lord through the means of instruction; and the more so, as it is a fundamental of their creed, that God is visible in a human form. These are the greater number [of the appointed for heaven]; and the best of them are from Africa."[45]

Had Blake also at this time begun to read the works of Boehme? Near the beginning of *Aurora*, the first book in Volume I of the famous four-volume edition known as Law's Boehme, which Blake praised so highly, is the passage:

> Most certainly *there is but One God*; but when the Veil is put away from thy Eyes, so that thou seest and knowest *him*, then thou wilt also see and know *all* thy Brethren, whether they be *Christians, Jews, Turks*, or *Heathens*. Or dost thou think that God is the God of you *Christians* only? Do not the *Heathens* also live in God, *whosoever doth* Right or *Righteousness, God* loves and *accepts him*. . . . Is he only *thy* King? Is it not written, *he is the Comfort of all the Heathen!*[46]

.   .   .

It is easy to argue that such poems as "The Little Boy Lost" and "Found" are symbolist in intention, for read as realistic they are unintelligible. "The Chimney Sweeper"[47] is entirely satisfactory as a poem about real London chimney sweepers (as of course it is), full of human sympathy and of social indignation. But this poem, also, can be read on several levels. It necessarily follows from the doctrine of influx and correspondence that every happening of earth has its counterpart in the world of spirit; and it is easy to see in the chimney sweepers—boys forced into a despised and oppressed class, just as the Africans are an enslaved and outcast race—yet another group belonging to the Blakean conception of the devils, the unjustly outcast spirits whose cause he was presently to embrace. Like the black African, the sweep (the wage slave) may say, "And I am black, but O my soul is white." These seemingly black sheep are really innocent lambs:

> There's little Tom Dacre, who cried when his head,
> That curl'd like a lamb's back, was shav'd: so I said
> "Hush, Tom! never mind it, for when your head's bare
> You know that the soot cannot spoil your white hair."

The "soot" is the earthly mire and clay that cannot defile the spirit:

And as the gold is deformed by the adherence of earthly clods, which are no sooner removed than on a sudden the gold shines forth with its native purity; and then becomes beautiful when separated from natures foreign from its own, and when it is content with its own purity for the possession of beauty: so the soul, when separated from the sordid desires engendered, by its too great immersion in body; and liberated from the dominion of every perturbation, can thus and thus only, blot out the base stains imbibed from its union with body.[48]

Whether or not Blake had in mind these words of Plotinus concerning the incorruptibility of the soul, this is the essential meaning of the poem; and moreover the symbolic language of Neoplatonism is in this poem unmistakable in the symbol that Blake here uses for the body, a denser envelope than Swedenborgian cloud or Paracelsus' smoke; here it is for the first time called a "coffin," the first of many such homonyms in Blake's later works, as a funeral urn, grave, or shroud. This symbol he probably knew from several sources. Everard's translation of the Hermetica, *The Divine Pymander*, contains a striking passage in which the body is called "the Sepulchre carried about with us." Taylor in his *Dissertation on the Mysteries* explains the symbol and the doctrine in a passage that gives also some idea of its widespread use:

And to begin with the obscure and profound Heraclitus, speaking of souls unembodied: "We live," says he, "their death, and we die their life" . . . And Empedocles, blaming generation, beautifully says of her [i.e. material nature]:

The species changing with destruction dread,
She makes the living *pass into the* dead.

And again, lamenting his connection with this corporeal world he pathetically exclaims:

For this I weep, for this indulge my woe,
That e'er my soul such novel realms should know.

Plato, too, it is well known, considered the body as the sepulchre of the soul; and in the *Cratylus* consents with the doctrine of Orpheus, that the soul is punished through its union with the body. . . . The Pythagorean Philolaus [writes] "that the soul is united with body for the sake of suffering punishment, and that it is buried in the body as in a sepulchre." And lastly, Pythagoras himself confirms the above sentiments, when he beautifully observes . . . "that whatever we see when awake, is death; and when asleep, a dream."[49]

Such is the condition of the "thousands of sweepers" all locked up in "coffins of black," for whom life in this world is no better than a living death.

It is a saying of Heraclitus that the waking are illuminated from dreams, and dreamers from the dead (that is, from those whose death we live); in Tom Dacre's dream the chimney sweepers enter the spiritual world, where their bodies are no longer coffins but clouds that ride on the wind:

Then naked & white, all their bags left behind,
They rise upon clouds and sport in the wind.

Blake, however, may not have gone to Heraclitus for the belief that dreams give access to the world of spirits, for Swedenborg's visions of other worlds were often revealed in dreams or in trance. The value of dreams as revelations of some order of reality is, after all, older and more normal than the myopic concentration upon waking experience as the only reality, characteristic of the concrete mind, of which Watts, the hymn writer, is so typical a representative. Watts's Sluggard is a dreamer: "You'd have wak'd me too soon, I must slumber again."

For Watts virtue was industry in the tasks of this world. Blake's chimney sweeper he would not have encouraged to tell his dream, but sent him about his business. Blake knew otherwise:

> Father, O Father! what do we here
> In this Land of unbelief & fear!
> The Land of Dreams is better far,
> Above the light of the Morning Star.[50]

The difference between the child dreamer and the adult dreamer is that the child naturally accepts the Land of Dreams as a plane of reality. Children come and go freely, and because they do not question the truth of their visions, the dreams of the night give comfort for the day. In the poem "The Land of Dreams" the child does not doubt that he has really walked with his dead mother in the Elysian fields—as Swedenborg, no less than Heraclitus and Pythagoras, taught:

> Among the Lambs, clothed in white,
> She walk'd with her Thomas in sweet delight.
> I wept for joy, like a dove I mourn;
> O! when shall I again return!

But the father can no longer come and go so freely:

> Dear Child, I also by pleasant Streams
> Have wander'd all Night in the Land of Dreams;
> But tho' calm & warm the waters wide,
> I could not get to the other side.

The sweeps, poor half-starved slaves in working life, are in spirit still gifted with the prerogative of childhood; their "angels behold the face of their heavenly Father" and are not wholly confined to this world. The world of Innocence includes the Land of Dreams. Some might say that Blake realized the nature of dreams in somewhat the same way as did Freud, who interprets dreams as the fulfillment of the vain desires of waking life. In fact he meant much more and saw dreams as states of real insight into the world of imagination, of "what eternally exists, really and unchangeably."

The world into which the chimney sweepers are freed suggests very strongly the landscape of Vergil's Elysium; and it is possible that Vergil has part in the inspiration of the lines,

> Then down a green plain leaping, laughing, they run,
> And wash in a river, and shine in the Sun.

If "The Chimney Sweeper" was written after Blake had read Thomas Taylor's *Dissertation on the Eleusinian and Bacchic Mysteries*[51] (we have evidence in the two "Lyca" poems of the deep impression made on him by that work), it is likely that his attention would have been drawn by Taylor to Vergil's description of Elysium:

> Nulli certa domus. Lucis habitamus opacis
> Riparumque toros, et prata recentia rivis
> Incolimus. . . .

translated by Dryden:

> In no fix'd place the Happy Souls reside.
> In Groves we live; and lye on mossy Beds
> By Crystal Streams, that murmur through the Meads.[52]

Taylor comments on this passage in terms that might well have suggested to Blake the freeing of the chimney sweepers from their "coffins" into Elysian existence: "By the blessed being confined to no particular habitation, the liberal condition of their existence is plainly implied; since they are entirely free from all material restraint, and purified from all inclinations to the dark and cold tenement of the body." The opening lines of "London" suggest very strongly Vergil's account of the damned in Hades:

> Nor Death itself can wholly wash their Stains;
> But long-contracted Filth ev'n in the Soul remains.
> The Reliques of inveterate Vice they wear;
> And spots of Sin obscene in ev'ry Face appear.[53]

Not like the chimney sweepers who "wash in the river" and are cleansed of the soot that has never defiled their souls, the people of London are spiritually defiled:

> I wander thro' each charter'd street,
> Near where the charter'd Thames does flow,
> And mark in every face I meet
> Marks of weakness, marks of woe.[53]

Vergil describes the gradual purgation of the souls as a washing; and "To cleanse the Face of my Spirit . . ." and "To bathe in the Waters of Life, to wash off the Not Human"[54] is a return to an image that Blake first used of the chimney sweepers.

A passage in Swedenborg suggests an additional meaning that is not immediately apparent in this poem. Swedenborg in one of his "memorable relations" writes the following strange account of chimney sweepers:

> There are also Spirits amongst those from the Earth Jupiter, whom they call Sweepers of Chimnies, because they appear in like Garments, and likewise with sooty Faces. . . . One of these Spirits came to me, and anxiously requested that I would intercede for him to be admitted into Heaven; he said, that he was not conscious of having done any Evil. . . . He was likewise of a black Colour in the Light of Heaven, but he himself said that he was not of a black Colour, but of a darkish brown. I was informed that they are such at first, who are afterwards received among those who consititute the province of the Seminal Vessels in the Grand Man or Heaven.[55]

This unlooked-for link between the chimney sweepers and the sexual instinct would have seemed singularly apt to Freud. The symbol, for Swedenborg, seems to have no social significance; it is, so far as we can judge, purely personal. There is all the difference in the world between Swedenborg's use of the chimney-sweeper figure and Blake's far more human sympathy with the real London boys, to whom he gives names—Tom, Dick, Joe, Ned, and Jack—lest we should forget that it is in these "minute particulars" that alone universal life is expressed. But that Blake made use of Swedenborg's "Relation," even that this provided the initial impulse of the poem, seems beyond doubt, for the passage continues:

> He came again to me, in vile Raiment, and again said, that he had a burning desire to be admitted into Heaven . . .At that Instant the Angels called to him to cast off his Raiment, which he did immediately, with inconceivable Quickness from the Vehemence of his Desire; whereby was represented what is the Nature of their Desires, who are in the Province to which the seminal Vessels correspond. I was informed that such, when they are prepared for Heaven, are stripped of their own Garments, and are clothed with new shining Raiment, and become Angels.

Is this the source of the angel in Blake's poem,

> And by came an Angel who had a bright key,
> And he open'd the coffins & set them all free;

calling to them, like the Angel in Swedenborg, to strip off their foul garments and rise free, "naked & white, all their bags left behind"?

There is, if this be so, a direct link between the chimney sweepers and Orc, who is Blake's Eros. He, too, chained to his rock and burning in his own flames, is set free in dreams, and the images used are the same ones we have already found in "The Chimney Sweeper:"

> Yet thou dost laugh at all these tortures, & this horrible place:
> . . .
> . . . feeding thyself
> With visions of sweet bliss far other than this burning clime.
> Sure thou art bath'd in rivers of delight, on verdant fields
> Walking in joy, in bright Expanses sleeping on bright clouds[56]

There is nothing improbable in the suggestion that the figure of Orc-Eros has its beginning—or one of its beginnings—in this strange and uncouth fable of the erotic figure of the sweeper of chimneys.

·　　·　　·

When we come to Songs of Experience, Swedenborg is giving place to more powerful influences, which were by now at work. But his influence is still present; in "The Clod & the Pebble," "The Garden of Love," and perhaps "The Human Abstract" and "The Angel" we may still find the mark of Swedenborgian symbolism.

"The Clod & the Pebble"[58] seems to have been suggested by a passage in *Divine Love and Wisdom* (though there are similar passages elsewhere), a book upon which Blake had drawn freely for several of the *Songs of Innocence*. The passage is one of Swedenborg's habitual black and white contrasts between the angelic and diabolic points of view. This characteristic Swedenborgian presentation has certainly left its mark upon Blake. One might say that the very conception of *Innocence* and *Experience* as "contrasting states of the human soul" is essentially Swedenborgian, as is the structure of the *Marriage*, with its angels and devils. In this case the theme is love:

Love consists in this, that what it hath may be another's, and that it may feel his Delight as Delight in itself; this is to Love; but for a Man to feel his own Delight in another, and not the other's Delight in himself, is not to Love, for in the latter case he loves himself, but in the former he loves his Neighbour: These two Kinds of Love are diametrically opposite to each other: They both indeed effect Conjunction, and it doth not appear, that for a Man to love his own, that is, himself in another, disjoineth, when nevertheless it so disjoineth, that in Proportion as any one hath thus loved another, so much does he afterwards hate him.[59]

Blake's poem follows the pattern closely, clod and pebble symbolizing Swedenborg's two kinds of love:

> "Love seeketh not Itself to please,
> Nor for itself hath any care,
> But for another gives its ease,
> And builds a Heaven in Hell's despair."
>
> So sang a little Clod of Clay
> Trodden with the cattle's feet,
> But a Pebble of the brook
> Warbled out these metres meet:
>
> "Love seeketh only Self to please,
> To bind another to Its delight,
> Joys in another's loss of ease,
> And builds a Hell in Heaven's despite."[60]

Hell and Heaven are strictly Swedenborgian in this context. What Blake has added is the poetic vision—the murmuring cold voice of the brook, the magical coldness of the vowels, "Warbled out these metres meet." There is nothing peculiar to Swedenborg in the symbol of a stone for hardness of heart, although one may point to plenty of examples of objects that turn to stone in the hands of those who have "removed themselves from the good of love." But the little Clod of Clay is a more interesting figure. She first appears in *The Book of Thel* as matron Clay, and later as Enion the Earth Mother (matter), one of the most beautifully characterized figures of Blake's mythology. I believe she has her genesis in an image in the *Universal Theology*, whose animation might well have delighted Blake. Swedenborg is expounding the spiritual and indeed human nature of every expression of life, and thus describes a particle of mold: "The Internal of a Particle of mould, whereby its External is impelled, is its Tendency to make the Seeds of Plants vegetate, exhaling somewhat from its little Bosom, which insinuates itself into the inmost [Parts] of the Seeds, and produceth this wonderful Effect."[61]

Blake's Clod of Clay in *Thel*, who nourishes the worm, is surely based upon this humblest of things. Blake's use of the word "exhale" in this context makes it almost certain:

> *The Clod of Clay heard the Worm's voice & rais'd her pitying head:*
> *She bow'd over the weeping infant, and her life exhal'd*
> *In milky fondness: then on Thel she fix'd her humble eyes.*
>
> *"O beauty of the vales of Har! we live not for ourselves.*
> *Thou seest me the meanest thing, and so I am indeed."*[62]

Her actions and her words are altogether in keeping with the Clod of Clay and with Swedenborg's mold.

·   ·   ·

In the "Garden of Love".... Blake is following the Swedenborgian formula of constructing a symbolic landscape in terms of correspondences.

Among the several influences traceable in "The Garden of Love," Swedenborg's predominates. Blake is following the Swedenborgian formula for constructing a symbolic landscape in terms of correspondences. The two states of the garden correspond respectively to the freedom of love in childhood and its suppression, in the name of religion, in the sexual expression that it naturally takes on in adult life. Or one might read the poem without a specifically sexual meaning, as a simple contrast between the freedom of a religion of love and the restraints of a religion consisting only of moral laws; for this is all that is implied in the passage of Swedenborg upon which it seems to be based:

> Faith separate from Charity deadens all Things, and Faith joined with Charity enlivens all Things. The nature of such

Deadening, and Enlivening, may be seen visibly in our spiritual World .... for where Faith is joined with Charity, there are paradisaical Gardens, flowry Walks, and verdant Groves, gay and delightful, in Proportion to such Conjunction; but where Faith is separate from Charity, there doth not grow so much as a blade of Grass, nor any green Thing, except it be on Thorns and Briers.[63]

That the garden of love must obviously bear sweet flowers, and the garden of cold faith only thorns and briars, follows by the logic of correspondence. The "priests in black gowns" are evidently taken from the same "Memorable Relation," which continues: "There were standing at a little Distance

from us, some of the Clergy, whom the Angel called Justifiers and Sanctifiers of Men by Faith alone, and also *Arcanists*, that is, Dealers in Mysteries." These clergy refused to listen to the teaching that "Faith without Charity Kills all things," and turned away so as not to hear it.

There is also a strong dig here at Isaac Watts, who describes the Sluggard's garden as overgrown with "nettles and briars" because its owner is an idle dreamer. Blake sees the matter otherwise: on the spiritual plane it is the moralistic clergy like Watts himself who make a wilderness of thorns, where the happy play of childhood plants bright gardens.

By a natural association of images, a passage from Boehme possibly comes into the complex whole of Blake's garden of love: "the Devil has built his Chapel close by the Christian Church, and has quite destroyed the Love of Paradise, and has in the Stead of it set up mere covetous, proud, self-willed, faithless, sturdy, malicious Blasphemers, Thieves and Murderers,"[64] a description of the clergy quite after Blake's own heart.

The "graves" in the garden, Gothic as imagery, have obvious Neo-platonic overtones. They are the bodily sepulchers of souls who have lost all access to eternity. They are, by the logic of the symbol, the graves of the children who once played in the garden, but are now its dead.

Notes

Works by Blake and Swedenborg are abbreviated in the following notes. See Abbreviations for complete titles.

1. *T.C.R.*, Vol 11, § 623, pp. 237-39.

2. *D.C.*: K. 581.

3. *H.H.*, § 89, p. 53.

4. Coleridge's definition of a symbol will make this clear. His symbol in no way differs from a Swedenborgian "correspondence," translated into literary terms:

> Now an Allegory is but a translation of abstract notions into a picture-language which is itself nothing but an abstraction from objects of the senses; the principal being more worthless even than its phantom proxy, both unlike unsubstantial, and the former shapeless to boot. On the other hand a Symbol is characterized by a translucence of the Special in the Individual or of the General in the Especial or of the Universal in the General. Above all by the translucence of the Eternal through and in the Temporal. It always partakes of the Reality which it renders intelligible; and while it enunciates the whole, abides itself as a living part in that Unity, of which it is the representative.
> [*The Statesman's Manual*, pp. 36-37. In Kathleen Coburn, ed., *Inquiring Spirit*, pp. 103-104.]

5. *T.C.R.*, Vol. I, § 200, pp. 275-76.

6. *A.C.*, Index, and Vol. I, § 273, p. 105.

7. Notebook 115; K. 162.

8. The relevant passage is in *Mysterium Magnum*, III, Chap. 33, § 27, p. 178:

> For the *Rainbow* has the *Colour* of all the three Principles, *viz.* The Colour of the *first* Principle is *red* and *darkish-brown*, which denotes the dark and Fire-world, that is, the first Principle, the Kingdom of God's Anger. The Colour of the *second* Principle is *white* and *yellow*: this is the majestical Colour, signifying, as a Type of the holy World, God's Love. The *Colour* of the *third* Principle is *green* and *blue*; blue from the Chaos, and green from the Water or Salt-petre; where, in the Flagrat or Crack of the Fire, the *Sulphur* and *Mercury* seperate themselves, and produce distinct, various and

several Colours, which denote to us the inward spiritual Worlds.

[References to the writings of Jacob Boehme are to *The Works of Jacob Behmen*, ed. Ward and Langcake (4 vols., London, 1764-81), known as "Law's Boehme", and herafter abbreviated as *Works*.]

9. *Annotations to D.L.W.* 12; K. 90.

10. Wicksteed interprets the two postures as representing the spiritual and the material sides of man. This is, I believe, a near approximation; the alternatives are wisdom and love. The difference in interpretation is slight but nevertheless important. This interpretation of right and left is traditional—the two pillars of justice (or severity) and mercy of the cabalistic tree, and these in turn derived from Jachin and Boaz, the pillars of Solomon's Temple. Blake knew of these pillars, and refers to them in his description of *A Vision of the Last Judgment*, "Jesus seated between the Two Pillars, Jachin & Boaz" (*V.L.J.* 76; K. 606). The context suggests their symbolic meaning.

11. Notebook 114; K. 164.

12. *Aurora*, Chap. 26, § 92; *Works*, I, 264.

13. *J.* 22; K. 622.

14. *D.L.W.*, K 292, pp. 266-67.

15. *Infant Sorrow, S.E.*; K. 217. The image was evidently one that had great power in Blake's imagination, for he chose to illustrate the same archetypal figure from *Macbeth*, in one of his finest paintings:

> And pity like a naked new born babe
> Striding the blast. . . .

There is surely in the "fiend hid in a cloud" also a reminiscence of that other, more sinister babe who summons Hecate:

> My little Spirit see
> Sits in a Foggy cloud, and stayes for me.

16. *S.I.*; K. 125.

17. Paracelsus, *Philosophy Reformed & Improved in four Profound Tractates . . . Discovering the Wonderfull Mysteries of the Creation, By Paracelsus: being his Philosophy to the Athenians*, translated by R. Turner (London, 1657), Bk. III, text 3-4, p. 58.

18. *D.C.* IV; K. 576.

19. *T.C.R.*, Vol. II, § 787, p. 419.

20. *D.L.W.*, § 11, p. 12.

21. *Annotations to D.L.W.* § 12; K. 90.

22. *D.L.W.*, § 157, p. 128.

23. Ibid., § 129, p. 105. Cf. the orientation of churches to the east.

24. Ibid., § 120, p. 99.

25. Notebook 105, K. 179.

26. *D.L.W.*, § 5, p. 5.

27. *Auguries of Innocence*; K. 434, 129-32.

28. *S.I.*; K. 120.

29. *S.I.*; K. 121.

29a. 1, 24 ff.

30. *Blake's Innocence and Experience*, p. 39.

31. *The Last Judgement* §§ 3-6, pp. 3-5.

32. *D.C.*; K. 577.

33. The exact date of *An Island in the Moon* is not known. Foster Damon suggested 1788, because it seems to lead on naturally to *Songs of Innocence*. Keynes formerly dated it approximately 1787, but in his 1957 edition moves the date back to 1784-85, on such evidence as the women's fashions mentioned by Blake that were "in" during those years. I question this earlier date because it seems to me that Blake was already familiar with Neoplatonic symbolism, which can most easily be explained by supposing he had read Taylor's translation of Plotinus' *Concerning the Beautiful* (1787). Both Damon and Keynes, however, allow that Sipsop the Pythagorean is (whatever the date of the *Island*) Taylor himself; so that my objection is not conclusive. Blake knew Taylor, and may have learned much from him in conversation.

34. Thomas Taylor, *Concerning the Beautiful, or a paraphrased translation from the Greek of Plotinus, Ennead I, Book 6* (London, 1787); p. 24; *Ennead* I.6.5. [Hereafter Plotinus' *Concerning the Beautiful* is abbreviated as *P.C.B.*]

35. For further discussion of this reference, see Kathleen Raine, *Blake and Tradition* Bollingen Series XXXV-11 (Princeton: Princeton University Press, 1968), Vol. 1, pp. 84-5, 108, 153.

36. *H.H.*, § 78, p. 47.

37. *T.C.R.*, Vol. I, § 33, p. 48.

38. Ibid., Vol II, § 470, p. 93.

39. *F.Z.*, VIIa; K. 329, 359-60.

40. *F.Z.* IX; K. 374, 641-42.

41. *J.* 91; K. 738, 30-31.

42. *P.C.B.*, pp. 11-12 n.; *Ennead* VI.3.7.

43. Ibid., pp. 36-37; *Ennead* I.6.8.

44. *S.I.*; K. 117.

45. *H.H.*, § 514, p. 353.

46. *Aurora*, Chap. 11, §§ 58-60,; *Works*, I, 97.

47. *S.I.*; K. 117.

48. *P.C.B.*, p. 25; *Ennead* I.6.5.

49. *Dissertation*, pp. 6-8. Cf. "I should not wonder if Euripides spoke the truth when he says, 'Who knows whether to live is not to die, and to die, is not to live?' And we, perhaps, are in reality dead. For I have heard from one of the wise, that we are now dead; and that the body is our sepulchre." (Plato, *Gorgias* 492E; *Works*, tr. Taylor, IV, 410. All translations from Plato in the present book are by Taylor.)

50. *The Land of Dreams*; K. 427.

51. See *Blake and Tradition* I, pp. 129 ff.

52. *Aenid* VI. 673-75; from Virgil. *Works: containing his Pastorals, Georgics, and Aeneis, translated into English Verse by John Dryden* (London, 1697), p. 389.

53. Ibid. 998-1001; p. 392.

54. *London*; K. 216.

55. *M.* 40; K. 533, 37-41, 1.

56. Swedenborg, *Concerning the Earths in our Solar System*, translated by John Clowes (London, 1787), § 79, pp. 87-88.

57. *F.Z.* VIIa; K. 321, 59-66.

58. *S.E.*; K. 211.

59. *D.L.W.*, § 47, p. 39.

60. Cf. also Milton, *Paradise Lost* I. 254-5: "the Mind is its own place and in itself/Can make a Heav'n of a Hell, a Hell of Heav'n."

61. *T.C.R.*, Vol. II, § 785, p. 417. See continuation of this passage in *Blake and Tradition* II, p. 127.

62. *B.T.* 4; K. 129, 7-12.

63. *T.C.R.*, Vol. I, § 385, P. 456.

64. *Three Principles of the Divine Essence*, Chap. 20, § 28; *Works*, I, 201.

The Human Face of God

KATHLEEN RAINE

IN her preceding essay, "The Swedenborgian Songs," Kathleen Raine demonstrated the Swedenborgian roots of Blake's early engraved poems. In the following, Dr. Raine presents extensive evidence which "confutes the often propounded view of Blake scholars that Swedenborg's influence is to be found only in Blake's early works."

Dr. Raine had begun to articulate Swedenborg's continued influence on Blake's later works in her 1982 book, *The Human Face of God* (Thames and Hudson, 1982), a study of Blake's 1823-6 *Job* engravings.

> Fortunately a valuable record exists (apart that is from his own writings) of some of Blake's most deeply held convictions, faithfully set down by Crabb Robinson, Wordsworth's friend and diarist. . . . [Blake] told Crabb Robinson that Swedenborg was "a divine teacher"—an important record since it is evidence of Blake's continued admiration for Swedenborg to the end of his life. . . . In fact Blake's "system" which has bewildered so many is in essence the Doctrine of Swedenborg's Church of the New Jerusalem. . . .
>
> No Blake scholar has yet done justice to the extent and importance of Swedenborg's influence on Blake. . . . Scholars have been misled by Blake's strictures on Swedenborg in *The Marriage of Heaven and Hell* in which he says Swedenborg has taught, not "one new truth," but "all the old falsehoods". . . .
>
> It is tempting to conclude from these intemperate words that Swedenborg had little or no influence on Blake's later writings. This is not the case. . . . Swedenborg's "leading doctrines" are in fact the ground of Blake's own unusual form of Christianity which has puzzled so many who have deplored its heresy or admired its originality. He uses Swedenborg's terms and adheres to his doctrines throughout the Prophetic Books, and a late work, *The Everlasting Gospel*, is an impassioned summary of the most distinctive and controversial of Swedenborg's leading doctrines.

In the following text of her previously unpublished 1985 Paris lecture (also titled "The Human Face of God"), Dr. Raine expands on her thesis that "the influence of Swedenborg, if anything, is clearer in the last works [of Blake] than in the first."   —Ed.

I will begin by reading a poem, perhaps known to many of you. It is entitled "The Divine Image," and comes from *Songs of Innocence*, a collection of poems written for children and published in 1789, when its author, the poet William Blake, was thirty-two years old. No one, of whatever place, time, or religion, could fail to understand and to assent to the simple directness of its message:

From a lecture delivered to l'Université St-Jean de Jérusalem, May, 1985, on the occasion of an annual conference established by Henry Corbin, by permission of the author. Copyright © 1985 by Kathleen Raine.

To Mercy, Pity, Peace and Love
All pray in their distress;
And to these virtues of delight
Return their thankfulness.

For Mercy, Pity, Peace, and Love
Is God, our father dear,
And Mercy, Pity, Peace, and Love,
Is Man, his child and care.

For Mercy has a human heart,
Pity a human face,
And Love, the human form divine,
And Peace, the human dress.

Then every man, of every clime,
That prays in his distress,
Prays to the human form divine,
Love, Mercy, Pity, Peace.

And all must love the human form,
In heathen, turk or jew;
Where Mercy, Love, & Pity dwell
There God is dwelling too.

For all the apparent simplicity of this poem the depth of its resonance leads us into deep eschatological mystery. At first sight it might appear to be a simple statement of the Christian doctrine of the Incarnation, but there is much in the poem that might be unacceptable to the Apostolic church, Catholic and Protestant alike; for Blake is not writing of the historical Jesus but of "the human form in heathen, turk or jew"—a comprehensive phrase which embraces all the races and religions of mankind without exception.

How did it come about that Blake was able to make, with such luminous simplicity, this affirmation which goes far beyond any conventional declaration of faith in Jesus Christ? He was a mystic, to be sure, but mystics are of their time and place. He was a reader of the Bible, and in the first chapter of Genesis it is written that God said, "Let us make man in our image, after our likeness . . . . So God created man in his own image, in the image of God created he him." (I:26) But these words have been variously interpreted. According to the Gospel of St. John the first-created man who was "in the beginning with God" "was made flesh and dwelt

amongst us" in the person of Jesus Christ, but not otherwise. There have been certain mystics—Eckhardt for example— who have understood the mystery of the Incarnation in a more universal sense but these have generally been frowned upon. At the end of the eighteenth century Blake spoke openly a realization which had hitherto been the secret knowledge of a few. He was—and knew himself to be— prophetically inspired, and "The Divine Image" is the quintessence of his prophetic message—that God is "in the form of a man" and that the Incarnation is not particular but universal. Such is the power and certainty of Blake's genius that in simple words he cuts through all theological tangles to the mysterious heart of the Christian revelation. When

Jesus affirmed "I and the father are one" and "he who has seen me has seen the father" his words were deemed blasphemous and led to his condemnation. Blake's religion, as he constantly declared, is "the religion of Jesus" (by which he does not necessarily mean as taught by the Christian church) and under the guise of "poetic license" the radical, not to say revolutionary content of his affirmation passes unnoticed. Such poems as "The Divine Image" win the assent of the heart before their doctrinal implications become apparent. "Knowledge is not by deduction, but Immediate by Perception or Sense at once. Christ addresses himself to the Man, not to his Reason." (Annotations to Berkeley's *Siris*; K.774) In Blake's terms Jesus, "the true man," is the Imagination present in all. That innate Imagination assents to Blake's words as being as self-evident as the light of day.

It is . . . the doctrines of Swedenborg that Blake's works embody and to which they lend poetry and eloquence.

Yet they embody the spirit of a new age, a new apprehension of the Christian revelation. But when in *The Marriage of Heaven and Hell* Blake wrote that "a new heaven is begun" he spoke not on his own authority but as a follower of Emanuel Swedenborg, as a member of the Swedenborgian Church of the New Jerusalem. Wonderful as are Blake's poems, his visionary paintings, his aphorisms, it is, in essence, the doctrines of Swedenborg that Blake's works embody and to which they lend poetry and eloquence. So, unawares, the teachings of Swedenborg's Church of the New Jerusalem have permeated the spiritual sensibility of the English nation, through Blake. Few of the ever-growing numbers who regard Blake as a prophet of the New Age are aware that the coherent and revolutionary interpretation of the Christian Mysteries which underlies Blake's prophecies is that of Swedenborg.

·   ·   ·

The writings of Swedenborg, stilted and voluminous, written in Latin at a time when Latin was ceasing to be the common language of the learned, have none the less had a profound influence throughout Protestant Europe and beyond; Henry

Corbin himself saw the seminal significance of Swedenborg, whom he went so far as to describe as "the Buddha of the west." He was by profession neither philosopher nor theologian but a man of science, assessor of minerals to the Swedish government. He spent much time in London where he had a small but devoted following, and might even have been seen by Blake as a boy, for Swedenborg died in London in 1772, when Blake was fifteen. Doubtless Swedenborg had predecessors in the millennial tradition, stemming from Joachim of Flora; but we must accept Swedenborg's word that his extraordinary prophetic insight came to him not by study but by what he described as an "opening" of his consciousness which revealed to him the inner worlds which he calls the "heavens" and the "hells"; and which those who follow the terminology introduced by Henry Corbin would call the *mundus imaginalis*; worlds not in space, but in mankind's inner universe. In his visions it was shown to Swedenborg that a "new church" had been established in the heavens, following a "Last Judgment" passed on the Apostolic church, which was to be superseded by the "Church of the New Jerusalem," the last and perfect revelation of the nature of Jesus Christ as the "Divine Humanity"; a mystery which had hitherto been imperfectly understood, but which was, in the New Church, to be fully revealed in the epiphany of the "Divine Human." This New Church, of which Swedenborg's writings are the scriptures, is to be the last in the six thousand years of the world's history from the creation to the end of days and the coming of the Kingdom. There have already been, according to Swedenborg, twenty-six such churches,* from the time of Adam, through a succession of prophetic revelations made to the Patriarchs, to Noah, Abraham, Moses, Solomon, and within the Christian era the churches of Paul, Constantine, Charlemagne and Luther; each of these representing some new realization—or revelation—which is to reach its term and perfect fulfillment in a total affirmation of the humanity of God and the divinity

---

*Swedenborg's standard scheme identifies five stages, or "dispensations," which he defines in terms of churches—the Most Ancient Church (antediluvian), the Ancient Church (pre-Decalogue), the Jewish Church, the Christian Church, and the New Christian Church (New Jerusalem). Blake seems to have derived his model of twenty-seven churches by adding up the sub-stages which Swedenborg identified, but did not total. —The Editors

of man, their unity and identity. In his setting out of the Leading Doctrines of the Church of the New Jerusalem Swedenborg declares that: "The Lord is God from eternity" and the divine Human is not merely the Son of God but God himself. "God and man, in the Lord . . . are not two, but one person, yea, altogether one . . . He is the God of heaven and earth." The Divine Humanity is almighty; or, as Blake simply says, "God is Jesus." (Laocoön; K.777) Since in this teaching the oneness of the human and the divine is total, it follows that the Christian revelation can go no farther, man and God being one, not only in the historic person of Jesus Christ but totally for the Christ within the whole human race.

Jung has written in criticism of the Christian Church that, if not in principle, at all events in practice, the divine Being has been envisaged as outside man and the Redemption (in the doctrine of the Atonement) also as an occurrence outside man, occurring once only in history. It is true that the Mass is held to be not a commemoration of that event, but a timeless re-enactment; but even so, that Mystery, as commonly taught and understood, is an external and historical event. Jesus Christ, moreover, is an exceptional being, virtually a demi-god in the Pagan sense, not fully human. Jung in his remarkable work, *Answer to Job*, admired by Henry Corbin,* and expressing the mature thought of a lifetime on the meaning of Christianity, writes that

> Christ, by his descent, conception and birth, is a half-god in the classical sense. He is virginally begotten by the Holy Ghost and, as he is not a creaturely human being, has no inclination to sin. The infection of evil was in his case precluded by the preparations for the Incarnation. He therefore stands more on the divine than on the human level. (*Answer to Job*, p. 669)

The same is true of the Virgin Mary:

> As a consequence of her immaculate conception Mary is already different from other mortals, and this fact is confirmed by her assumption. (Ibid., note.)

Thus salvation is available to humankind through the external intervention of these superhuman personages. In making

*Reviewed by Henry Corbin in *La Revue de Culture Européen*, No. 5, 1953.

this criticism of Christianity Jung makes no mention of Swedenborg's teachings, which did in fact raise and respond to many of his own criticisms, in calling for an interiorization of the Christian mysteries of the Incarnation, Passion and Resurrection. Swedenborg gives an actual date—1757 (which was, incidentally, the date of Blake's birth)—when a "Last Judgment" had been passed on the Apostolic Church "in the heavens"—that is to say in mankind's inner worlds—to be followed by an epiphany of the Divine Humanity in his full glory in the inner worlds of "heavens." With this inner event a new kind of realization, a new kind of consciousness, began to dawn within Christendom, following the interiorization of the Apostolic teaching. This Last Judgment was not an outer event, in time and in history, but an inner event, which would, not dramatically, but gradually, make itself apparent also in the outer world of history. A new church is thus a new consciousness. Without invoking the idea of "evolution" (as understood by materialist science) we are to understand Swedenborg's concept of the twenty-seven churches as a progressive revelation in time and history. This is entirely in keeping with the linear view of time common to all the Abrahamic religions (Judaism, Christianity and Islam) and indeed without such a conception time and history become meaningless. Blake indeed saw the twenty-seven churches as cyclic rather than linear, a progressive darkening of the paradisal vision from Adam to Jesus Christ, followed by a progressive recovery to be fulfilled in the "second coming" in the inner worlds. This event completes the cycle which leads humankind back to the Paradisal state from which we have fallen.

What is under consideration is not in its nature an event to be pinned down like an event in history to a certain date, but is rather a subtle change of awareness. It seems that such a change in the understanding of the nature of spiritual events did begin to manifest itself at that time, which has continued to grow like a plant from a small seed. Swedenborg's seed fell on fertile ground in the spirit of William Blake; and our presence here at the University of St. John of Jerusalem, dedicated to an understanding of the Imaginal universe, the inner universe, is an expression—one amongst others—of this new understanding, in a world where the old foundations seem inadequate. It may well be that in the future our own time will be seen not as the age of the triumph of materialist

"Then the Lord answered Job out of the Whirlwind"; *Job* **13 (detail)**

science but as the breakdown of that phase and the beginning of just such an "opening" of humanity's inner worlds as Swedenborg prophetically experienced and foresaw.

This theme is a central one for Jung, who in his *Answer to Job* sets forth at length a view of the Bible in which, from Job to the Incarnation of Jesus Christ, there is what he calls "a tendency for God to become man." This tendency is already implicit in Genesis, when by a special act of creation Jahweh created man, who was the image of God. Jung is, of course, using the terms not of theology but of psychology and is therefore writing of changes in human consciousness of the Divine Being, and not of changes in God himself in an absolute sense. Jung writes:

> In omniscience, there had existed from all eternity a knowledge of the human nature of God or of the divine nature of man. That is why, long before Genesis was written, we find corresponding testimonies in ancient Egyptian records. Preparations, however, are not in themselves creative events, but only stages in the process of becoming conscious. It was only quite late that we realized (or rather, are beginning to realize) that God is Reality itself and therefore—last but not least—man. This realization is a millennial process. (para. 631, p. 402)

Jung sees this process foreshadowed in the story of Job—the type of the human encounter with the divine. The God of the Book of Job is so totally other that Job seems to himself to be insignificant, powerless, without recourse—except to God himself; and Jung is in agreement with theologians who have seen in Job's words, "I know that my redeemer liveth, and that he shall stand in the latter day upon the earth . . . yet in my flesh shall I see God," a foreshadowing of the Incarnation:

> The life of Christ is just what it had to be if it is the life of a god and a man at the same time. It is a *symbolus*, a bringing together of heterogenous natures, rather as if Job and Yahweh were combined in a single personality. Yahweh's intention to become man, which resulted from his collision with Job, is fulfilled in Christ's life and suffering. (para. 648, p. 409)

On the way to this realization, Jung points out, we have Ezekiel's vision of the "Son of Man," which reappears in the Book of Daniel, and later (about 100 B.C.) in the Book of Enoch. Ezekiel is himself addressed as "Son of Man"—the man on the throne whom he beheld in his vision; and hence a prefiguration of the much later revelation in Christ. Daniel had a vision of the "Ancient of Days," to whom "with the clouds of heaven there came one like the son of man." Here the "son of man" is no longer the prophet himself but a son of the "Ancient of Days" in his own right.

The power of Swedenborg's revelation, and of Blake's prophetic writings lies in the reality of what they describe, a growing inner awareness on which we cannot go back.

I suggest that the power of Swedenborg's revelation, and of Blake's prophetic writings lies in the reality of what they describe, a growing inner awareness on which we cannot go back. Jung, and even Freud, were aware of this process of interiorization of the Mysteries, but they were not the first to challenge the externalised consciousness of post-Cartesian science; "The Divine is not in Space," Swedenborg affirmed, "although the Divine is omnipresent with every man in the world, and with every angel in heaven." (DLW 7) This, it may be said, has always been so and is implicit in every religious tradition; yet as a fact of the history of two thousand years of Christendom, the realization has been progressive and come but slowly. Seen in another way, Swedenborg's teaching can be seen as a return to a lost traditional norm at the height of the age of Deism or "natural religion" as a philosophic creed; whose effects in every sphere of life are still dominant in our own world. Materialist science has identified "reality" as the natural order, conceived to be an autonomous mechanism external to mind; and in his denial of this view of the "real," Swedenborg, it might be said—and Blake no less—restored a lost norm which understands that mind is not in space but space in mind.

The divine, (Swedenborg declared) is everywhere, yet not in space; and insists

> that these things cannot be comprehended by a natural idea because there is space in that idea; for it is formed out of such things as are in the world; and in each and all these things, which strike the eye, there is space. Everything great and small is of space; everything, broad and high there is of space; in short every measure, figure and form there is of space.

Swedenborg strove to remove the identification of reality with an external material order. Space is a function of the natural body but the human spirit is capable of the omnipresence of the non-spatial.

Furthermore, it is not God who is omnipresent spirit while man exists in space, because "God is Very Man" the human universe is likewise boundless spirit, as God is. He writes:

> In all the heavens there is no other idea of God than the idea of a man; the reason is, that heaven as a whole, and in every part is in form as a man and the Divine, which is with the angels, constitutes heaven; and thought proceeds according to the form of heaven; wherefore it is impossible for the angels to think of God otherwise. Hence it is that all those in the world who are conjoined with heaven (that is with the inner worlds) when they think interiorly in themselves, that is, in their spirit, think of God in a like manner. For this cause that God is a Man. . . . The form of heaven affects this, which in its greatest and its least things is like itself. (DLW 11)

Heaven in its whole and in every part is "in form as a man"; and because man was created "after the image and likeness of God," "the ancients, from the wise to the simple"—from Abraham to the primitive Africans—thought of God as a man. This is not anthropomorphism in the sense in which the word is currently understood, as a projection of the human image upon the divine mystery, but rather the reverse, a recognition of the divine image imprinted on the inner nature of humankind, as "the Divine Human," to use Swedenborg's term. "All is Human, Mighty, Divine," Blake writes; and summarizes the Swedenborgian teaching in a quatrain:

> God Appears & God is Light
> To those poor Souls who dwell in Night,
> But does a Human Form Display
> To those who dwell in Realms of day.
> (Auguries of Innocence; K.434)

These lines are the reversal of the "enlightened" view that we cease to see God in human form as we learn more about "the universe" as natural fact. The ultimate knowledge, according to Blake and Swedenborg, is that the universe is contained in mind—a view to be found also in the Gnostic writings, in the Vedas, and in other spiritually profound cosmologies of the East, but long forgotten in the West with its preoccupation with externality.

The ultimate knowledge, according to Blake and Swedenborg, is that the universe is contained in mind.

Thus we are given a conception of man totally other than that of a materialist science: Man in his spiritual being is boundless and contains not a part of his universe but its wholeness and infinitude. The "body" of the Divine Human is not contained in natural space but contains all things in itself. Swedenborg writes:

> His human body cannot be thought of as great or small, or of any stature, because this also attributes space; and hence He is the same in the first things as the last and in the greatest things and the least; and moreover the Human is the innermost of every created thing, but apart from space. (DLW 285)

Swedenborg uses a strange but cogent argument for the humanity of the Divine: that the attributes of God would be inconceivable except in human terms; and since God is knowable only in human terms He must therefore possess human attributes:

> . . . that God could not have created the universe and all things thereof, unless He were a Man, may be very clearly comprehended by an intelligent person from this ground that . . . in God there is love and wisdom, there is mercy and clemency, and also there is absolute Goodness and Truth, because these things are from Him. And because he cannot deny these things, neither can he deny that God is a Man: for not one of these things is possible abstracted from man: man is their subject, and to separate them from their subject is to say that they are not. Think of wisdom and place it outside man. Is there anything? . . . It must be wisdom in a form such as man has, it must be in all his form, not one thing can be wanting for wisdom to be in it. In a word, the form of wisdom is a man; and because man is the form of wisdom, he is also the form of love, mercy, clemency, good, and truth, because these make one with wisdom. (DLW 286)

It is for these reasons, Swedenborg argues, that Man is said to be created in the image of God, that is, into the form of love and wisdom. It cannot be that man invented God in his own image, since that image is already imprinted in us in our very being. The argument is a subtle one; and although it could be asked, could not God have created beings and universes other than man, the same argument would in every case apply: whatever their attributes these too would bear the image and imprint of their creator and source. Blake, who had read and annotated Swedenborg's *Divine Love and Wisdom* with evident delight might, when he wrote his poem "To Mercy, Pity, Peace and Love" have been thinking of this very passage.

Swedenborg dismisses the idea of those who think of God as other than as a Man, and "of the divine attributes otherwise than as God as a man; because separated from man they are figments of the mind. God is very Man, from whom every Man is a man according to his reception of love and wisdom." (DLW 289)

So it is that

> . . . *Mercy has the human heart,*
> *Pity a human face,*
> *And Love, the human form divine,*
> *And Peace, the human dress.*

"The human form divine" is not the natural body idolatrously glorified but the spiritual form of our human nature.

In understanding that when he wrote these words, so luminously simple, Blake is propounding Swedenborgian doctrine, it becomes perfectly clear that no humanism is implicit in his assigning the human attributes to God, the source and author of our humanity. Swedenborg wrote that *"in all forms and uses there is a certain image of man,"* and that "all uses from primes to ultimates, from ultimates to primes, have relation to all things of man and correspondences with him, and therefore man in a certain image is a universe; and conversely the universe viewed as to its uses is man in an image." (DLW 317) Swedenborg draws the conclusion that it is for this reason that man is called a microcosm; since the universe is totally present in all its parts. Or again, in Blake's words, "One thought fills immensity." What Swedenborg is saying in his stilted style, and Blake is repeating in what to his contemporaries seemed "wild" poetic ravings, is in fact of extreme subtlety and great profundity—that human consciousness contains its universe. This is a return to the ancient teaching, as found for example in the *Hermetica*, that mind is not in space but all spaces and whatever these contain, in mind; "Nothing is more capacious than the incorporeal." To have reaffirmed this realization in the eighteenth century attests to an insight so extraordinary that it can only be described—and Swedenborg did so describe it—as a prophetic revelation.

·   ·   ·

But if for Swedenborg the true man is not the natural body, he nevertheless insists in great detail on the minutiae of the spiritual anatomy:

> . . . because God is a Man, He has a body, and everything belonging to the body; consequently He has a face, a breast, an abdomen, loins, feet; for apart from these he would not be a Man. And having these, he has also eyes, ears, nostrils,

mouth, tongue; and further the organs that are within a man, as the heart and lungs, and the parts which depend on these . . . but in God Man they are Infinite . . . (DLW 21)

He insists "that the angelic spirits are in every respect human . . . they have faces, eyes, ears, hearts, arms, heads and feet; they see, hear and converse with one another and, in a word, that no external attribute of man is wanting, except the material body." (HH 75) In describing realities of the imaginal world Swedenborg insists on the clarity and distinctness of the spirits:

> I have seen them in their own light, which exceeds by many degrees the light of the world, and in that light I have observed all parts of their faces more distinctly and clearly than ever I did the faces of men on earth. (HH 75)

It is hard to know whether Blake possessed this faculty or if he is paraphrasing Swedenborg, so closely do their accounts tally:

> A Spirit and a Vision are not, as the modern philosophy supposes, a cloudy vapour, or a nothing: they are organized and minutely articulated beyond all that the mortal and perishing nature can produce. He who does not imagine in stronger and better lineaments, and in stronger and better light than his perishing, and mortal eye can see, does not imagine at all. The painter of this work asserts that all his imaginations appear to him infinitely more perfect and more minutely organized than any thing seen by his mortal eye. Spirits are organized men. (D.C.; K.576-7)

This is pure Swedenborg; but it may be that we have to conclude that those gifted with the clear vision of the imaginal world are in essential agreement because describing the same reality.

To return to Swedenborg, he affirms continually that the universal heaven is in the form of a man, and "each society in heaven, be it large or small, is so likewise; hence also an angel is a man, for an angel is heaven in its least form." Thus every part down to the smallest "heaven in its least form" is infinite, and the Divine Human an infinite whole made up of infinite wholes, and "the universal heaven consists of myriads of myriads of angels." (Here it must be said that Swedenborg's angels are also men, but discarnate. The

word angel, as he uses it, is not to be understood in the sense of the Near Eastern religions, or indeed of the Christian Fathers and Dionysius the Areopagite's Celestial Hierarchies.)

The human form is present throughout the universe alike in its greatest and in its least parts. Swedenborg writes that "In God Man infinite things are distinctly one. It is well known that God is Infinite, for he is called the Infinite. He is not infinite by this alone, that He is very Esse and Existere in Himself, but because there are Infinite things in Him." (DLW 17) The "vision of light" Blake described in a letter to a friend is purely Swedenborgian; every infinitesimal part of nature is human—and this is his answer to Newton's theory that light is made of "particles":

The "vision of light" Blake described in a letter to a friend is purely Swedenborgian; every infinitesimal part of nature is human.

> In particles bright
> The jewels of Light
> Distinct shone & clear.
> Amaz'd & in fear
> I each particle gazed,
> Astonish'd, Amazed;
> For each was a Man
> Human-form'd. Swift I ran,
> for they beckon'd to me
> Remote by the Sea,
> Saying: Each grain of Sand,
> Every Stone on the Land,
> Each rock & each hill,
> Each fountain & rill,
> Each herb & each tree,
> Mountain, hill, earth & sea,
> Clour, Meteor & Star,
> Are Men Seen Afar.
> (Letter, 2 Oct. 1800; K.804-5)

Swedenborg's Grand Man of the Heavens is a concept of great splendour. In this Divine Man or Human Divine all lives are contained, individually and as angelic societies within the one life of the Divine Humanity; and so down to every inhabitant of heaven who is "every one in his own heaven" and the whole is reflected in each. "The Lord leads all in the universal heaven as if they were one angel" and in the same way "an angelic society sometimes appears as one man in the form of an angel." (HH 51) So "when the Lord himself appears in the midst of the angels, he does not appear encompassed by a multitude but as one in an anglic form." "I have seen," he writes of a visionary society, that "when at a distance it appears as one, and on its approach, as a multitude." And again it is hard to know whether Blake is describing his own vision or paraphrasing Swedenborg when he writes:

> The various States I have seen in my imagination; when distant they appear as One Man but as you approach they appear multitudes of nations. (VLJ; K.609)

Blake summarizes the essence of the Swedenborgian vision of the Grand Man in a passage several times repeated in the Prophetic Books:

> Then those in Great Eternity met in the Council of God
> As one man. . . .
> . . . .
> As One Man all the Universal Family; & that One Man
> They call Jesus the Christ, & they in him & he in them
> Live in Perfect harmony, in Eden the land of life. (FZ; K.277)

Eden the land of life is the *Mundus imaginalis*, the "bosom of God," our native place and state.

·   ·   ·

In affirming the humanity of God Swedenborg is nevertheless remote from what is now called "humanism"; for man is (in Blake's words) only "a form and organ of life" and the life of every individual, of every community, of the whole creation, is "from the Lord." No man's life belongs to himself, each is a recipient of the one life. Thus, whereas Blake wrote that "God is Man & exists in us & we in him" (On Berkeley; K.775), this is no more or less than the teaching of St. John's Gospel and the words of Jesus, "as thou, Father, art in me, and I in thee, that they also may be one in us." Created beings and men exist by virtue of what Swedenborg

calls the "influx" of the one divine life. This influx is through the inner worlds; the outer world of natural appearances is the mirror of spiritual realities, but has itself no substance. (This is of course the teaching of Plotinus on Nature, and of other Platonic writers.) But the outer form—whether of human being or animal, plant or mineral—is the "correspondence" of their living nature. Nothing in nature is, as for materialist science, a self-existent physical entity subject to natural causes; indeed for Swedenborg there is no such thing as a natural cause, all causes being spiritual and "nature" the lowest effect. Again Blake is giving expression to this doctrine when he writes that

> . . . every Natural Effect has a Spiritual Cause, and Not
> A Natural; for a Natural Cause only seems: it is a Delusion
> Of Ulro & a ratio of the perishing Vegetable Memory.
> (Milton 27; K.513)

The realities mirrored in nature belong to the imaginal world—in Blake's terms the Imagination.

> This world of Imagination is the world of Eternity; it is the divine bosom into which we shall all go after the death of the Vegetated body. This World of Imagination is Infinite and Eternal, whereas the world of Generation, or Vegetation, is Finite & Temporal. There Exist in that Eternal World the Permanent Realities of Every Thing which we see reflected in this Vegetable Glass of Nature. All Things are comprehended in their Eternal Forms in the divine body of the Saviour, the True Vine of Eternity, the Human Imagination. . . . (VLJ; K.605-6)

Blake insists that the Imaginal world is a plenitude of forms, and in the same work writes:

> Many suppose that before the Creation All was Solitude & Chaos. This is the most pernicious Idea that can enter the Mind, as it . . . Limits All Existence to Creation & to Chaos, to the Time & Space fixed by the Corporeal Vegetative Eye . . . Eternity Exists & all things in Eternity, Independent of Creation . . . (VLJ; K.614)

While Blake's account of the Imaginal World bears a more platonic stamp than does Swedenborg's, with his emphasis on the inner forms of the Imagination as the originals of which the natural forms are images or copies, yet it is evident that Swedenborg's accounts of heavenly scenery are describing the same imaginal reality. The destination of the discarnate soul is not an empty *nirvana* but comparable to the Far Eastern paradises which await the discarnate soul after death, and the similar paradises and hells of the Near Eastern religions. In *The Divine Love and Wisdom of the Angels* Swedenborg writes:

> ...The spiritual world in external appearance is quite similar to the natural world. Lands appear there, mountains, hills, valleys, planes, fields, lakes, rivers, springs of water, as in the natural world.... Paradises also appear there, gardens, groves, woods, and in them trees and shrubs of all kinds bearing fruit and seeds; also plants, flowers, herbs and grasses.... Animals appear there, birds and fish of every kind. (DLW 321)

Thus in his systematic manner Swedenborg spells out the presence in the "heavens" of the mineral, vegetable and animal kingdoms. In Swedenborg's "heavens" and Blake's Imagination, which both call the Divine Human, the whole universe is contained in its infinite variety as the diversification of the single being of the Divine Humanity. In an early work, *Vala, or The Four Zoas*. Blake describes the whole natural creation striving—"groaning and travailing," in the words of St. Paul (Romans 8:22) to bring forth the human:

> ... *Man looks out in tree & herb & fish & bird & beast*
> *Collecting up the scatter'd portions of his immortal body*
> *Into the Elemental forms of every thing that grows.*
> ....
> *In pain he sighs, in pain he labours in his universe*
> *Screaming in birds over the deep, & howling in the wolf*
> *Over the slain, & moaning in the cattle & in the winds*
> ....
> *And in the cries of birth & in the groans of death his voice*
> *Is heard throughout the Universe: wherever a grass grows*
> *Or a leaf buds, The Eternal Man is seen, is heard, is felt*
> *And all his sorrows, till he reassumes his ancient bliss.*
> (FZ; K.355)

Humanity, the immortal body "distributed" as the Platonist would say, in the "many" must be reassumed into the "one," the bosom of God, the Human Imagination. In that universe

microcosm and macrocosm are one.

·   ·   ·

I mentioned earlier C.G. Jung's highly significant criticisms of the Christian Church for its conversion of the figures of Jesus Christ, and in the Catholic Church the Virgin Mary likewise, into what have been to all intents and purposes pagan demigods. Jung's criticisms of Christianity have indeed been cogent, and he has played a significant part in calling for an interiorization of the Christian Mysteries. In the Introduction to his work on *Psychology and Alchemy* he writes:

> We can accuse Christianity of arrested development if we are determined to excuse our own shortcomings. In speaking therefore not of the deepest and best understanding of Christianity but of the superficialities and disastrous misunderstandings that are plain to see. The demand made by the *imitatio Christi*—that we should follow the ideal and seek to become like it—ought logically to have the result of developing and exalting the inner man. In actual fact, however, the ideal has been turned into an external object of worship, and it is precisely this veneration for the object that prevents it from reaching down into the depths of the soul and transforming it into a wholeness in keeping with the ideal. Accordingly the divine mediator stands outside as an image, while man remains fragmentary and untouched in the deepest part of him. (para. 7, p. 7)

—and later in the same work

> It may easily happen, therefore, that a Christian who believes in all the sacred figures is still undeveloped and unchanged in his innermost soul because he has "all God outside" and does not experience him in the soul.... Yes, everything is to be found outside—in image and in word, in Church and Bible—but never inside.... Too few people have experienced the divine image as the innermost possession of their own souls. Christ only meets them from without, never within the soul. (para. 12)

This summons to our time to discover the God within may be seen as perhaps Jung's greatest contribution—and a very great one it is. But Jung seems not to have been aware of Swedenborg as a predecessor and prophet of just such a transformation of consciousness as he himself wished to see. Swedenborg, on his part, would have seen Jung as one fulfilment of his prophecy, his vision of a Last Judgment in the heavens passed on the Apostolic Church, to be followed by the appearance of the Lord in the inner heavens. Jung writes of the "God-image," the divine signature or archetype, imprinted in every soul. Accused by theologians of "psychologism" for making his appeal to this God-image (whose presence is testified nevertheless in the first chapter of Genesis) and thereby of "deifying the soul," Jung replied, "when I say as a psychologist that God is an archetype, I mean by that the 'type' in the psyche. The word 'type' is, as we know, derived from τύπος', to 'blow' or 'imprint'; thus an archetype pre-supposes an imprinter." (para. 15) The argument is very close to that of Swedenborg, that human qualities must mirror divine qualities. In this respect Henry Corbin, in the review already cited, defends Jung, he himself being deeply concerned with defining and discovering the "imaginal" world.

> True, C.G. Jung chooses not to speak otherwise than as a psychologist, and deals only with psychology; he does not claim to be a theologian or even a philosopher of religion. But having said "Only a psychologist, only psychology" one has the sudden sense of having committed a grave injustice, of associating oneself by that way of speaking with all those who, mistrusting for one reason or another the implications of Jung's works, close the matter after each one with the comment "it is *nothing but* psychology". But one may well ask oneself what they have done with their *soul*, with their *Psyche* to dismiss it in this way and to dare to speak of it in terms of being "nothing but that." So why when one has shown that there are psychological factors which correspond to divine figures, do some people find it necessary to cry blasphemy as if all were lost and those figures devalued? (Cf *Psychology and Alchemy*, p. 21)

Swedenborg too had insisted that the imprint of the infinite and eternal is within every form; and moreover that the infinite and eternal is present in the infinite variety of things, "in that no substance, state or thing in the created universe can ever be the same or identical with any other." So that in none of the things that fill the universe can any sameness be produced to all eternity. This (he continues) is perspicuously evident in the variety of faces of all human beings;

"not one face exists in the whole world which is the same as another, neither can exist in all eternity; nor therefore one mind for the face is the type of the mind." (DLW 315) Here Swedenborg is using the word "type"—imprint—in exactly Jung's sense. Yet by influx all these are forms of the divine image, in Blake's words

> . . . the Divine—
> Humanity who is the Only General and Universal Form
> To which all Lineaments tend & seek with love & sympathy.
> (J. 43:19; K.672)

There is not one image or face of God but an infinity of images, an infinity of faces. The implications are overwhelming for it follows that every human face in the world is, insofar as it is open to the divine influx, one of the myriad faces of God. Was it not this Mystery that Jesus himself sought to impart in the parable which tells how the "Son of Man" says to the Just,

> I was an hungered and ye gave me meat, I was thirsty and ye gave me drink; I was a stranger and ye took me in, naked and ye clothed me: I was in prison and ye came unto me. (Matt. 25:35-37)

The Just ask,

> Lord, when saw we thee an hungered, and fed thee? Or thirsty and we gave thee drink? When saw we thee a stranger and took thee in? Or naked, and clothed thee? . . . and the King shall answer and say unto them . . . inasmuch as ye have done it unto one of the least of these my brethren, ye have done it unto me. (Matt. 25:37-40)

and so with the Unjust who have rejected in all these the "Son of Man." Whereas the conventional reading may be that to serve the hungry and thirsty, strangers and prisoners, is equivalent to serving the Lord in person, the plain reading of the text is that it actually *is* the Divine Humanity who is present in all these.

Swedenborg claimed for his Church of the New Jerusalem that it is to be the ultimate Christian revelation and understanding of the Son of God in his Divine Humanity; and indeed it is not possible to conceive a closer union of God and Man than in this universal influx of divinity in all creation and in all humankind.

. . .

To turn once again to Jung's remarkable diagnosis of our present situation, *Answer to Job*: He describes the gradual emergence, in the Bible, of the idea of God as Man, becoming ever clearer from Job to Ezekiel to Daniel, to the Book of Enoch, and finally to the Incarnation of Jesus Christ. But Jung, like Swedenborg, does not see the gradual realization as ending there. As Swedenborg in the symbol of his twenty-seven Churches sees, from the time of Jesus, not one but several successive churches emerging and falling into decay, so does Jung see the Christian Revelation as incomplete. As a psychologist he had witnessed, over a long lifetime, the pressure within the human soul itself towards some further understanding. Whereas Swedenborg saw the awaited completion as a perfected understanding of the nature of Jesus Christ as omnipresent in all, Jung saw it as an awaited incarnation within poor imperfect earthly humankind; which indeed was what Swedenborg himself understood by his New Church but saw it as already accomplished. Jung points out that Jesus himself in sending to his disciples "the spirit of truth," the Holy Ghost, envisages a continuing realization of God in his children, which amounts to a continuance of the Incarnation. He reminds his disciples that he had told them that they were "gods." The believers or the chosen ones are children of God, all "fellow-heirs with Christ." Of this teaching the Fourth Gospel is full; " 'the indwelling of the Holy Ghost' means nothing less than an approximation of the believer to the status of God's son. One can therefore understand what is meant by the remark 'you are gods.' The deifying effect of the Holy Ghost is naturally assisted by the *imago Dei* stamped on the elect. God, in the shape of the Holy Ghost, puts up his tent in man, for he is obviously minded to realize himself continually not only in Adam's descendants, but in an indefinitely large number of believers, and possibly in mankind as a whole." (para. 656)

Only in suffering the limitations of the "empirical human being," Jung insists, can God truly suffer the human condition, for in a Christ exempt from sin he could not do so. Jung points out that throughout the history of the Church, both Catholic and Protestant, whereas the worship of the Son has been practised and encouraged, the presence of the Holy Spirit within the soul has been played down, to say the least. Jung cites the instance of the banning of the writings of Eckhart on account of certain passages in which this teaching is made too clear for the liking of the apostolic heirarchy. Again Corbin supports Jung, commenting that

> The action of the Paraclete, metaphysically so important, is wholly undesirable for the good organisation of the Church, for it eludes all control. In consequence there was to be energetic affirmation of the uniqueness of the event of the Incarnation, and the progressive indwelling of the Holy Spirit in man either discouraged or ignored. Whoever felt himself to be inspired by the Holy Spirit to "deviations" was a heretic, his extirpation and extermination both necessary and in accordance with Satan's liking.

This is the Protestant point of view, shared by Jung, son of a Lutheran Pastor, by Henry Corbin, by Swedenborg and by William Blake. It is at the heart of the great and unresolved division within Christendom.

The Millennial prophesies of Joachim of Flora have echoed throughout subsequent history his foretelling of a third phase of Christendom which he called the Age of the Holy Spirit, which was to follow the ages of the Father and of the Son. Within this tradition Swedenborg and Blake are situated, and indeed so is Jung himself. Jung writes on the sending of the Paraclete:

> Since he is the Third Person of the Deity, this is as much as to say that *God will be begotten in creaturely man*. This implies a tremendous change in man's status, for he is now raised to sonship, and almost to the position of a man-god. With this the prefiguration in Ezekiel and Enoch, where, as we saw, the title "Son of Man" was already conferred on the creaturely man, is fulfilled. But that puts man, despite his continuing sinfulness, in the position of the mediator, the unifier of God and creature. Christ probably had this incalculable possiblity in mind when he said, ". . . he who believes in me, will also do the works I do," and referring to the sixth verse of the Eighty-second Psalm, "I say, 'You are gods, sons of the Most High, all of you,' " he added, "and scripture cannot be broken." (para. 692)

I have quoted Jung at length because his understanding of Christianity as a progressive revelation stands within the mystical mainstream represented by Joachim of Flora, Eckhardt, Swedenborg and Blake; even though Jung seems to have known little of the latter two, who certainly had no direct influence on Jung's own conclusions.

.   .   .

In some respects Swedenborg's Christianity lies within the mainstream of orthodoxy; he believed, for example, that Jesus Christ alone among humankind was resurrected in the natural body. Blake indeed reproached Swedenborg because he had not in fact taught anything new. In *The Marriage of Heaven and Hell* Blake writes:

> *Now hear a plain fact: Swedenborg has not written one new truth. Now hear another: he has written all the old falsehoods.* (MHH; K.157)

What Blake chiefly held against Swedenborg was that he laid excessive stress on moral virtue, placing the virtuous in the heavens and the evil-doers in the hells. Blake himself saw Divine Humanity as embracing the wholeness of life, both heaven and hell, reason and energy, the darkness and the light in a holiness and a wholeness beyond what humankind calls good and evil in terms of the moral laws of this world. Like Jung, Blake understood that there can be no completeness if any part of the totality of the Divine Human is excluded. It is probable that Blake did not, either, share Swedenborg's view of the unique and exceptional nature of the historical Jesus Christ. He does profess "the religion of Jesus" but by this he may not have meant Apostolic Christianity but the religion that Jesus himself practiced. Blake's view is that "Jesus, the Imagination," the Divine Human, is born, lives and dies in every life, and the Resurrection is not of, but from, the carnal body. God is born in every birth, not one only; when Jehovah

> *. . . stood in the Gates of the Victim, & he appeared a weeping Infant in the Gates of Birth in the midst of Heaven.*

—he is born not in one but in all:

> *. . . a little weeping Infant pale reflected Multitudinous in the Looking Glass of Enitharmon . . .* (J.63; K.697)

—that is, in the "mirror" of the natural world. The one Babe of the eternal Incarnation is reflected not in one but in multitudes of births, in every birth. For Blake's Divine Humanity says,

> *. . . in Me all Eternity Must pass thro' condemnation and awake beyond the grave.* (K.662)

Man is not once but continually redeemed in "the Body of Jesus"—that is, in the Divine Humanity in whom all participate; and the "Divine Similitude"—the face of God—is seen

> *In loves and tears of brothers, sisters, sons, fathers and friends Which if Man ceases to behold, he ceases to exist.* (K.664)

Jerusalem 33 (detail)

The "Divine Family" is "as one Man"

> *. . . and they were One in Him. A Human Vision! Human Divine, Jesus the Saviour, Blessed for ever and ever.* (K.667)

Thus the "Divine Humanity" is not a single individual but a family; and Blake goes so far as to condemn explicitly the teaching that the Lord, or any of the "eternal states" which constitute the human universe is or ever could be represented by any single individual. In this Blake certainly goes beyond Swedenborg at least in relation to the Jesus Christ of history. How strongly Blake held this view is clear from these lines from *Jerusalem*:

Los cries: "No Individual ought to appropriate to Himself
"Or to his Emanation [his feminine counterpart] any of the
    Unitive real Characteristics
"Of David or of Eve, of the Woman or of the Lord,
"Of Reuben or of Benjamin, of Joseph or Judah or Levi.
"Those who dare appropriate to themselves Universal
    Attributes
"Are the Blasphemous Selfhoods, & must be broken asunder.
"A Vegetated Christ & a Virgin Eve are the Hermaphroditic
"Blasphemy, by his Maternal Birth he is that Evil-One
"And his Maternal Humanity must be put off Eternally,
"Lest the Sexual Generation swallow up Regeneration.
(J,90; K.736)

—and the passage ends with the invocation,

"Come, Lord Jesus, take on thee the Satanic Body of
    Holiness."

The Divine Humanity is invoked to put on a generated body
in order to transcend his natural humanity, transmitted by
the mother. To Blake mortal generation is a binding of an
immortal spirit into the cruel bondage of mortality:

Thou, Mother of my Mortal part,
With cruelty didst mould my Heart,
And with false self-deceiving tears
Didst bind my Nostrils, Eyes, & Ears:

Didst close my Tongue in senseless clay,
And me to Mortal Life betray.
The Death of Jesus set me free.
Then what have I to do with thee? (K.220)

This poem from *Songs of Experience* is far indeed from those
Christmas lullabies of the Nativity to which we are accustomed, but is a concise summary of Swedenborg's teaching.
Readers unfamiliar with Swedenborg's view of the place of
the Mother in the Mystery of the Incarnation must find
Blake's treatment of the Incarnation in this and other passages extremely puzzling. But the Leading Doctrines of the
Church of the New Jerusalem, far from supporting the view
of the Immaculate Conception of the Virgin Mary, see the
Mother as the means through which Jesus Christ took on
sin. Both Swedenborg and Blake had confronted the question

which was later to present itself to Jung, of how the not-quite-
human son of a mother herself born without sin could experience the human condition. If, as Swedenborg taught, Jesus
came to "glorify his human" by overcoming the successive
temptations "admitted into his human from the mother" in
order to "put on a human from the Divine within him, which
is the Divine Human, and the Son of God" (LD 4 & 64)*
then the mother is indeed, as in Blake's poem, "cruel" and
the source of evil not of good. Swedenborg is quite categorical
in his insistence that the natural humanity inherited by Jesus
Christ from his earthly mother "cannot be transmuted into
the Divine Essence nor can it be commixed with it . . . thus
it follows that the Lord put off the human from the mother
which, in itself, was like the human of another man, and
thus material, and put on the human from the Father, which,
in itself, was like His Divine, and thus substantial; and from
which the Human was also made divine" (77)—not, be it
understood, by the elevation of what Blake calls "a Vegetated
Christ" but, on the contrary, by putting off his natural humanity. Blake summarizes the Swedenborgian teaching
when he writes, of Jesus,

He took on Sin in the Virgin's Womb,
And put it off on the Cross & Tomb (K.749)**

Thus in his doctrine that "The Lord put off the human from
the Mother, and put on the Human from the Divine in himself which is called the father" Swedenborg anticipated and
resolved Jung's later question as to the incompleteness of
the Incarnation. What Jung saw as a future possibility
Swedenborg and Blake saw as already accomplished in the
Mystery of the Incarnation, which had not hitherto been
properly understood. The two lines just quoted are taken
from a late poem by Blake entitled *The Everlasting Gospel*,
a series of fragments which are in fact all expositions of

---

*LD is Dr. Raine's abbreviation for *Four Leading Doctrines of the New
Church* (London, 1907), which consists of excerpts from the 1781 English
translation of Swedenborg's *True Christian Religion* (1771).   —The Editors

** Blake concludes this passage with the line: "To be worship'd by the church
of Rome." He is in this sense right that the Roman Church specifically
teaches the ressurection of the physical body and that the natural man
ascends to heaven.

The influence of Swedenborg, if anything, is clearer in the last works than in the first.

Swedenborg's Leading Doctrines; which fact entirely confutes the often-propounded view of Blake scholars that Swedenborg's influence is to be found only in Blake's early works. This is by no means the case; the influence of Swedenborg, if anything, is clearer in the last works than in the first. One fragment expands at length the necessity that the Mother of Jesus should be a vehicle of sins and not "a Virgin pure / With narrow Soul & looks demure." He comes very close indeed to Jung when he writes

> Or what was it, which he took on
> That he might bring salvation?
> A body subject to be tempted
> From neither pain or grief Exempted?
> Or such a body as might not feel
> The passions that with sinners deal?

Yet in affirming the indwelling of the Divine Human in mankind, and the total humanity of Jesus in taking on a fully human, fully sinful inheritance, how far are Swedenborg, and Blake, and Jung also for that matter, from any humanistic intent of exalting the natural humanity—the mortal selfhood—to a god-like status, usurping the name of humanity from the divine principle in man and affirming the supremacy of the natural man. Swedenborg insists that it is only through putting off his natural humanity through temptations overcome, and finally on the Cross, that Jesus glorified the Divine Humanity of the Father. Blake, who saw the divine image in every human face, wrote:

> The Spirit of Jesus is continual forgiveness of Sin: he who waits to be righteous before he enters into the Saviour's kingdom, the Divine Body, will never enter there. I am perhaps the most sinful of men. I pretend not to holiness: Yet I pretend to love, to see, to converse with daily as man with man, & the more to have an interest in the Friend of Sinners. (K.621)

And finally Jung, who has most powerfully carried into our own day the mystery of the divine presence in every man, concludes his *Answer to Job* with these words, on the paradox

"When the morning Stars sang together, & all the Sons of God shouted for joy"; *Job* 14 (detail)

of the divine presence that indwells "the ordinary mortal who is not free from original sin":

> . . . Even the enlightened person remains what he is, and is never more than his limited ego before the One who dwells within him, whose form has no knowable boundaries, who encompasses him on all sides, fathomless as the abyss of the earth and vast as the sky.

HISTORICAL CONTEXTS

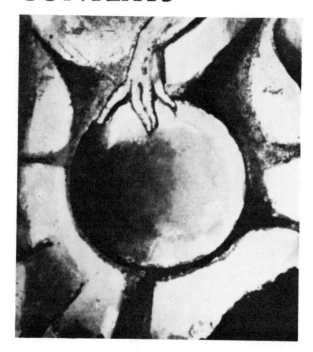

"Met Unwittingly in London Streets"

ALEXANDER GILCHRIST

Blake, *Songs of Experience* 46 (detail)

Excerpted from Alexander Gilchrist's *Life of William Blake, 'Pictor Ignotus'*, completed after Gilchrist's death by D. G. Rossetti (London and Cambridge: Macmillan and Co., 1863), Vol. 1, pp. 15-16.

DURING most of his life, and after his death, Blake remained relatively unknown. His obscurity faded with the 1863 publication of *Life of William Blake*, by the Victorian Barrister-at-Law, Alexander Gilchrist. The following brief excerpt, which speculates on Blake and Swedenborg having "met unwittingly in London streets" in 1772, is representative of Gilchrist's style and approach to the enigmatic poet-artist, William Blake. —Ed.

Another still more memorable figure, and a genius singularly germane to Blake's own order of mind, the 'singular boy of fourteen,' during the commencement of his apprenticeship, *may* 'any day have met unwittingly in London streets, or walked beside: a placid, venerable, thin man of eighty-four, of erect figure and abstracted air, wearing a full-bottomed wig, a pair of long ruffles, and a curious-hilted sword, and carrying a gold-headed cane,—no Vision, still flesh and blood, but himself the greatest of modern Vision Seers,—Emanuel Swedenborg by name; who came from Amsterdam to London, in August 1771, and died at No. 26, Great Bath Street, Coldbath Fields, on the 29th of March, 1772.' This Mr. Allingham pleasantly suggests, in a note to his delightful collection of lyrical poems, *Nightingale Valley* (1860), in which (at last) occur a specimen or two of Blake's verse. The coincidence is not a trivial one. Of all modern men the engraver's apprentice was to grow up the likest to Emanuel Swedenborg; already by constitutional temperament and endowment was so: in faculty for theosophic dreaming, for the seeing of visions while broad awake, and in matter of fact hold of spiritual things. To *savan* and to artist alike, while yet on earth, the Heavens were opened. By Swedenborg's theologic writings, the first English editions of some of which appeared during Blake's manhood, the latter was considerably influenced; but in no slavish spirit. These writings, in common with those of Jacob Boehmen, and of the other select mystics of the world, had natural affinities to Blake's mind, and were eagerly assimilated. But he hardly became a proselyte or 'Swedenborgian' proper; though his friend Flaxman did. In another twenty years we shall find him freely and—as true believers may think—heretically criticising the Swedish seer from the spiritualist, not the rationalist point of view: as being a Divine Teacher, whose truths however were 'not new,' and whose falsehoods were 'all old.'

New Light on C. A. Tulk, Blake's 19th Century Patron

RAYMOND H. DECK, JR.

RAYMOND DECK, who earned his Ph.D from Brandeis University in 1978 with a thesis on Blake and Swedenborg, has written extensively on the historical context of Blake's relationship to early English Swedenborgians. The following concerns C. A. Tulk (1786-1849), a little known Swedenborgian and progressive Member of Parliament. Tulk was a frequent patron during the last decade of Blake's life. He introduced Blake to Coleridge; helped foster Blake's posthumous fame, and according to Dr. Deck, "Their friendship suggests that Blake's moderating attitudes toward Swedenborg in the nineteenth century may have resulted from their acquaintance."   – Ed.

CHARLES Augustus Tulk (1786-1849) not only played an important role as Blake's patron and in promoting Blake's cause both during and after the poet's lifetime, but he was also closely enough associated with the poet that we might reasonably speculate upon his personal significance for the last decade of Blake's thought and work. To date we have had fragmentary evidence sufficient only to suggest some interesting possibilities. This essay will report on new evidence about Tulk's activities and will also survey the previously available evidence in an attempt to establish the documentary foundation for a more substantial consideration of Tulk's relationship to Blake and of his contribution to Blake's fame.

Charles Augustus Tulk was a leisured gentleman known chiefly for his interests in Swedenborg and for his political activities. He served as a Member of Parliament (1820-26, 1835-37) and as a county Magistrate for Middlesex (1836-47). His progressive social philosophy is reflected in his newspaper articles arguing for better conditions in factories and in his special interest in prisons and asylums.[1] But our chief concern here is, like Tulk's, his interest in Swedenborg, which led to his association with Blake—and Coleridge as well. Almost from the day of his birth, Tulk's Swedenborgianism places him in some relationship to Blake. Tulk's father, John Augustus Tulk, had been one of the very earliest

Almost from the day of his birth, Tulk's Swedenborgianism places him in some relationship to Blake.

From *Studies in Romanticism* 16, no. 2, pp. 217-36, by permission of the publisher. Copyright © 1977 by the Trustees of Boston University.

English readers of Swedenborg, founding with Robert Hindmarsh and a few others "The Theosophical Society" in 1783 and opting to establish in 1787 the New Church as a distinct institution based upon Swedenborg's teachings.[2] Toward the end of this decade, Blake began to read Swedenborg's works, and in 1789 he attended the First General Conference of the New Church, which was held at Eastcheap from April 13 to 17, 1789.[3] Here we might speculate on a "first meeting" of Tulk and Blake; though this suggestion is less than serious, it provides the occasion for making two important points about the significance of Swedenborg and Swedenborgians for Blake and his work in the nineteenth century. Tulk's father and mother attended the first General Conference with Blake,[4] and during the five days of the Conference, Blake might possibly have met the very young Charles Augustus. The first point is that, although we first find Blake and Charles Augustus Tulk together at the genesis of a sectarian religious establishment based upon Swedenborg's writings, Blake soon terminated his relationship with the New Church, and C.A. Tulk refused ever to join, preferring instead Sunday discussions of the Lord's Prayer and Swedenborg's writings in his own home. Tulk believed that Swedenborg's works contained truths of incalculable importance but he also believed that a spiritual "New Church" effected by those truths was every day progressing in the hearts and minds of men everywhere and that the exclusive and doctrinaire nature of a sectarian establishment, even one based upon the writings themselves, might just impede the development of what Swedenborg really meant by a New Church on earth. The second point raised by our supposed "first meeting" is that Blake's institutional involvement in 1789, although it is a commonplace of modern scholarship, was not remembered in the nineteenth century either by Tulk, (who might be excused because he was only two years old) or by any other Swedenborgian.

Tulk's first appearance with Blake probably came through John Flaxman,* Blake's close friend who regularly helped to find patrons for Blake's work. The link between Tulk and Flaxman was Swedenborg. Flaxman had attended one or more meetings of the Theosophical Society between 1784 and 1787 (Hindmarsh, p. 23), but his extended travel in Italy, from 1787 to 1794, removed him from the divisive arguments about sectarianism in England. After his return to London,

Flaxman actually joined the sectarian New Church congregation of Joseph Proud at the Hatton Garden "Temple," where he was a member of the governing committee of laity from about 1797 to 1799.[5] Sufficiently dismayed by the endless squabbling of the various sectarian factions, Flaxman in subsequent years was not associated with any sectarian Swedenborgian group. Tulk's and Flaxman's shared interest in Swedenborg and their common disenchantment with the sectarian New Church may have brought them together before 1810, and in that year we find both men associated as founding members of "The Society for Printing and Publishing the Writings of the Hon. Emanuel Swedenborg," which was known after 1855 as the "Swedenborg Society."[6] Tulk was a prominent member of the Society for Printing, serving as president for most of the years from 1812 to 1826 and again in 1843. Flaxman served as a member of the Society's governing committee in 1811, 1815, and 1817, and he continued as a subscribing member until his death in 1826, although he was seldom present at the Society's meetings in later years (*Report*, 1827, pp. 13-14). We also know that during the years of Flaxman's active membership, he was associated with Tulk in the examination of Swedenborg's skull in 1819 ("Mr. Flaxman observed, that 'the skull was worthy of [having a cast made] for its mere beauty' ")[7] and that Flaxman designed a cameo of Swedenborg for Tulk.[8] We also have evidence of a personal relationship between the Tulks and the Flaxmans during the years of Flaxman's active involvement with the Society for Printing. On October 3, 1815, Flaxman wrote to his wife, Nancy, about the Tulk's

---

*JOHN FLAXMAN (1755-1826) was a respected British sculptor, also widely known for his book illustrations and designs for Wedgewood ware. According to the noted art historian, W. H. Janson, Flaxman transformed British funereal sculpture with his Swedenborgian depictions of the soul of the departed in the form and likeness of the deceased, rather than in allegorical guise. Many later sculptors followed his innovation. Flaxman met Blake in 1779, when they were students at the Royal Academy School in London; and, except for an 1806-14 period of estrangement, he was among Blake's closest friends and supporters until his death in 1826. Flaxman introduced Blake into cultured London society, helped pay for the 1783 publication of Blake's early *Poetical Sketches*, and secured several patrons and commissions for Blake in later years. Blake deemed Flaxman "the Sculptor of Eternity," and in a letter of 1800, wrote, "I bless thee, O Father of Heaven and Earth, that ever I saw Flaxman's face./ Angels stand round my Spirit in heaven; the blessed of Heaven are my friends upon Earth."—The Editors

new baby,[9] and testimony from Tulk's daughter suggests that admiration for this baby was the "origin of the friendship between the Tulk family & the Flaxmans & the Poet Coleridge."[10] We then find dated in the next year, 1816, Flaxman's portraits of Mrs. Tulk and the children (*Records*, p. 242).

By 1816 Flaxman appears to have convinced Tulk to patronize Blake. In July of that year we have the earliest documentation of Tulk's actual patronage in a letter from Nancy Flaxman to her husband about "our Friend," who Bentley thinks may well have been Tulk, and one of his encounters with Blake:

> . . .I have had some discourse with our Friend about Blakes book & the *little drawings*—It is true he did not give him anything for he thought It would be wrong so to do after what pass'd between them, for as I understand B—— was very violent[,] Indeed beyond *all credence* only that he has served you his *best friend* the *same trick* [some]time back as you must well remember—but he *bought a drawing* of him, I have nothing to say in this affair[.] It is too tickilish, only I know what has happened both to yourself & me,& other people are not oblig'd to put up with *B s* odd humours—but let that pass[.] (*Records*, pp. 241-242)

The point of this rather confused report seems to be that Tulk and Blake argued about "Blakes book & the *little drawings*" for which Tulk would not pay Blake, but that despite Blake's "odd humours" and actions (involving a "*trick*," which suggests to me Blake's interpretation of some financial arrangement about the "*little drawings*") Tulk "*bought a drawing* of him." The important point is that by this time, 1816, Tulk seems to have become a patron of Blake.

Bentley cannot identify the "*little drawings*," for they do not correspond to any of Blake's works which Tulk is known to have owned; perhaps they are examples of a number of works which Tulk purchased during his years of patronage but which we cannot now identify. We do know that by 1818 Tulk had purchased the copy of the *Songs* which he loaned to Coleridge in that year, as discussed below. Tulk's copy of *Poetical Sketches* bears Blake's personal inscription, something Blake usually reserved as an attestation of his friendship.[11] Tulk eventually owned a copy of *No Natural Religion*, and if Tulk was the author of an 1830 article, "The

Inventions of William Blake, Painter and Poet," which includes extensive quotation from the *Book of Thel*, then probably he also acquired that work (*Records*, p. 242). With this evidence of Tulk's patronage we have the claim of his daughter that "William Blake, the Poet & Painter, with his wife, were rescued from destitution by Mr. C. A. Tulk," (*Records*, p. 250). Although this may be an exaggeration, we cannot doubt that Tulk's patronage must have been of some importance in the difficult financial circumstances of Blake's last years.

While we can reasonably suspect that Tulk's financial patronage continued intermittently until Blake's death, the remaining documented connections between Tulk and Blake, which will show their personal association to have extended into the last months of Blake's life, concern Tulk's efforts to introduce Blake and Blake's works to Samuel Taylor Coleridge. In September, 1817, Coleridge met Tulk at Littlehampton,[12] and from that point until 1826 they carried on an extensive correspondence, of which we have thirty-three letters from Coleridge to Tulk. As we have mentioned, Tulk introduced Coleridge to Blake's works by sending him a copy of the *Songs* which Coleridge returned with a commentary on February 12, 1818. The commentary has been reprinted frequently,[13] and for our purposes the most interesting part of Coleridge's comment is the evidence that Tulk seems to have presented Blake as a non-sectarian Swedenborgian. In his commentary Coleridge links Blake with the "scholars of Emanuel Swedenborg" (*Letters*, IV, 837), and in a slightly earlier letter to H. F. Cary, Coleridge reports that he understands Blake to be "a Swedenborgian—certainly" (*Letters*, IV, 834; cf. *Records*, p. 38).

It is also possible that Tulk's loan of the *Songs* to Coleridge may reflect what Tulk took to be the common *social* as well as Swedenborgian concerns of himself, Coleridge, and Blake. Coleridge and Tulk sought passage of a "Bill for the Relief of the Children employed in Cotton Factories," which was before Parliament in early 1818; their mutual interest is apparent in Coleridge's letter to Tulk on February 21, 1818—only nine days after his commentary on Blake's poems—about Coleridge's ideas for fostering passage of the bill (*Letters*, IV, 843). David Erdman suggests that "one side effect of this agitation seems to have been Tulk's lending him [Coleridge] a copy of Blake's *Songs*," and he ventures the speculation that "what Coleridge called Blake's 'mood of mind in this wild poem ["The Little Vagabond"],' read in February, contributed to Coleridge's wild mood of mind" as the author of a letter about the Children's Relief Bill to the *Courier* on March 31, 1818.[14] To the case for the shared social concerns of Coleridge and Tulk we can add the claim of Tulk's later protegee, Mary Catherine Hume, that during this period Tulk "used, in conjunction with Coleridge and others, to write newspaper articles in behalf of the workers in factories, children especially," a claim consistent with other details of Tulk's association with Coleridge in early 1818.[15] Nevertheless, their shared interest in Swedenborg remained the central theme of Coleridge's letters to Tulk before and after February, 1818. Given Coleridge's comments about Blake's supposed Swedenborgian interests, we can judge that Tulk had in mind Blake's Swedenborgian concerns at least as clearly as an idea of Blake's social concerns in the *Songs* when he loaned the poems to Coleridge in 1818, although the distinction may not have seemed a very important one to Tulk, who subscribed to Swedenborg's teaching that faith and social concerns are one according to the doctrine of "use."[16]

> **Given Coleridge's comments about Blake's supposed Swedenborgian interests, we can judge that Tulk had in mind Blake's Swedenborgian concerns . . . in the *Songs* when he loaned the poems to Coleridge.**

Tulk's continued friendship with both Blake and Coleridge led, not surprisingly, to his introduction of the two poets. The evidence of this meeting is a statement by James Spilling in one of two articles he wrote about Blake for the *New Church Magazine* of 1887:

> We are informed that Charles Augustus Tulk took Coleridge to see Blake's picture of "The Last Judgement" and that the author of Christabel poured forth concerning it a flood of eloquent commentary and enlargement.[17]

Considered together, the two articles make clear that the authority for Spilling's claim is Tulk himself. For example,

we read that "Dr. Garth Wilkinson tells us that Charles A. Tulk averred that Blake told him that he wrote it ["The Divine Image"] in the New Jerusalem Church, Hatton Garden."[18] Although this is certainly a mistaken statement about the poem's composition[19] (perhaps made by Blake for the special edification of his Swedenborgian patron), we have no reason to question the sincerity of the Swedenborgians—Tulk, Wilkinson, and Spilling in turn—in their efforts to transmit accurately to us Blake's claims. From this and other references to Tulk and Wilkinson in the articles,[20] we may conclude that Spilling is being "informed" by Wilkinson about the meeting of Tulk, Coleridge, and Blake and that Wilkinson had his description of the meeting directly from Tulk.[21]

We can then combine this evidence with Crabb Robinson's statement about Blake and Coleridge to conclude that this meeting occurred in 1825 or very early in 1826. In Robinson's only mention of this matter, he writes to Dorothy Wordsworth on February 19, 1826: "Coleridge has visited B. & I am told talks finely about him" (*Records*, p. 325). I do not think it overly rash to conclude that Crabb Robinson and Tulk (via Wilkinson) are reporting the same meeting between Coleridge and Blake, that they are describing the same reaction by Coleridge, and that Tulk did indeed take Coleridge to Blake's rooms at Fountain Court in late 1825 or early 1826 to see "The Last Judgement" and to meet Blake. Coleridge's letters give only a fragmented story of his meeting with Tulk, but they do show that they were meeting at about this time. In June, 1826, Tulk dined at Highgate (*Letters*, VI, 583-84), and, most significantly, Coleridge wrote to H. N. Coleridge on May 8, 1826, that "I shall be in town tomorow—& any time between 5 o'clock and 10 you would find me at Mr. Tulk's, 19 Duke St., Westminster. If I sleep in town, it will be at Mr. Hart's [Tulk's father-in-law] in Mecklenburg Square" (*Letters*, VI, 682). We have no letters from Coleridge to Tulk between that of March 15, 1825, and that of August 17, 1826; nevertheless, their continued association during 1825 is suggested by the attention of the London Swedenborgians to Coleridge's offer—as conveyed to them by C. A. Tulk—"to write a 'Life of the Mind of Swedenborg,' if 200 pounds were raised for him."[22] As for the Last Judgement, we can also be certain that during the last years of his life Blake had at his residence a large painting of this subject, probably the one described by J. T. Smith in *Nolle-kens and His Times*:

> Had he fortunately lived till the next year's exhibition at Somerset-house, the public would then have been astonished at his exquisite finishing of a Fresco picture of the Last Judgement, containing upwards of one thousand figures, many of them wonderfully conceived and grandly drawn. The lights of this extraordinary performance have the appearance of silver and gold; but upon Mrs. Blake's assuring me that there was no silver used, I found, upon a closer examination, that a blue wash had been passed over those parts of the gilding which receded, and the lights of the forward objects, which were also of gold, were heightened with a warm colour, to give the appearance of the two metals.[23]

In 1825 Coleridge would have seen this very large and impressive picture hanging amidst the "good number [of frescos, temperas, and drawings] in his show-room, which was rather dark,"[24] and in this setting he would have met and talked with Blake when he accompanied Tulk to Fountain Court.

A final connection during Blake's lifetime is Tulk's previously unnoticed publication of two of Blake's poems in *The Dawn of Light, and Theological Inspector*,[25] a Swedenborgian monthly published only during 1825. Tulk's leading role in the magazine is clear from the prominence and number of his contributions; in fact, the journal almost certainly had its genesis in Tulk's disputes with the orthodox majority of Swedenborgians, who by 1825 controlled the *Intellectual Repository*, the leading Swedenborgian journal.[26] I have found no evidence that any of the other few Swedenborgians contributing to *The Dawn of Light* had any connection with Blake; this fact together with Tulk's known interest in Blake and his preeminent role as a contributor and supporter of the periodical strongly suggests that he was the individual responsible for the insertion of Blake's poems. The very fact of Blake's poems appearing in letterpress during his lifetime was an extremely unusual occurrence[27] and in *The Dawn of Light* we find the first letterpress version of "On Another's Sorrow." "The Divine Image" had previously appeared in Malkin's *Memoirs* (1806),[28] but the text in *The Dawn of Light* differs in accidentals from the earlier letterpress version. The texts in *The Dawn of Light* also differ from Blake's original, chiefly in the capitalization of

words referring to God, and in accidentals of punctuation—most notably the addition of question marks in "On Another's Sorrow"; substantial emendations are "Who" for "That" in line 14 of "The Divine Image," and "wish" for "seek" and "griefs" for "grief" in line 34 of "On Another's Sorrow." It is even possible that Blake himself authorized the texts in *The Dawn of Light*, for we know from the report of Coleridge's visit that the acquaintance of Blake and Tulk continued in 1825. "The Divine Image" was printed on the last page of the issue for April, 1825:

> To Mercy, Pity, Peace and Love,
> All pray in their distress,
> And to these virtues of delight
> Return their thankfulness.
>
> For Mercy, Pity, Peace and Love,
> Is God our Father dear;
> And Mercy, Pity, Peace and Love,
> Is man his child and care.
>
> For Mercy has a human heart,
> Pity a human face,
> And Love the Human Form Divine,
> And Peace the human dress.
>
> Then every man of every clime,
> Who prays in his distress,
> Prays to the human Form Divine,
> Love, Mercy, Pity, Peace.
>
> And all must love the human form,
> In Heathen, Turk, or Jew;
> Where Mercy, Love and Pity dwell,
> There God is dwelling too.

"On Another's Sorrow" was printed on the last page of the issue for July, 1825 (Vol. I, No. 7, p. 252):

> Can I see another's woe,
> And not be in sorrow too?
> Can I see another's grief,
> And not wish for kind relief?
>
> Can I see a falling tear,
> And not feel my sorrow's share?

Can a father see his child
Weep, nor be with sorrow fill'd?

Can a mother sit, and hear
An infant groan, an infant fear?
No! no! never can it be,
Never, never can it be.

And can He who smiles on all,
Hear the wren with sorrows small;
Hear the small birds grief and care,
Hear the woes that infants bear;

And not sit beside the nest,
Pouring pity in their breast;
And not sit the cradle near,
Weeping tear on infant's tear?

And not sit both night and day,
Wiping all our tears away?
Oh! no, never can it be!
Never, never can it be!

He doth give his joy to all;
He becomes an Infant small;
He becomes a man of woe,
He doth feel the sorrow too.

Think not thou canst sigh a sigh,
And thy Maker is not by;
Think not thou canst weep a tear,
And thy Maker is not near;

Oh! He gives to us his joy,
That our griefs he may destroy,
'Til our grief is fled, and gone,
He doth sit by us and moan.

Unfortunately for the furtherance of Blake's reputation, even among the periodical's small readership, neither poem carries any indication of authorship. In fact, attribution is not given with any of the other poems in *The Dawn of Light*, although some, apparently original works by the magazine's contributors, are signed with one or more initial.

Much of what can be said about Tulk's personal association with Blake and about his interest in Blake's posthumous reputation depends upon our establishing more positively his authorship of "The Inventions of William Blake, Painter and Poet," in the *London University Magazine* for March, 1830.[29] About this article in the context of Blake's nineteenth-century reputation we have Suzanne Hoover's cogent evaluation:

First, the author has made a modest effort to explain one of Blake's major symbols, the giant Albion, and has done it, moreover, with interest and respect. Further, he has not only quoted "A Cradle Song" and "The Divine Image" from *Songs of Innocence*, and "Introduction," "The Poison Tree," and "The Garden of Love" from the *Songs of Experience*, but also he has printed, for the first time in letterpress, part (exactly one-third) of *The Book of Thel*. Most remarkable is the author's grasp of Blake's idea of the artist as prophet. (Even his most enthusiastic admirers of the Revival of the sixties would not have such a sympathetic insight into Blake's moral purposes; they would tend rather to read his Prophecies as a new kind of psychological or aesthetic experiment—or an attempt *epater les bourgeois*.) For all of these reasons, the *London University Magazine* article may rightly be said to be "in most respects. . .the most important criticism of Blake's poetry to appear before the 1860's."[30]

In addition to having importance as a critical document, the *London University Magazine* article is especially interesting for its implications about the personal relationship of Tulk and Blake. Tulk's responsibility for this article, the case for which I will present at some length, suggests that during the last decade of Blake's life Tulk was more than a charitable patron who appreciated but was incapable of understanding Blake's art and thought; instead Tulk emerges as a reader not only of the shorter poems but probably also of *Jerusalem*, in which the figure of Albion emerges with prominence, and we might speculate that the conversations of Tulk and Blake turned to such concerns as Blake's conception of history and of the artist's role as prophet. If Tulk was indeed the author, we have in the *London University Magazine* article substantial evidence to suppose that there was a sharing of ideas between Tulk and Blake, and we would have reasonable grounds upon which to consider the possible influence of Tulk's thought and his peculiar brand of Swedenborgianism upon Blake's later development. For that matter, from the perspective of Swedenborgian history one might then reasonably speculate upon Blake's influence on Tulk, possibly an influence of some importance as Tulk's idealistic interpretation (the orthodox called it the "Tulkite Heresy") helped to shape the course of Swedenborgian thought in the nineteenth century.[31]

In making a case for Tulk's authorship of the *London University Magazine* article, we must first recognize that there were very few people who had sufficient familiarity with or interest in Blake's works to have written the piece. That Tulk was one of the small number familiar with Blake and his works has been demonstrated, and his interest in Blake's posthumous reputation will be shown to extend beyond the article in question. Likewise, we know that Tulk stood in fairly close relationship to the newly-established London

University. In the preceding volume of the *London University Magazine*, he had been among those listed for honors and prizes at the University.[32] His name also appears on a list of "Proprietors" of London University apparently dating from 1827; this record indicates that he was not seated on any of the official councils of the school but that he was one of the several hundred individuals who contributed the capital for the institution's foundation.[33]

In 1829 we have yet another suggestion of Tulk's interest in the University in the offer of the Swedenborgian Society for Printing's governing committee—of which Tulk was a member—to donate a complete set of Swedenborg's writings to London University. About this offer we read in the Society's report for 1829: "It appears by the newspapers, that, at a meeting of the proprietors of the University, the announcement of this gift was followed by loud laughter" (*Report*, 1829, p. 6). Most importantly, the circumstances of this offer bear upon a possible reservation about Tulk's proposed authorship: why, if he was such an enthusiastic reader of Swedenborg and if he considered Blake to be something of a Swedenborgian, does he make no reference to Swedenborg in the article? The answer must lie in the hostility of London University officials to Swedenborg (Tulk, as a proprietor of the University, presumably found himself in the midst of the laughing throng when the gift of Swedenborg's works was announced) and in Tulk's fear that mention of Swedenborg in the article about Blake would not be well received by the magazine's unsympathetic readership. Having been a Member of Parliament for six years before 1830, Tulk must have had sufficient experience with popular reaction to Swedenborg to have learned discretion in making claims for the master's wisdom and influence.

Further evidence for Tulk's authorship of the *London University Magazine* article is the concluding footnote in it, that "Blake and Coleridge, when in company, seemed like congenial beings of another sphere, breathing for a while on our earth; which may easily be perceived from the similarity of thought pervading their works."[34] Who might have seen Blake and Coleridge "in company"? In Blake scholarship we have documentary evidence about only one candidate, Charles Augustus Tulk, as discussed earlier in this essay. That the article writer singles out Flaxman in addition to Coleridge and Blake also suggests Tulk's authorship. The linking of Blake with Flaxman was uncommon enough to have suggested Tulk's authorship to some readers,[35] but the circle of Blake, Flaxman, and Coleridge is even more indicative of Tulk's special interests. The article writer's statements about Flaxman and Coleridge are consistent with Tulk's attitudes toward these two men. Much of Coleridge's correspondence with Tulk concerns an application to Swedenborg of the philosophy he was developing from contemporary German sources. Through Coleridge, Tulk would have seen the categorical difference between the reception in England and Germany of "a more elevated and purer system." With the article writer's belief that Coleridge had "laid the foundation . . .for the development of a more internal philosophy,"[36] we should compare Tulk's idealistic interpretation of Swedenborg—for which he argued so vehemently against Swedenborg's other English interpreters—which was largely the application of such idealistic principles as Coleridge propounded to the interpretation of Swedenborg's writings.

That Tulk's opinion of Flaxman was consistent with the article writer's is apparent in a final piece of evidence. In the *Times* of London for December 15, 1826, there appeared Tulk's brief article on the occasion of Flaxman's death:

John Flaxman, R.A.—(From a Correspondent.)[37]

—Flaxman, as an artist, has been long esteemed by the best judges of art in Italy and Germany, the first of his profession; and is cited by an illustrious living author, Augustus Schlegel, as a bright example among the few men of genius of whom England at the present day can boast. His works are before the world, and time, which undermines many a fashionable reputation, will serve to show the country of his birth what a surpassing genius it possessed in Flaxman. But as a man, he was known only to the few who had the privilege of his friendship. Among these there is but one sentiment, that of admiration at his singular worth, the purity, the inflexible integrity of his mind, and his unaffected piety. But notwithstanding these great qualities, Flaxman did not escape detraction. His mind was incapable of stooping to those servile arts usually required by Court flatterers, and he was therefore represented as a favourer of republican opinions. But never was there a more unfounded calumny than this. He was warmly and upon principle, attached to the political institutions of the country, abhorred all kinds of anarchy and disorder, and was, in the only true sense of the word, loyal, for his loyalty was founded on the love of freedom, and a thorough independence both of thought and action. His attachment to monarchy and to the monarch was best known to those who knew him best. He could not make an ostentatious display of it to serve his interest, but was content that his family should know and profit by his sentiments. In those sentiments he remained unchanged to the end of his life, and whether in the unrestrained moments of friendly conversation, or in the simple duties of family devotion, he gave abundant proofs that while he served his God with all his heart, he did not neglect to honour his King. His religious sentiments had for many years been framed entirely on the doctrines of Swedenborg. To those whom he employed in his profession, his manners were gentle, kind, and unassuming; constantly treating them as if he were the person who was receiving a favour by their service, and not conferring one. In his domestic circle he was loved and revered as a father and a friend. His charity was shown not only in numerous instances of private beneficence, but in that which is of far greater moment—the undeviating justice of all his actions, and the uniform sacrifice of himself to the happiness, comfort, and interest of those around him.

The general similarities between Tulk's article in the *Times* and the article in the *London University Magazine* are corroborative evidence for Tulk's authorship of the later piece. In the first sentences of the *Times* article we should note Tulk's emphasis upon the German adulation of Flaxman's productions and upon the belief that the English will grow more appreciative of his "surpassing genius," a sentiment much like that in the *London University Magazine*: the philosophy appreciated in Germany is beginning "to take root in the breast of the English nation" through such "forerunners" as "Coleridge, Blake, and Flaxman."[38] In the *Times* article, Tulk defends Flaxman against charges of republicanism; the writer of the *London University Magazine* article expresses a similar opinion of republican principles in his observation that Europe can "break forth into eruptions, like the French revolution."[39] In the *Times* article, Tulk's brief mention of Swedenborg is really a very moderate advertisement considering that Tulk does not claim Flaxman's Swedenborgianism was necessary or even helpful for the many other praiseworthy characteristics Tulk discusses. If Tulk makes only this modest claim for Flaxman, who attended meetings of the early Theosophical Society, who was a governing member of the New Jerusalem Church at Hatton Garden, and who was a longtime member of the Society for Printing, we should not be surprised that in the later article he does not even mention Blake's Swedenborgianism. Again, this perhaps reflects Tulk's very realistic view of public attitudes toward Swedenborg. A final point about the *Times* article—although not directly related to our argument about Tulk's authorship of the later piece—is that the final sentence may serve as an eloquent comment on Flaxman's lifelong loyalty to his occasionally very trying friend, William Blake.

For the ten years after Blake's death, we have little documentary evidence of Tulk's interest aside from the *London University Magazine* article of 1830 and the possibility, suggested by Bentley, on the basis of unstated evidence, that Tulk purchased Blake's "Good and Evil Angels" from Blake's widow (*Records*, p. 354). For these ten years we can reasonably suspect that Tulk's interest in Blake's work continued, probably extending to the purchase of a few of his works, and that, to those whom he could interest in Blake, he continued to promote the idea of Blake's Swedenborgianism. Particularly important in this last respect is the meeting in 1837 of Tulk and the young Swedenborgian J. J. Garth Wilkinson, who would publish an edition of Blake's *Songs* with a Swedenborgian preface in 1839.[40] Wilkinson's interest in Swedenborg had developed during the middle of the 1830's, and in 1837 he had joined the Society for Printing, where he was introduced to many current and conflicting interpretations of Swedenborg (*Report*, 1837, p. 21). His own interpretation had been idealistic, and therefore he was strongly attracted to Tulk's position. Wilkinson therefore sought out Tulk, one result apparently being Wilkinson's first introduction to Blake's writings, at least to those which Tulk owned (*Memoir*, pp. 190, 25). Wilkinson's interest in Blake proceeded in a somewhat independent direction as he sought out many other available examples of Blake's poetry and art and sought financing for an edition of the *Songs*.[41] For the 1839 edition itself, Tulk was very probably one of the "subscribers" Wilkinson found (*Memoir*, p. 26).

Given Tulk's and Wilkinson's connection with each other through the Society for Printing and their common reading of Swedenborg, we can expect that Tulk must have introduced Blake's works to Wilkinson in a Swedenborgian context. As discussed in connection with Coleridge, Tulk did think Blake something of a Swedenborgian and was accustomed to presenting Blake thus to others, at least to those who, like Coleridge and Wilkinson, had already manifested a great interest in Swedenborg's writings. Most importantly, in James Spilling's "Blake the Visionary" we have some of Tulk's testimony to Wilkinson on the subject of Blake's Swedenborgianism:

Tulk did think Blake something of a Swedenborgian and was accustomed to presenting him thus to others.

"Blake," says Dr. Wilkinson, "informed Tulk that he had two different states; one in which he liked Swedenborg's writings, and one in which he disliked them. The second was a state of pride in himself, and then they were distasteful to him, but afterwards he knew that he had not been wise and sane. The first was a state of humility, in which he received and accepted Swedenborg."[42]

Tulk's significance, then, for the 1839 edition is that his Swedenborgian introduction to Blake predisposed Wilkinson to a certain interpretation of the poems and channeled some of Wilkinson's great enthusiasm for Swedenborg into his publication of the *Songs*. Tulk apparently could not bring Wilkinson to share his admiration, indicated in the *London University Magazine* article of the genius of Blake's poems, for in his preface Wilkinson condemns most of Blake's later works.

Tulk's special interest in a letterpress edition of the *Songs* was manifested in 1843, when he had printed privately twelve copies of the *Songs*, following, as did Wilkinson, the order of the poems in his own copy.[43] The evidence for the circumstances of Tulk's edition, as first noted by Keynes, is again the testimony of Garth Wilkinson, who wrote on the unbound sheets of one copy:

This copy of Blake's *Songs of Innocence and Experience* was printed by Mr. Charles Augustus Tulk, a Friend of Blake's, and a dear friend of my Wife's and mine;—and spaced as in the Original, in order that any one who chose, might copy in the paintings with which the original is adorned. Twelve copies only were printed.

April 9, 1886—J. J. Garth Wilkinson[44]

Tulk's apparent intention was to provide this edition to friends who manifested special interest in Blake's original designs, which they might have seen at Tulk's home. No doubt there did exist some such interest which prompted Tulk's printing, and from this we may conclude that he continued to introduce Blake's works to his acquaintances during the 1840s. Unfortunately, only two surviving copies of Tulk's unique edition have been reported,[45] and these give us no clue about the friends other than Wilkinson for whom he may have intended the work. Nevertheless, we might reasonably expect that Tulk's testimony about Blake's Swedenborgianism sparked the interest of other Swedenborgians, just as it had sparked Wilkinson's interest.

We have one last indication of Tulk's interest in Blake—yet another printing of "The Divine Image," in *The New Church Advocate* for December, 1844.[46] Like *The Dawn of Light*, the *Advocate* was a short-lived periodical founded and edited by Tulk in company with others whose views differed from the orthodox Swedenborgian majority. Evidence of Tulk's important editorial position are his twenty or more lengthy contributions from 1842 to 1845, many of them occupying the leading position in a month's issue, including the very first issue of the *Advocate* and the issue containing Blake's poem.[47] It is possible but less likely that Wilkinson, who was then active in Swedenborgian circles, was responsible for the insertions of the poem, but he does not seem to have attained an important editorial position in the *Advocate* until very late in 1845.[48] We might add that by the time of this printing, December, 1844, any one of the many individuals associated with *The New Church Advocate* might have been responsible for the insertion of Blake's poem; notably, however, we entertain this possibility because Tulk had been indirectly or directly responsible for two editions of Blake's *Songs* available to other Swedenborgians and because he no doubt continued to testify to Blake's Swedenborgian interests.

The assembled evidence of Blake's relationship with Tulk records their continuing acquaintance and Tulk's patronage at least during the last ten years of Blake's life. During these years Tulk visited Blake, purchased some of his works, and was singularly influential in interesting Coleridge in Blake, first by lending him Blake's *Songs* in 1818 and later by actually introducing the two poets in 1825 or early 1826. The evidence is sketchy but coherent, and it suggests that there is much about Blake's enduring relationship with Tulk which we have yet to determine. After Blake's death, Tulk proved a unique figure in the development of Blake's reputation. Showing for all of Blake's works an approval very rare in the pre-Gilchrist years, Tulk argued publicly in 1830 that all Blake's works were sane. Tulk was also responsible for Swedenborgian interest in Blake and for Blake's reputation as a Swedenborgian during the nineteenth century. In this connection, Tulk's interest in Blake led to the publication of Blake's *Songs* with a Swedenborgian preface by J. J. Garth Wilkinson in 1839; and Wilkinson, who had Tulk's testimony about Blake's Swedenborgianism, proved in turn responsible for the Blakean interests of Carlyle, Emerson, and Henry James, Sr.[49] The extent of Tulk's personal acquaintance with Blake and of his interest in Blake's posthumous reputation also indicates that much remains to be said in a more interpretive vein about Tulk's significance for Blake.

Their friendship suggests that Blake's moderating attitude toward Swedenborg in the 19th century may have resulted from [his aquaintance with Tulk].

Their friendship suggests that Blake's moderating attitudes toward Swedenborg in the nineteenth century may have resulted from their acquaintance, Tulk's was also a very peculiar brand of Swedenborgianism which centered upon a Christology not so very different from that expressed in *Jerusalem*; perhaps Tulk's position had some significance for Blake's later theology—or perhaps Tulk may have learned from Blake the idealistic interpretation of Swedenborg's theology which Tulk began to promulgate at about the time of his first patronage of the poet. Finally, about Blake's posthumous reputation, Tulk's testimony to Blake's Swedenborgian sympathies may have had an importance for Blake's reputation which has not yet been appreciated sufficiently in Blake scholarship.

Notes

1. The *Dictionary of National Biography* contains a brief sketch emphasizing matters other than Tulk's Swedenborgianism.

2. Robert Hindmarsh, *Rise and Progress of the New Jerusalem Church* (London: Hodson, 1861), pp. 14, 54-58. Further references to this work are cited in the text by author.

3. G.E. Bentley, Jr., *Blake Records* (Oxford: Clarendon, 1969), pp. 34-38. Further references to this work are cited in the text as *Records*.

4. John Augustus Tulk was a signer of the printed minutes: *Minutes of a General Conference of the Members of the New Church Signified by the New Jerusalem in the Revelation* (London: R. Hindmarsh, 1789), p. 42. The wife of J.A. Tulk was also an active member of the New Church, and it seems to have been the custom for both spouses to attend the General Conference, e.g. the joint attendance of William and Catherine Blake.

5. William White, *Emanuel Swedenborg: His Life and Writings*, 2 vols. (London: Simpkin, Marshall, 1867) II, 607-08.

6. *Plan of the Society for Printing and Publishing the Writings of the Hon. Emanuel Swedenborg* (London: Hodson, 1810); *Report of the First Annual Meeting of the Society for Printing and Publishing the Writings of the Hon. Emanuel Swedenborg* (London: Hodson, 1810). These reports were issued annual. The name change in 1855 is significant for bibliographical purposes because the Society for Printing is often called the "Swedenborg Society" in later studies. Further references to the reports are cited in the text as *Report* and by date.

7. "Testimony Collected by J.J. Garth Wilkinson, M.D.," *Documents Concerning the Life and Character of Emanuel Swedenborg*, ed. R.L. Tafel, 2 vols. (London: Swedenborg Society, 1875, 1877),II, 557-58; for the circumstances and date of this examination of the skull, see Hindmarsh's *Rise and Progress*, pp. 398-403.

8. The cameo is reported by Charles Pooley in Mary Catherine Hume, *A Brief Sketch of the Life, Character and Religious Opinions of Charles Augustus Tulk*, 2nd ed., ed. Charles Pooley (London: Speirs, 1890), p. 17n; also about this cameo we read in the manuscript testimony of Caroline Tulk, discussed in the second following note, that "Mr. Flaxman by your Grandfather's [C.A. Tulk] desire, employed the celebrated Cameo cutter, Caputi of Rome to cut a cameo of the head of Swedenborg."

9. I have been informed by G.E. Bentley, Jr. (in a letter of October 12, 1976), about the substance of Flaxman's letter, which is now at the Fitzwilliam.

10. The testimony of Caroline Tulk is recorded in a manuscript now at the Swedenborg Society, London. Bentley discusses the circumstances of this manuscript and quotes the material directly relevant to Blake in *Records*, p. 250, 250n. Bentley very generously has provided me with a transcription of the complete manuscript, which begins: "The origin of the friendship between the Tulk family & the Flaxman's & the Poet Coleridge was the admiration of both Sculptor & Poet for Marmaduke Tulk (brother of C[aroline]. A.T. [ulk].) when an infant of a few months old. They saw him in his nurse's arms, at the sea-side, & fell in love with him. The acquaintance thus begun quickly ripened into an intimate friendship between the families, especially with the Flaxmans & Denmans—(sisters of Mrs. Flaxman). They often came to Marble Hall, Twickenham, where Mr. Charles Augustus Tulk then lived, & Flaxman made many sketches of his large family." Some of these drawings of the family are mentioned in my text. Bentley informs me about a sketch by Flaxman of Marmaduke Tulk in the Rosenwald Collection. About the mentions of Coleridge, see my note 12, below.

11. Geoffrey Keynes, "Blake, Tulk and Garth Wilkinson," *The Library*, 4th ser. 26 (1945), 191.

12. Lucy E. Watson (nee Gillman), *Coleridge at Highgate* (London: Longmans, 1925) pp. 55-56. The testimony of Caroline Tulk, quoted in my note 10, suggests that the first acquaintance of Tulk and Coleridge was contemporaneous with Flaxman's interest in Marmaduke Tulk, for which Flaxman's letter about Tulk's baby suggests 1815 as a date. I have found no other evidence to support the possibility of their meeting before 1817, nor does a common friendship seem to have evolved among Tulk, Coleridge, and Flaxman. Coleridge's sole letter to Flaxman (January 24, 1825) does indicate, however, through its mention of the death of Tulk's wife, that Coleridge and Flaxman were at least aware of their mutual acquaintance with Tulk: *Collected Letters of Samuel Taylor Coleridge*, ed. Earl Leslie Griggs (Oxford: Clarendon, 1956, 1959, 1971), v,

409. Further references to the letters are cited in the text as *Letters*.

13. E.g., Geoffrey Keynes, *Blake Studies* (London: Rupert Hart, 1949), pp. 96-97. Coleridge, *Letters*, IV, 835, 838; *Discussions of William Blake*, ed. John E. Grant (Boston: Heath, 1961), pp. 3-4; the text with manuscript corrections in *Records*, pp. 251-53.

14. *The Collected Coleridge*, Part 3 in 3 vols.: *Essays on His Times*, ed. David V. Erdman (Princeton U. Press [the volume is forthcoming; Erdman very kindly has provided me with a copy of the page proofs of relevant material]), I, clxxvii.

15. Hume, *A Brief Sketch*, p. 14. Perhaps among their collaborations are two letters about the Children's Relief Bill which Erdman thinks "Coleridge seems to have inspired or may have assisted in" and which immediately preceded Coleridge's letter of March 31, 1818: Erdman, Introduction to *Essays on His Times*, I, clxxvii. Hume writes that their collaborations occurred "before he [Tulk] had entered Parliament [1820 according to the *Dictionary of National Biography*; Hume gives 1821]". Given that Coleridge and Tulk first met in 1817, that Coleridge's letter to the *Courier* of March 31, 1818, seems to be his last such production, and that Hume describes the substance of their collaborations as concerning "workers in factories, children especially," their joint "newspaper articles" seem likely to have concerned the Children's Relief Bill and to have been prepared in the first months of 1818.

16. See Chapter 7 of Swedenborg's *True Christian Religion*, "Charity or Love to the Neighbor, and Good Works."

17. James Spilling, "Blake, Artist and Poet," *New Church Magazine*, 6 (1887), 253. Both this article and "Blake the Visionary" (*New Church Magazine*, 6 [1887], 204-11) have been noted in *A Blake Bibliography*, #1985 and #1986, and Bentley, (*Records*, p. 38) includes a quotation from the former about Tulk's testimony that Blake had "two different states" in which he alternately liked and disliked Swedenborg. Tulk's testimony, which I argue should be considered reliable, about the meeting of Blake and Coleridge has not been noticed in either Blake or Coleridge scholarship.

18. Spilling, "Blake, Artist and Poet," p. 254.

19. The Hatton Garden "Temple" was opened only in 1797, Carl Theophilus Odhner, *Annals of The New Church*, (Bryn Athyn, Pa.: Academy of the New Church, 1904), I, 169-70. "The Divine Image" was written in 1789.

20. Spilling's other articles in this and the earlier volume of the *New Church Magazine* are even more dependent upon Wilkinson's testimony: "Dr. Wilkinson's Reminiscences of Carlyle," 5, 107-12; "Emerson and Dr. Wilkinson," 6, 529-33.

21. I argue below that Tulk was very probably the author of "The Inventions of William Blake, Painter and Poet," *London University Magazine*, 2 (1830), 318-23, which conludes with the note: "Blake and Coleridge, when in company, seemed like congenial beings of another sphere, breathing for a while on our earth, which may easily be perceived from the similarity of thought pervading their works." If Tulk was indeed the author of the *London Univeristy Magazine* article, a case for which we have several different evidences, then we might take Tulk's later statement as corroborating evidence of his role in their meeting.

22. The quotation comes from a manuscript note by the Rev. William Mason printed in J.H. "Biographical Sketch of the late Rev. William Mason," *Intellectual Repository*, "enlarged series" 10 (1863), 320.

23. John Thomas Smith, *Nollekens and His Times*, 2 vols. (London, 1828), II, 473, rpt. in *Nineteenth-Century Accounts of William Blake*, ed. Joseph Anthony Wittreich, Jr. (Gainsville, Fla.: Scholar's Facsimiles and Reprints, 1970), pp. 112-46; also in *Records*, pp. 455-76. For Blake's several renditions of the Last Judgement, more than one of which may have been at Fountain Court in 1825, see Bentley's entries under "Last Judgement" in his index to *Blake Records*.

24. Richmond's pencil annotation of Gilchrist's *Life*, in G.E. Bentley, Jr., "William Blake, Samuel Palmer, and George Richmond," *Blake Studies*, 2, No. 2 (Spring, 1070), 44.

25. [William Blake], "The Divine Image," "On Another's Sorrow," *The Dawn of Light, and Theological Inspector*, 1 (London, 1825), 144, 252.

26. Tulk had long been involved in the publication of Swedenborgian periodicals, in large part, no doubt, because his non-sectarian position denied him a place in the official councils of the New Church. In 1812, Tulk had been one of the initial editors of the newly-established *Intellectual Repository*, the longest-lived Swedenborgian periodical of the nineteenth century. However, within six months he had withdrawn from his editorial role to be replaced by Samuel Noble, who became an ordained Minister of the New Church in 1820 (*Intellectual Repository*, 5 [1820-21], 199); nevertheless, Tulk continued to make regular contributions to the periodical through 1813 (this information is adduced from an examination of the periodical; into my copy someone has transcribed the notes which Noble added to his copy, chiefly information about editors and contributors from 1812 to 1825). From the last number for 1817 to the last number for 1819, Tulk contributed four articles which develop an idealistic interpretation of Swedenborg's writings (3 [1816-17], 455-57; 4 [1818-19], 106-11, 440-42, 511-15) and which found little favor with the editors, particularly Samuel Noble, who adds a critical note to Tulk's last article. Clearly an important interpretational dispute had arisen between Tulk and the editors of the *Intellectual Repository*, and this dispute explains the lack of Tulk's subsequent connection with that periodical. In fact, behind this public scene was an extensive personal dispute between Tulk and Noble, which had arisen out of the translation of Swedenborg's *True Christian Religion* which they had undertaken jointly in 1819 (*Intellectual Repository*, N.S. 3 [1828-29], 403, 513). In connection with Coleridge's Swedenborgian interests, we should note that the personal dispute between Noble and Tulk may explain Coleridge's very critical stance in his annotations to Noble's *Appeal*, published in 1827. Coleridge's annotations are reprinted in *The Literary Remains of Samuel Taylor Coleridge*, ed. H.N. Coleridge (London: Pickering, 1839), IV, 415-24. One result of this dispute was that Tulk sought to establish throughout the remainder of his life an alternative periodical to the *Intellectual Repository*. In the 1820's Tulk first sponsored *The Light of Dawn* in 1825 and then the *New Jerusalem Magazine and Theological Inspector* from 1826 to 1828, and finally a "new series," simply entitled the *New Jerusalem Magazine*; in the "new series," we find an editorial policy which excludes articles written by the editors themselves. Tulk's financial and editorial role in this series of periodicals and particularly

his frequent contributions to *The Dawn of Light* all suggest his responsibility for the insertion of Blake's poems.

27. Malkin printed a few selections from Blake's verse, and Crabb Robinson included some of these and others in his German article of 1811. Besides these printings, only two of Blake's *Songs* appeared in letterpress during his lifetime: "The Chimney Sweeper" in *The Chimney Sweeper's Friend* (1824 and 1825) and "Holy Thursday" in *City Scenes* (1818) (*Records*, pp. 427-28, 432-47, 284n, 254n).

28. Rpt. in *Nineteenth-Century Accounts*, pp.35-36, Malkin pp. xxxiii-xxxiv; also in *Records*, pp. 427-28.

29. Tulk's authorship was first suggested in 1949 by Geoffrey Keynes, *Blake Studies*, p. 98; Keynes offers no evidence for his speculation. Some evidence for this case had been presented by Deborah Dorfman, *Blake in the Nineteenth Century* (New Haven: Yale U. Press, 1969), p. 42-43; my notes indicated Dorfman's contributions incorporated into the present argument.

30. Suzanne R. Hoover, "William Blake in the Wilderness: A Closer Look at his Reputation 1827-1863," in *William Blake: Essays in Honour of Sir Geoffrey Keynes*, ed. Morton D. Paley and Michael Phillips (Oxford: The Clarendon Press, 1973), pp. 317-18, quoting *A Blake Bibliography*, p. 11.

31. Among others, Wilkinson and Henry James, Sr., were deeply affected by Tulk's interpretation. See J.J.G. Wilkinson's letter to Henry James, Sr., excerpted in Clement John Wilkinson, *James Garth Wilkinson: A Memoir of his Life, with a Selection from his Letters* (London: Kegan Paul, 1911), pp. 188-195. Future references to the work are cited as *Memoir*.

32. Dorfman, *Blake*, p. 43. Dorfman writes that this is "an 'Augustus Tulk' of Duke St., Westminster"; we can add that this was indeed the residence of Blake's patron.

33. *University of London: Proprietors of Shares* (London: n.p., "S. Holdsworth, Printer, 66, Paternoster Row, London," n.d.), p. 18; in a volume of early documents from London University at the Boston Athenaeum, this twenty-page pamphlet is bound immediately after *Statement of the Council of the University of London* (London: Longman, 1827); the other documents in the collection date from the period 1826-30.

34. "The Inventions of William Blake," p. 323. This seems to be the author's, not the editor's note. Bentley also judges this the author's note (*Records*, p. 386).

35. Dorfman, *Blake*, p. 42.

36. "The Inventions of William Blake," p. 318; *Records*, p. 381.

37. About Tulk's authorship, we read in a review of the *Times* article (*Intellectual Repository*, N.S. 2 [1826-27], 435) that the editors "think [they] recognize the pen of an avowed friend of those [Swedenborg's] doctrines—the President of the London Printing Society [i.e., Tulk]."

38. "The Inventions of William Blake," p. 319; *Records*, p. 382.

39. Ibid., p. 319; Bentley does not reprint this section.

40. William Blake, *Songs of Innocence and of Experience* (London: Pickering, Newbery, 1839).

41. Wilkinson saw at least the collections of Tatham and William Clarke; see *Memoir*, pp. 29 and 30.

42. Spilling, "Blake the Visionary," p. 210.

43. Keynes, "Blake, Tulk, and Garth Wilkinson," pp. 190-192.

44. Ibid., p. 191.

45. Ibid., pp. 190-191; Wilkinson's copy is at the British Museum, and the second copy is at Liverpool University.

46. [William] Blake, "The Divine Image," *The New Church Advocate. A Magazine and Review of Theology, Science, Art, and Literature*, 2 (1844-45), 191. Wilkinson's 1839 edition differs from this text in that the nouns mercy, pity, peace, and love are capitalized in lines 1,5,7,9,11, and 12, and Tulk's text of 1825 differs in these and other accidentals.

47. During 1845, bitter contention again flared among English Swedenborgians over the questions of "Tulkism" through articles and letters published both in the *Advocate* and in the *Intellectual Repository*, the long-established Swedenborgian periodical which was now the official organ of the New Church. Tulk's idealistic interpretation of Swedenborg was apparently much too radical even for most other non-sectarian Swedenborgians. One result of the debate was that Tulk withdrew—or was excluded—from the editorial borad of the *Advocate*, for in 1846 the *Advocate* appears in a "new series" as the *New Church Advocate and Examiner*, in which we find no articles by Tulk and an unfavorable review of his major work, *Spiritual Christianity* (*New Church Advocate and Examiner*, 1 [1846] 159-62). Nevertheless, Tulk was certainly in a position of editorial prominence in December, 1844, and was probably personally responsible for the insertions of Blake's poems.

48. As early as 1842, excerpts from Wilkinson's translation of Swedenborg's *Animal Kingdom* had begun to appear in the *Advocate*, and from 1843 through 1846 the magazine consistently noticed the proceedings of the "Swedenborg Association," which Wilkinson formally organized in 1845 for the support of translations and publication of Swedenborg's scientific writing. Only very late in 1845 and especially in the reorganized *Advocate* of 1846, however, do we find evidence of Wilkinson's editorial role in the increasing notice of American Swedenborgian publications, particularly notices of the *Harbinger*, which would have been supplied to Wilkinson by his friend, Henry James, Sr.

49. Wilkinson sent to Carlyle a copy of his 1839 edition of the *Songs* in 1839 (*Memoir*, p. 35); the intimacy of Wilkinson with James and Emerson, documented in C.J. Wilkinson's *Memoir*, passim, suggests Wilkinson as the most likely candidate to have introduced Blake's poems to them.

An Account of the First General Conference of the Members of the New Jerusalem Church

London, April 13 - 17, 1789

ROBERT HINDMARSH

Excerpted from Robert Hindmarsh's *The Rise and Progress of the New Jerusalem Church in England, America and Other Parts*, ed. Edward Madely (London: Hodson, 1861), pp. 79-84, 97, 101-08.

THE MOST frequently cited evidence of Blake's early Swedenborgian connections was his attendance with his wife at the 1789 General Conference for establishing a new church based upon the theological writings of Swedenborg (who had died in 1772). Although Blake soon severed his ties with the New Jerusalem Church—perhaps, in large part, because of the events at the General Conference—the proceedings of the Conference are an important record of the intentions of the Swedenborgian movement with which Blake interacted.

The author of the following account, Robert Hindmarsh, was one of the men most responsible for convening the General Conference. In 1783, he had been instrumental in founding the "Theosophical Society Instituted for the Purpose of Promoting Heavenly Doctrine by Translating, Printing and Publishing the Theological Writings of the Honorable Emanuel Swedenborg." Effective in distributing Swedenborg's books to subscribers around the world, the Theosophical Society included Blake's close friend, the sculptor, John Flaxman, among its membership.

Hindmarsh led a faction of Swedenborgians dedicated to creating a new religious denomination. In 1787, he obtained a formal license for public worship, and in January 1788 the New Jerusalem Church held its first service in a chapel in Great East Cheap, London. The ceremony, written by Hindmarsh, was conducted by his father, a former Methodist minister, expelled by Wesley for his interest in Swedenborg.

On December 7, 1788, Hindmarsh's group issued five hundred copies of a Circular Letter announcing a General Conference of Swedenborgian readers who wished to participate in the establishment of an on-going New Jerusalem Church. Among those who heeded the call were William and Catherine Blake.   – Ed.

THE London Society, having proceeded thus far in their exertions, first, to bring the Church into an actual external existence, then to introduce into it a regular and orderly Ministry, and afterwards to invite their brethren in other parts of the kingdom to unite with them in giving more full effect to their humble endeavours to propagate the truth among mankind, — now proceeded to take into consideration the propriety of calling a General Conference of all the readers of the Theological Writings of Emanuel Swedenborg, in order that the measures to be hereafter adopted might be the acts, not of one Society only, but of the New Church in general. For this end a Meeting was convened of all the members of the London Society, who appointed a Committee to prepare a Circular Letter, to be addressed to all the Societies of the New Church in Great Britain, and to such individuals, not united in any Society, as were known to be receivers of the new doctrines, and friendly to the formation of an external visible Church. This Meeting was held in the Chapel in Great East Cheap, London, on the 7th day of December, 1788; when the following Circular Letter, containing Forty-two Theological Propositions, taken from the Writings of Emanuel Swedenborg, with a general invitation for all the readers to attend the proposed Conference, was submitted to the Meeting, approved of, and ordered to be forthwith sent to all Societies and individuals, that might be supposed interested in the establishment and prosperity of the New Jerusalem.

Copy of a Circular Letter, addressed to all the Readers of the Theological Writings of the Honourable Emanuel Swedenborg, who are desirous of rejecting, and separating themselves from, the Old Church, or the present Established Churches, together with all their Sectaries, throughout Christendom, and of fully embracing the Heavenly Doctrines of the New Jerusalem.

NEW JERUSALEM CHURCH, GREAT EAST CHEAP, LONDON.
Dec. 7, 1788.

At a full Meeting of the members of the New Jerusalem Church who assemble at the above place, for the purpose of considering the most effectual means of promoting the establishment of the New Church, distinct from the Old, both in this and other countries, it was unanimously agreed, that a GENERAL CONFERENCE of all the readers of the Theological Writings of EMANUEL SWEDENBORG, who are desirous of rejecting, and separating themselves from, the Old Church, or the present Established Churches, together with all their Sectaries, throughout Christendom, and of fully embracing the Heavenly Doctrines of the New Church, be held in Great East Cheap, London, on Easter Monday, the 13th day of April, 1789; when the following Propositions, containing the principal Doctrines of the New Church, will be taken into serious consideration, and such Resolutions submitted to the said Meeting, as may be found necessary to promote the above design.

PROPOSITIONS

I. That Jehovah God, the Creator of heaven and earth, is One in Essence and in Person, in whom is a Divine Trinity, consisting of Father, Son, and Holy Ghost, like Soul, Body, and Operation in Man; and that the Lord and Saviour Jesus Christ is that God. *True Christian Religion*, n. 5 to 24, 25, 164 to 171, 180.

II. That Jehovah God himself came down from heaven as Divine Truth, which is the Word, and took upon him Human Nature for the purpose of removing hell from man, of restoring the heavens to order, and of preparing the way for a New Church upon earth, and that herein consists the true nature of redemption, which was effected solely by the omnipotence of the Lord's Divine Humanity. *True Christ. Rel.* n. 85, 86, 115 to 117, 124, 125.

III. That a Trinity of Divine Persons existing from eternity, or before the creation of the world, when conceived in idea, is a Trinity of Gods, which cannot be expelled by the oral confession of One God. *True Christ. Rel.* n. 172, 173.

IV. That to believe Redemption to have consisted in the passion of the cross, is a fundamental error of the Old Church; and that this error, together with that relating to the existence of Three Divine Persons from eternity, hath perverted the whole Christian Church, so that nothing spiritual is left remaining in it. *True Christ. Rel.* n. 132, 133.

V. That all Prayers directed to a Trinity of distinct persons, and not to a Trinity conjoined in One Person, are henceforth not attended to, but are in heaven like ill-scented odours. *True Christ. Rel.* n. 108.

VI. That hereafter no Christian can be admitted into heaven, unless he believeth in the Lord God and Saviour Jesus Christ, and approacheth him alone. *True Christ. Rel.* n. 26, 107, 108.

VII. That the doctrines universally taught in the Old Church, particularly respecting Three Divine Persons, the Atonement, Justification by Faith alone, the Resurrection of the material Body, &c., &c., are highly dangerous to the rising generation, inasmuch as they tend to ingraft in their infant minds principles diametrically opposite to those of the New Church, and consequently hurtful to their salvation. *True Christ. Rel.* n. 23, 173.

VIII. That the Nicene and Athanasian doctrine concerning a Trinity have together given birth to a faith, which hath entirely overturned the Christian Church. *True Christ. Rel.* n. 177.

IX. That hence is come that abomination of desolation, and that affliction, such as was not in all the world, neither shall be, which the Lord hath foretold in Daniel, and the Evangelists, and the Revelation. *True Christ. Rel.* n. 179.

X. That hence too it is come to pass, that unless a New Heaven and a New Church be established by the Lord, nor flesh can be saved. *True Christ. Rel.* n. 182.

XI. That the Word of the Lord is Holy; and that it containeth a Three-fold Sense, namely, Celestial, Spiritual, and Natural, which are united by Correspondences; and that in each sense it is Divine Truth, accommodated respectively to the angels of the three heavens, and also to men on earth. *True Christ. Rel.* n. 193 to 213.

XII. That the Books of the Word are all those which have the Internal Sense, which are as follow, viz. in the Old Testament, the five Books of Moses, called Genesis, Exodus, Leviticus, Numbers, and Deuteronomy; the Book of Joshua, the Book of Judges, the two Books of Samuel, the two Books of Kings, the Psalms of David, the Prophets Isaiah, Jeremiah, Lamentations, Ezekiel, Daniel, Hosea, Joel, Amos, Obadiah, Jonah, Micah, Nahum, Habakkuk, Zephaniah, Haggai, Zechariah, Malachi; and in the New Testament, the four Evangelists, Matthew, Mark, Luke, John, and the Revelation. And that the other Books, not having the Internal Sense, are not the Word. *Arcana Cœlestia*, n. 10325. *New Jer.* n. 266. *White Horse*, n. 16.

XIII. That in the Spiritual World there is a Sun distinct from that of the Natural World, the essence of which is pure love from Jehovah God, who is in the midst thereof: that the heat also proceeding from that Sun is in its essence love, and the light thence proceeding is in its essence wisdom; and that by the instrumentality of that Sun all things were created, and continue to subsist, both in the Spiritual and in the Natural World. *True Christ. Rel.* n. 75. *Influx*, n. 5.

XIV. That immediately on the Death of the material body, (which will never be re-assumed,) man rises again as to his spiritual or substantial body, wherein he existeth in a perfect human form; and thus that Death is only a continuation of Life. *New Jer.* n. 223 to 228.

XV. That the State and Condition of man after death is according to his past life in this world; and that the Predominant Love, which he takes with him into the Spiritual World, continues with him for ever, and can never be changed to all eternity; consequently, that if this Predominant Love be good, he abides in heaven to all eternity, but if it be evil, he abides in hell to all eternity. *Heaven and Hell*, n. 480, 521 to 527. *True Christ. Rel.* n. 199. *Arc. Cœl.* n. 10596, 10749. *De Amore Conjug.* n. 524. *Apoc. Explic.* n. 745, 837, 971, 1164, 1220.

XVI. That there is not in the universal heaven a single Angel that was created such at first, nor a single Devil in all hell, that had been created an angel of light, and was afterwards cast out of heaven; but that all both in heaven and hell are of the human race, in heaven such as had lived in the world in heavenly love and faith, and in hell such as had lived in hellish love and faith. *Last Judgment*, n. 14. *Heaven and Hell*, n. 311 to 317.

XVII. That man is not Life in himself, but only a Recipient of Life from the Lord, who alone is Life in Himself; which life is communicated by influx to all in the Spiritual World, whether in Heaven or in Hell, or in the intermediate state called the World of Spirits, and to all in the Natural World; but is received differently by each, according to the quality of the recipient subject. *True Christ. Rel.* n. 470 to 474.

XVIII. That man hath power to procure for himself both Faith and Charity, and also the Life of Faith and Charity; but that nevertheless nothing belonging to Faith, nothing belonging to Charity, and nothing belonging to the Life of each, is from man, but from the Lord. *True Christ. Rel.* n. 356 to 359.

XIX. That Charity and Faith are mere mental and perishable things, unless they be determined to Works, and exist therein, whensoever it is practicable. And that neither Charity alone, nor Faith alone, produces good Works; but that both Charity and Faith together are necessary to produce them. *True Christ. Rel.* n. 375 to 377, 450 to 453.

XX. That there are three universal Loves, viz. the Love of Heaven, the Love of the World, and the Love of Self, which, when in right subordination, make man perfect; but when they are not in right subordination, that they pervert and invert him. *True Christ. Rel.* n. 394 to 405.

XXI. That man hath Free-will in spiritual things, and that without this Free-will the Word would be of no manner of use, and consequently no church could exist; and that without Free-will in spiritual things there would be nothing about man, whereby he might join himself by reciprocation with the Lord, but God himself would be chargeable as the Author of evil, and all would be mere absolute predestination, which is shocking and detestable. *True Christ. Rel.* n. 479 to 485. *New Jer.* n. 141 to 149.

XXII. That Miracles are not to be expected at this day, because they carry compulsion with them, and take away man's Free-will in spiritual things. *True Christ. Rel.* n. 501, 849. *Div. Prov.* n. 130.

XXIII. That Repentance is the beginning and foundation of the Church in man; and that it consisteth in a man's examining not only the actions of his life, but also the intentions of his will, and in abstaining from evils, because they are sins against God. *True Christ. Rel.* n. 510 to 566.

XXIV. That Regeneration or the New Birth is effected of the Lord alone, by charity and faith, during man's co-operation; and that it is a gradual, not an instantaneous work, the several stages thereof answering to those of man's natural birth, in that he is conceived, carried in the womb, brought forth, and educated. *True Christ. Rel.* n. 576 to 578, 583 to 586.

XXV. That in proportion as man is regenerated, in the same proportion his Sins are removed; and that this Removal is what is meant in the Word by the Remission of Sins. *True Christ. Rel.* n. 611 to 614.

XXVI. That all have a Capacity to be regenerated, because all are redeemed, every one according to his state. *True Christ. Rel.* n. 579

to 582.

XXVII. That both evil Spirits and good Spirits are attendant upon every man and that the evil Spirits dwell in and excite his evil affections, and that the good Spirits dwell in and excite his good affections. *True Christ. Rel.* n. 596 &c.

XXVIII. That spiritual Temptations, which are Conflicts between good and evil, truth and falsehood, are a means of purification and regeneration, and that the Lord alone fighteth for man therein. *Ibid.*

XXIX. That the Imputation of the Merit and Righteousness of Christ, which consist in Redemption, is a thing impossible; and that it can no more be applied or ascribed to any angel or man, than the Creation and Preservation of the Universe can; Redemption being a kind of Creation of the Angelic Heaven anew, and also of the Church. *True Christ. Rel.* n. 640.

XXX. That the Imputation, which really takes place, and which is maintained by the New Church from the Word, is an Imputation of Good and Evil, and at the same time of Faith; and that the Lord imputeth Good to every man, and that Hell imputeth Evil to every man. *True Christ. Rel.* n. 643 to 646.

XXXI. That the Faith and Imputation of the New Church cannot abide together with the Faith and Imputation of the Old Church; and in case they abide together, such a collision and conflict will ensue, as will prove fatal to every thing that relates to the Church in man. *True Christ. Rel.* n. 647 to 649. *Brief Expos.* n. 96, 103.

XXXII. That there is not a single genuine Truth remaining in the Old Church, but what is falsified; and that herein is fulfilled the Lord's prediction in Matthew xxiv. 2, that 'one stone of the Temple shall not be left upon another, that shall not be thrown down.' *True Christ. Rel.* n. 174, 177, 180, 758.

XXXIII. That Now it is allowable to enter intellectually into the Mysteries of Faith, contrary to the ruling maxim of the Old Church, that the Understanding is to be kept bound under Obedience to Faith. *True Christ. Rel.* n. 185, 508. *Apoc. Rev.* n. 564, 914.

XXXIV. That external Forms of Worship, agreeable to the doctrines of the New Church are necessary, in order that the members of the New Church may worship God in One Person, according to the dictates of their own consciences, and that their acknowledgment of the Lord may, by descending into the ultimates, be confirmed, and thus their external man act in unity with their internal. *Apoc. Rev.* n. 533, 707. *True Christ. Rel.* n. 23, 55, 177, 508.

XXXV. That the two Sacraments of Baptism and the Holy Supper are essential institutions in the New Church, the uses of which are now revealed, together with the spiritual sense of the Word. *True Christ. Rel.* n. 667 to 730.

XXXVI. That the Kingdom of the Lord, both in heaven and on earth, is a Kingdom of Uses. *True Christ. Rel.* n. 387, 459. *Arc. Cœl.* n. 5395.

XXXVII. That true Conjugial Love, which can only exist between One Husband and One Wife, is a primary characteristic of the New Church, being grounded in the marriage of goodness and truth, and corresponding with the marriage of the Lord and his Church; and therefore is more celestial, spiritual, holy, pure, and clean, than any other love in angels or men. *De Amore Conjug.* n. 57 to 73.

XXXVIII. That the Last Judgment was accomplished in the Spiritual World in the year 1757; and that the former heaven and the former earth, or the Old Church, are passed away, and that all things are become New. *Last Judgment*, n. 45. *True Christ. Rel.* n. 115, 772. *Apoc. Rev.* n. 886. *Brief Expos.* n. 95.

XXXIX. That Now is the Second Advent of the Lord, which is a Coming, not in Person, but in the power and glory of the Spiritual Sense of his Holy Word, which is Himself. *True Christ. Rel.* n. 776 to 778.

XL. That this Second Coming of the Lord is effected by means of his servant EMANUEL SWEDENBORG, before whom he hath manifested Himself in Person, and whom he hath filled with his Spirit, to teach the doctrines of the New Church by the Word from Him. *True Christ. Rel.* n. 779.

XLI. That this is what is meant in the Revelation by the New Heaven and New Earth, and the New Jerusalem thence descending, prepared as a Bride adorned for her Husband. *True Christ. Rel.* n. 781.

XLII. That this New Church is the Crown of all Churches, which have heretofore existed on this earthly globe, in consequence of its worshiping One Visible God, in whom is the Invisible, as the Soul is in the Body. *True Christ. Rel.* n. 786 to 790.

Sir,

As a friend to the establishment of the New Church, distinct from the Old, you are hereby invited to the above-mentioned Conference, to be held in Great East Cheap, London, on Easter Monday, the 13th of April next, at Nine o'clock in the morning. Any person within the circle of your acquaintance, whom you know to be a lover of the truths contained in the Theological Writings of Emanuel Swedenborg, and friendly to the formation of a New Church, agreeable to the doctrines contained in the said Writings, and consistent with the plan proposed in the Circular Paper, you are at liberty also to invite; as nothing but the real welfare and promotion of the New Jerusalem Church is Hereby intended; which end, it is thought, may be most effectually answered by a general concurrence of the members of the New Church at large.

Signed in behalf of the New Church at London,

Thomas Wright, *President*
Robert Hindmarsh, *Treasurer and Secretary*
John Augustus Tulk
Thomas Willdon
Richard Thompson
Isaac Hawkins
Manoah Sibly
Samuel Smith
James Hindmarsh

The Committee.

Great East Cheap, London
Dec. 7, 1788.

On the publication of this Circular Letter, and the Propositions accompanying it, by some means or other it came to the knowledge of the then Bishop of London, (Dr. Beilby Porteus), who immediately sent his Chaplain, the Rev. Mr. Sellon, Minister of St. James's Church, Clerkenwell, to my house for a copy of it, and at the same time to inquire of me what it all meant, or what our intentions were in summoning an Assembly of the above description. In answer to this application, I sent two or three copies of that Circular, with my compliments, to the Bishop, and begged the messenger to assure his Lordship, that no violence or disrespect was intended to any order of society; but that the design was to spread the doctrines of the New Jerusalem among mankind as publicly and extensively as possible. I heard no more from the Bishop after that. But I have reason to believe, that his Lordship was pretty well acquainted with the nature and tendency of those doctrines, and that he was far from entertaining an unfavorable opinion of them. His Chaplain, Mr. Sellon, who was a neighbour of mine, after that, frequently called on me, and purchased the books, as they came from the press, partly on his own account, and, as I understood, partly on account of the Bishop.

On the arrival of the appointed time for the meeting of the General Conference, which began on Easter Monday, the 13th, and continued till the 17th of April, 1789, a numerous assemblage of readers attended at the place of worship in Great East Cheap, London. Besides the Society in London, individuals were present from Kensington, in Middlesex, Rotherham, in Yorkshire, Derby, Liverpool, Salisbury, and other parts of England; also from Sweden, America, and Jamaica. All seemed desirous of promoting, to the utmost of their power, the great object for which they were convened; and though many of them had never before seen each other, they all rejoiced in the opportunity afforded them of testifying their sincere attachment to the cause which brought them together, and were anxious to manifest to the world their sense of the blessings, which awaited them in this new era of the Church.

The Meeting was opened in the manner described in the Minutes of the First General Conference of the Members of the New Jerusalem Church. After a prayer suited to the particular occasion of the day, and for the prosperity of the New Church at large, a member of the London Society (Mr. Robert Hindmarsh) addressed the Meeting in the following words:—

Friends and Brethren,

I am directed by the members of the New Jerusalem Church in London, to thank you, in their name, for the readiness you have shewn in accepting their invitation to this General Conference. It gives them unspeakable pleasure to find, that the heavenly doctrines of the New Jerusalem are now manifesting themselves in this land, and that in every quarter of the globe, the Lord's New Church is in some small degree beginning to make its appearance. May the Lord hasten the time, when righteousness shall cover the earth, as the waters cover the sea!

Be assured, that nothing but a sincere love to makind in general, and an ardent desire to promote their spiritual welfare, could have induced them to step forward on the present occasion, and call your attention to subjects, which, however new, or opposed to the prejudices and misconceptions of the present day, are nevertheless of the utmost moment and importance to all.

With hearts filled with gratitude to the most merciful Lord Jesus, for the greatest of all mercies, his Second Advent; and warmed with affection towards their brethren of the New Church, the Society of London can with freedom and confidence communicate their sentiments to all present; not doubting but the same charity and benevolence, which they trust actuate themselves, will be equally manifested on the part of the friends now assembled. Under this persuasion, and that all our proceedings may be conducted with harmony and good order, they have directed me to request, that the Meeting at large do now proceed to the election of a President and Secretary, to officiate in their respective capacities during the present Conference.

Hereupon the Meeting unanimously appointed Mr. Henry Peckitt, of London, to be President; and Mr. Robert Beatson, of Rotherham, in Yorkshire, to be Secretary.

When the President had taken his seat, he opened the business of the Conference in the following manner.

It is presumed, that all present are well acquainted with the design of the present Meeting, that it is, as stated in the circular letter, for the purpose of considering the most effectual means of promoting the establishment of the New Church, distinct from the Old, and for entering into such Resolutions, as may appear necessary in a work of so great importance. I trust, that the utmost harmony will be preserved during the whole of this Conference; and that each member, in delivering his sentiments, will ever keep in mind the necessity of humility, and guard against every domineering spirit that might attempt to infest his mind, by persuading him that he alone is in the true light, or that his judgment is superior to that of others; as knowing, that of himself he can neither think a good thought, nor speak a good word, but that every good and perfect gift proceeds from the Father of mercies, even the Lord God and Saviour Jesus Christ, who alone is the true fountain and source of all life and light. In his Name, and by the influence of his Holy Spirit, may all our proceedings be begun and carried on!

Sensible of the many difficulties we have to encounter, and of our inability, without divine assistance, to perform the task before us, let us remember, that whatever may be done in our present weak and imperfect state, can only be preparatory to the future complete and glorious establishment of the Lord's kingdom upon earth; to effect which great and blessed end, frequent Conferences will no doubt be necessary, in order that unanimity and harmony may prevail in all the Societies of the New Church, wheresoever they may be formed throughout the world. In the mean time, let us offer up our united prayers to the Omnipotent Jehovah Jesus, who is King of kings, and Lord of lords, that he would be pleased to preside in the present Assembly, and by his divine presence warm our hearts with love to himself and his kingdom, enlighten our understandings with the pure and genuine light of heaven, and so bless our feeble endeavours at this time, that they may tend to the further exaltation of his great and holy Name, and a more general reception of the glorious truths of the New Jerusalem.

Passages, extracted from the *True Christian Religion*, written by the Hon. Emanuel Swedenborg, were then read; wherein is contained an account of the New Angelic Heaven forming in the Spiritual World, and a view of the principal Arcana of the New Church now revealed to mankind. [TCR n. 108, n. 846-851.]

Having finished these Extracts, the Circular Letter, convening the Conference, was read. The Meeting then proceeded, with a solemnity and deliberation suited to the magnitude of the occasion, to take into serious consideration the various Propositions contained in the above Letter; and after a most interesting and instructive conversation on their important contents, the following Resolutions were moved, and unanimously agreed to.

RESOLUTIONS

I. **Resolved Unanimously:** That it is the opinion of this Conference, that the Theological Works of the Hon. Emanuel Swedenborg are perfectly consistent with the Holy Word, being at the same time explanatory of its internal sense in so wonderful a manner, that nothing short of Divine Revelation seems adequate thereto. That they also contain the Heavenly Doctrines of the New Church, signified by the New Jerusalem in the Revelation; which Doctrines he was enabled by the Lord alone to draw from the Holy Word, while under the Inspiration and Illumination of his Holy Spirit.

II. **Resolved Unanimously:** That it is the opinion of this Conference, that the First Proposition in the Circular Letter, asserting the Unity of Jehovah God, both in Essence and Person, is a truth founded in, and demonstrable from, the Holy Scriptures or Word of God, as well as consistent with sound rationality. That this Unity implies a Threefold Principle, consisting of Divine Love or Divine Good, Divine Wisdom or Divine Truth, and the Divine Proceeding or Operation, which in the Word are called Father, Son, and Holy Ghost; being so termed by way of accommodation to the capacity of man, in whom also exists a Trinity, though finite, of soul, body, and operation, corresponding with the Divine and Infinite Trinity, which alone exists in the Glorified Humanity of the Lord and Saviour Jesus Christ.

III. Resolved Unanimously: That it is the opinion of this Conference, that the second Proposition, asserting the nature and end of Redemption, together with the mode of its accomplishment, is agreeable to the genuine sense of the Holy Word.

IV. Resolved Unanimously: That it is the opinion of this Conference, that the Old Church, by which is meant the present Christian Church, so called, both as existing among Roman Catholics, and among Protestants of every description or denomination, is at this day arrived at its full period or consummation, in consequence of its destructive faith, the fatal effects of which are enumerated in the 3rd to the 10th, 32nd, and 38th Propositions.

V. Resolved Unanimously: That it is the opinion of this Conference, that the Faith of the Old Church is a Faith directed to Three Gods, the ultimate consequence of which is a belief either that Nature is God, or that there is no God at all.

VI. Resolved Unanimously: That it is the opinion of this Conference, that the Faith of the Old Church ought to be abolished from the mind of every individual, in order that the Faith of the New Church may gain admission, and be established.

VII. Resolved Unanimously: That it is the opinion of this Conference, that as long as men adhere to, and are influenced by, the Faith of the Old Church, so long the New Heaven cannot descend to them, and consequently so long the New Church cannot be established in and among them.

VIII. Resolved Unanimously: That it is the opinion of this Conference, that all Faith and Worship directed to any other, than to the One God Jesus Christ in his Divine Humanity, being directed to a God invisible and incomprehensible, have a direct tendency to overturn the Holy Word, and to destroy every thing spiritual in the Church.

IX. Resolved Unanimously: That it is the Opinion of this Conference, that the Doctrines and Worship in the Old Church are highly dangerous to the rising generation, inasmuch as they tend to implant in young people the idea of Three Divine Persons, to which is unavoidably annexed the idea of Three Gods; the consequence whereof is spiritual death to all those who confirm themselves in such an opinion.

X. Resolved Unanimously: That it is the opinion of this Conference, that it is the duty of every true Christian to train up his Children in the Principles and Heavenly Doctrines of the New Jerusalem Church alone, the two grand Essentials of which, as stated in the 1st, 23rd, and 42nd Propositions, are, I. That the Lord and Saviour Jesus Christ is the Only God of Heaven and Earth, and that his Humanity is Divine. II. That in order to salvation, man must live a life according to the Ten Commandments, by shunning evils as sins against God.

XI. Resolved Unanimously: That it is the opinion of this Conference, that for the above purpose it is expedient that a Catechism be drawn up for the use of the New Church; and that a deputation from this Conference be appointed to see the same put into execution.

XII. Resolved Unanimously: That it is the opinion of this Conference, that a complete and total Separation from the Old Church is warranted not only from the Theological Writings of Emanual Swedenborg, but also from the Holy Word; and that this Separatism ought to commence in every individual, on being fully convinced of the truth of the Heavenly Doctrines of the New Church, and of their opposition to those of the Old. *See Prop.* 29, 30, 31 *and* 33.

XIII. Resolved Unanimously: That it is the opinion of this Conference, that as the Doctrinals of the Old and New Church are in full and direct opposition to each other; and as the Faith of every Church does, or ought to, contain a clear, explicit, and determinate view of their Understanding of the Word; so no person, when once convinced of the truth of the Heavenly Doctrines of the New Jerusalem, ought to assent or conform to any of the Articles of Faith in the Old Church, or to Prayers directed to any other than to Jesus Christ alone.

XIV. Resolved Unanimously: That it is the opinion of this Conference, that the establishment of the New Church will be effected by a gradual Separation from the Old Church, in consequence of a rational conviction wrought in the minds of those, who are in search of Truth for the Sake of Truth, and who are determined to judge for themselves in spiritual things, without any regard to the influence or authority of the Clergy in the Old Church, or the hopes or preferment either in Church or State.

XV. Resolved Unanimously: That it is the opinion of this Conference, that the Establishment of the New Church distinct from the Old, is likely to be productive of the most eminent uses to mankind at large, inasmuch as thereby the communication betwixt the Angelic Heaven and the Church on earth will be rendered more full and complete; and consequently that it is greater charity to separate from the Old Church, than to remain in it.

XVI. Resolved Unanimously: That it is the opinion of this Conference, that the Eleventh Proposition, asserting the Sanctity and Divinity of the Word, and its Threefold Sense, is abundantly proved in the Works of Emanuel Swedenborg, by the clearest and most satisfactory evidence from the Word itself.

XVII. Resolved Unanimously: That it is the opinion of this Conference, that those Books only, which contain the Internal sense, and are enumerated in the Twelfth Proposition, ought to be received by the New Church as Canonical, or of Divine Authority, inasmuch as they treat of the Lord alone, and of the most holy things of

Heaven and the Church.[*]

XVIII. **Resolved Unanimously:** That it is the opinion of this Conference, that the existence of a Sun in the Spiritual World, distinct from that of the Natural World, as the primary instrumental Cause of Creation and Preservation, agreeably to the 13th and 17th Propositions, is highly rational to suppose, and at the same time perfectly consistent with the Holy Word.

XIX. **Resolved Unanimously:** That it is the opinion of this Conference, that the Doctines of the New Church concerning the nature of man's Resurrection, his eternal state and condition after Death, according to his past life in this world, and the Seminary from whence both Heaven and Hell are peopled; concerning Charity, Faith, and Good Works; concerning the Order whereby man's Life ought to be regulated; concerning Free-will, Repentance, and Regeneration; concerning Imputation, the exercise of the Rational Understanding in matters of Faith, and the necessity of a Life of Uses; and concerning true Conjugial Love, as described in the 14th to the 30th, 33rd, 36th, and 37th Propositions, are Doctrines drawn from the pure and genuine sense of the Holy Word, and calculated, through divine mercy, to instruct, reform, and bless mankind.

XX. **Resolved Unanimously:** That it is the opinion of this Conference, that the working of Miracles, which was necessary for establishing the first Christian Church, is now superseded by the plain Manifestation of Divine Truth in the Holy Word, and the Revelation of its Internal sense; the effect whereof is as much superior to that of Miracles, as the Understanding is superior to the bodily eye. *See Prop. 22.*

XXI. **Resolved Unanimously:** That it is the opinion of this Conference, that it is agreeable to Divine Order, that the New Jerusalem Church assume to itself an External Appearance, distinct from the Old Church, both in Doctrine and Worship; but that there may be many varieties of External Worship therein, provided they are all influenced by the genuine Doctrine of the Lord and of Charity. *See Prop. 34.*

XXII. **Resolved Unanimously:** That it is the opinion of this Conference, that as Baptism in the Old Church is a Baptism into the Faith of Three Gods, between which Faith and Heaven there can be no conjunction; so Baptism in the New Church, being a Baptism into the Faith of One God, between which Faith and Heaven there is conjunction, is highly necessary, inasmuch as the person baptized thereby takes upon him the badge and profession of genuine Christianity; and is at the same time inserted among Christians even in the Spiritual World. *See Prop. 35.* —— It is therefore recommended to all, who desire to become members of the New Jerusalem Church, to be baptized, both themselves and their children, in the Faith of that Church; and in case they have already been baptized in the Faith of the Old Church, to be re-baptized in the Faith of the New.

XXIII. **Resolved Unanimously:** That it is the opinion of this Conference, that the Holy Supper in the New Church is the most sacred and solemn of all Worship; but that it ought not to be received in the Old Church, by any who desire to be members of the New Church; because this would be a solemn acknowledgement of the existence of Three Gods, and that the sum and substance of redemption consisted in the passion of the cross, as a satisfaction or atonement made to appease the wrath of the Father. *See Prop. 3,4,7, and 35.*

XXIV. **Resolved Unanimously:** That it is the opinion of this Conference, that the state of Marriage, when under the influence of true Conjugial Love, is the most holy, chaste, and perfect state, that either Men or Angels are capable of attaining; being the ground or plane which receives the influx of the Lord into his New Church. *See Prop. 37.*

XXV. **Resolved Unanimously:** That it is the opinion of this Conference, that the Second Advent of the Lord, which a Coming in the internal sense of his Holy Word, has already commenced, and ought to be announced to all the world. That this Second Advent involves two things, namely, the Last Judgment, or Destruction of the Old Church, which was accomplished in the Spiritual World in the year 1757, and the consequent Formation or Establishment of the New Church. *See Prop. 38 to 41.*

XXVI. **Resolved Unanimously:** That it is the opinion of this conference, that the true Christian Religion is alone to be found in the New Jerusalem Church, because this is the Only Church that acknowledges and worships Jesus Christ Alone, as Father, Son, and Holy Ghost, in One Divine Person, and consequently as the Great Jehovah, the everlasting God of Heaven and Earth, in a Visible Human Form; which Church, being the Crown of all Churches, which have heretofore existed on this earth, will never have an end.

XXVII. **Resolved Unanimously:** That it is the opinion of this Conference, that men of every Religion or Persuasion throughout the whole world, even Pagans and Idolaters, are saved, after receiving instruction in the Spiritual World, provided they have lived a life of Charity, according to the best of their knowledge. That nevertheless the true Christian Religion, being founded on the Word, which is the Lord himself as to Divine Truth, is that to which all other Religions tend as to their Centre, and from which they receive all their Sanctity, together with all their Power of Salvation.

XXVIII. **Resolved Unanimously:** That it is the opinion of this Conference, that the Evidence of the Truth of Christianity arises chiefly

---

[*] The other Books, which have not the Internal Sense, as well as those which have an internal sense, but not in Series, are nevertheless useful in their place, so far as they inculcate the great Doctrine of the Lord, and the Doctrine of Charity.

from the Internal Sense of the Word; by virtue of which Sense, rationally understood, according to the Science of Correspondences, the New Church is in possession of more certain Evidence in favour of Christian Religion, than it is possible to obtain without it.

XXIX. **Resolved Unanimously:** That it is the opinion of this Conference, that, notwithstanding the apparent severity of some of these Resolution, which are intended to be directed chiefly against the Evils and Falses of the Old Church, and not against the Persons of any religious Body whatever; yet the greatest Charity ought to be maintained towards those in the Old Church, who, being in states of simplicity, and not confirmed in Falses of Doctrine, are the Remains, out of which the Lord will build his New Church, on their reception of the Heavenly Doctrines of the New Jerusalem.

XXX. **Resolved Unanimously:** That it be recommended to all the readers and lovers of the Theological Works of Emanuel Swedenborg, both in this and other countries, to form themselves into societies distinct from the Old Church, and to meet together as often as convenient, to read and converse on the said Writings, and to open a general correspondence for the mutual assistance of each other.

XXXI. **Resolved Unanimously:** That it is the opinion of this Conference, that the Writings of Emanuel Swedenborg are calculated to promote the Peace and Happiness of Mankind, by making them loyal subjects, Lovers of their Country, and useful Members of Society: And therefore that these Resolutions are not intended to militate against, or in the smallest degree to annul the Civil Authority in any Country; but only to emancipate mankind from the mental Bondage and Slavery, wherein they have so long been held captive by the Leaders and Rulers in the Old Church.

XXXII. **Resolved Unanimously:** That a General Conference of the Members of the New Church be again held in London, on Easter Monday, the 5th of April, 1790, when, by the Divine Mercy of the Lord, such further matters respecting the Establishment of the New Church distinct from the Old, as may at that time appear necessary, will be taken into serious consideration.

Signed in behalf of this Conference,

Henry Peckitt, of London, *President*
Robert Beatson, of Rotherham, *Secretary*
August Nordenskjöld, from Sweden
Charles Berns Wadstrom, from Sweden
Samuel Hands, of Derby
Henry Servanté, of London
Benjamin Banks, of Salisbury
Charles Harford, of Liverpool
John Willdon, of London

John Ashpinshaw, of London
Robert Jackson, from Jamaica
James Cruden, from America
John Augustus Tulk, of Kensington
Benedict Chastanier, of London

Great East Cheap, London,
    April 16, 1789.

Such were the proceedings of the *First General Conference* held in London; and as a singular circumstance it may be recorded, that, although the individuals composing it came from the east, the west, the north, and the south, and had been previously of almost every denomination of professing Christians, such as the unanimity which prevailed on all the subjects of discussion, that not a single dissentient voice was heard, but the whole of the proceedings was conducted in harmony, peace, and love.

As this was the first General Assemblage of the members of the New Church, met for the purpose of promoting the great interests of that Body at large, it was thought advisable to give a particular and circumstantial detail of what passed on that occasion; in order that the spirit of charity and affection, which influenced all present, and the zeal tempered with prudence, by which all were actuated, might never be lost sight of, nor departed from, by those who shall hereafter be engaged, either publicly or privately, in advocating and advancing the same cause. It was to be expected, that a Church, professing to derive its lineage and birth from heaven, should bring it into the natural world not only those doctrines of divine truth, which were seen by the beloved Apostle to descend in their aggregate as the holy city, New Jerusalem, from its celestial abode in the spiritual world, but also the still more valued principles of universal benevolence, which so particularly distinguish that Church. This expectation was fully realized during the time the General Conference held its sittings; and the harmony, which then prevailed, was justly regarded as a kind of pledge or earnest, that all future meetings of the New Church would in like manner be conducted in the true spirit of love to the Lord, and charity towards all mankind.

When the business of the Conference was completed, a Committee was appointed to prepare an Address to the Members of the New Church at large, informing them of the nature and design of the Meeting, the harmony that prevailed among them, and the result of their deliberations in the Resolutions which they had unanimously adopted. Of this address, which was prefixed to the printed Minute, the following is a copy.

The Members of the New Jerusalem Church, *assembled in General Conference, in Great East Cheap, London, the 13th of April, 1789, for the Purpose of taking into Consideration the most effectual Means of promoting the Establishment of the* New Church, *distinct from the Old,*

To all the Lovers of Truth, as contained in the Holy Word, and illustrated in the Theological Writings of the Hon. Emanuel Swedenborg.

Dear Friends and Brethren,

Impressed with a deep sense of the important business, in which we are engaged, and desirous that all the members of the New Church, wherever dispersed throughout the whole world, may be preserved in perfect harmony of sentiment, as well as united together in the bonds of mutual love and affection; we think it a duty incumbent upon us to communicate the result of our deliberations, by transmitting you such Resolutions, as appeared to us necessary to be adopted, in order to promote the above design. And it is with particular satisfaction that we can with truth declare, there was not a single dissentient voice among us, notwithstanding the Meeting was numerously attended, as well by the friends from different parts of England, and from abroad, as by the Members of the New Jerusalem in London.

We do not, however, hereby mean to dictate to you, or to any one, either how you must act or believe; as knowing that this would be contrary to the genuine principles of the New Church, which allows all men the free enjoyment of their religious persuasions, however various, without attempting even to *touch*, much less to *violate* the freedom of the human will. We would only recommend to you and to all, and this with the most sincere and affectionate desire for your spiritual good, a serious examination and search after truth for the sake of truth, that in all things our words and actions, as well as our thoughts and affections, our external man, as well as our internal, may be brought into a strict conformity to the divine laws.

The reasons, which have induced us to think it absolutely necessary for the New Jerusalem to assume to itself an external appearance, distinct from the Old Church, both as to doctrine and worship, are many and weighty, and may be seen partly in the Resolutions accompanying this Letter, but more fully in the works of our enlightened Author, Emanuel Swedenborg; whose testimony in this matter, authorized and confirmed by innumerable passages from the Holy Word itself, is so positive and clear, that, notwithstanding the weakness of the instruments, whom it may please the Lord to make choice of in so great a work, yet we have not the shadow of doubt, but even in our days *"the God of heaven hath begun to set up a kingdom, which shall never be destroyed; a kingdom, which shall not be left to other people, but shall break in pieces, and consume all these kingdoms, and shall stand for ever."*—Dan. ii. 44.

We desire with affection and thanks to acknowledge the receipt of sundry Letters from different societies and individuals, members of the New Church, in various parts of England, as likewise from abroad, who, by the necessary avocations of life, were prevented from a personal attendance. It has afforded us no small satisfaction to find, that the end proposed in the Circular Letter meets the approbation of so great a number of the lovers of pure and undefiled religion. May each of us in heart and life endeavour to promote the same, by examining the ends and motives of all our actions, by shunning evils continually as sins against God, and by living a life of genuine uses according to His Holy Word and commandments. So will the kingdom of the Lord be established in our hearts, and we ourselves prepared for admission into the holy city, the New Jerusalem, now descending from God out of heaven.

Signed, in behalf of the Conference,

Henry Peckitt, *President*
Robert Beatson, *Secretary*
August Nordenskjöld
Charles Berns Wadstrom
Samuel Hands
Henry Servanté
Benjamin Banks
Charles Harford
John Willdon
John Ashpinshaw
Robert Jackson
James Cruden
John Augustus Tulk
Benedict Chastanier

Great East Cheap, London
April 16, 1789

It ought not to be forgotten, that every day, during the sitting of Conference, the members dined together at a neighbouring tavern in Abchurch Lane, to the number of sixty or seventy, male and female; at which repasts the most cordial unanimity and brotherly affection were observable. It appeared as if the times of Primitive Christianity were restored among us, when all things were held in common. Natural and spiritual food were both dealt out with an unsparing hand; and while the body was refreshed with a rich supply of the good things of this world, the mind was at the same time replenished with the bread that cometh down from heaven. The tree of life, whose roots are planted in the gar-

Blake, *Jerusalem* 92 (detail)

dens and streets of the New Jerusalem, as well as on either bank of its river, spontaneously sprung up before our eyes, luxuriant in foliage, and laden with the sweetest fruits of paradise in endless variety and abundance. Filled to satiety with this delightful food, yet panting as it were and anxious for the return of the next meeting, the company retired at an early hour of the evening of each day, highly gratified with their own sumptuous entertainment, and no less so with the assurance from the Divine Word, that "the leaves of the tree of life were still left for the healing of the nations." Rev. xxii. 2.

The Church, in its aggregate capacity, having proceeded thus far, now took a survey of its relative situation since the commencement of public worship in 1788, compared with its former state before that event: and it was ascertained, that the increase of members in particular, and of readers in general, in *one year* after the opening of the Chapel in Great East Cheap, was at least seven-fold more than it was during the *four years* that the London Society held their meetings in the Temple. From this circumstance alone it is very evident, that the fears entertained by some sincere but timid minds, lest a separation from former Establishments should prove to be premature, and even injurious to the cause of truth, were entirely unfounded. On the contrary, the success, which had been anticipated by the friends to that measure, was realized beyond the fullest extent of their most sanguine expectations. Almost every week added to the number of recipients; the Writings of Emanuel Swedenborg came to be more in demand; and the doctrines of the New Church began to spread themselves far and wide both at home and abroad.

SWEDENBORGIAN
POSTSCRIPTS

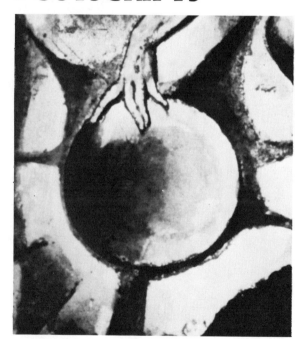

Swedenborgian Postscripts

Blake's connections with Swedenborg's theological works and with prominent early Swedenborgians sparked a reciprocal and on-going interest in Blake among (Swedenborgian) New Church writers, as represented in the following selections.

"William Blake's New Church Critics," by Donald C. Fitzpatrick, Jr., chronicles nineteenth and twentieth century Swedenborgian works about Blake, and concludes: "William Blake's New Church critics . . . reflect a sustained interest in one man which is probably unique in the church except for the interest in Swedenborg himself." This article is from the January, 1959 issue of *New Church Life*, a periodical founded by General Church Swedenborgians who have had an active community in Bryn Athyn, Pennsylvania since the early 1880s.

The second article, "Blake and Swedenborg" is excerpted from 1949 issues of *New Church Herald*, a publication of English Swedenborgians who are the successors of the group which convened the 1789 General Conference attended by Blake and his wife. The author, H. N. Morris (1872-1959), a Manchester chemist involved with mission work in Asia, writes within an orthodox interpretation of Swedenborg's theology to demonstrate his sincere belief that "Blake's attitude to Swedenborg and the doctrines revealed in his writings varied, but it cannot truly be said that he eventually rejected Swedenborg."

The third selection, "William Blake and the Writings of Swedenborg," is the text of a January, 1984 address by the Reverend Peter M. Buss, president of the Academy of the New Church, a Swedenborgian high school/college and theological school in Bryn Athyn, Pennsylvania. Like Morris, Buss views Blake from an orthodox New Church perspective; and he laments Blake's having severed his ties with the Swedenborgian church, since: "We suspect that our church might be much larger and richer in artistic talent had this one disciple held his candle on high for all the world to see." —Ed.

William Blake's New Church Critics

DONALD C. FITZPATRICK

The knowledge that Blake was acquainted with Swedenborg's theological writings has naturally led members of the New Church to be interested in him. This interest has been reflected in books and articles published in the church from time to time since shortly after his death in 1827. It will be our purpose here to examine a number of these publications in an effort to bring to light the criticism of Blake which has been produced in the New Church.

William Blake's life and work were first considered in a New Church publication when an editorial note entitled "Memoirs of William Blake" appeared in the *New Jerusalem Magazine* of Boston in January, 1832. This note was published in order that readers of the magazine might have the opportunity of contrasting Blake with John Flaxman, the sculptor, an early receiver of the teachings of Swedenborg and an intimate acquaintance of the poet's.

The editorial writer relied upon the then recently published work on the lives of the leading British artists by Allan Cunningham for most of the biographical material presented. His own introduction and conclusion, however, clearly indicate how he wished his readers to regard Blake.

That the poet was "pious, virtuous, sincere, and peaceful," as to his external life, the editor readily admitted. "But," he continued, "while Flaxman believed in the reality of a spiritual world, and in the actual and personal existence of spirits, as fully as Blake, in him this belief had nothing in it or with it of unregulated enthusiasm or of wild phantasy; he believed, and he knew why and what he believed."

This, then, was a fault in Blake's belief and understanding. He did not, as did Flaxman apparently, see the whole of the system of Swedenborg, but only certain broken parts which he mixed with falsities and used for his own selfish purposes. Here the writer sounded the note which we will hear repeated often in the criticism of later New Church writers.

Later in this long paragraph the editor softened his criticism somewhat by writing that he did not wish to imply that the influence of Swedenborg was destroyed completely in Blake. The poet's character seemed to him to show that this was not the case, and revealed a man more to be pitied than scorned.

In closing the memoirs the editor merely noted that Blake "became more and more fantastic, more and more removed

Excerpted from *New Church Life*, January 1959 (Bryn Athyn: General Church of the New Jerusalem), pp. 20-27, by permission of the publisher.

from the business and employments of actual life, and finally at an advanced age, he died in a state of poverty and almost of destitution."

Blake is certainly not presented here in a very favorable light. The editor relied upon Cunningham for the facts of the poet's life and may never have read any of Blake's poetry in a serious way. Whatever explanation might be given, it seems certain that the memoir itself could have no very favorable effect upon the average reader's opinion of Blake or his work.

Both the poet and his work were to receive better treatment at the hands of an English New Church man about seven

and one-half years after the appearance of these "Memoirs"; for in July, 1839, Dr. James John Garth Wilkinson published the first printed edition of the *Songs of Innocence* and *Songs of Experience*. Previous to this time, the works had "existed only in the prints struck off from the copper upon which Blake had himself engraved in relief both the text and the marginal illustrations."

Dr. Wilkinson had borrowed an original copy of the *Songs of Innocence and of Experience* from an acquaintance in 1838. Much impressed by it, he wrote a long preface, and with funds supplied by his brother William had a ninety-five page octavo volume published by Pickering and Newberry on July 9, 1839.

The preface opens with a biographical sketch which again relied upon Cunningham's work as the source of facts concerning Blake's life.

Then, having condemned in no uncertain terms the standards by which Cunningham had presumed to pass judgment on Blake's works, Dr. Wilkinson wrote: ". . .it is far indeed from our intention, to express an approbation of the spirit in which he conceived and executed his later works; or to profess to see good in the influences to which he then yielded himself, and from which his visional experiences proceeded."

For the poems he was arranging to print, Dr. Wilkinson had only good to say, however.

The present Volume contains nearly all that is excellent in Blake's Poetry; and great, rare, and manifest, is the excellence that is here. The faults are equally conspicuous, and he who runs may read them. They amount to an utter want of elaboration, and even, in many cases, to an inattention to the ordinary rules of grammar. Yet the "Songs of Innocence," at least, are quite free from the dark becloudment which rolled and billowed over Blake in his later days. He here transcended Self, and escaped from the isolation which Self involves; and, as it then ever is, his expanding affections embraced universal Man, and without violating, beautified and hallowed, even his individual peculiarities. Accordingly, many of these delicious Lays, belong to the Era as well as to the Author. They are remarkable for the transparent depth of thought which constitutes true Simplicity—they give us glimpses of all that is holiest in the Childhood of the World and the Individual— they abound with the sweetest touches of that pastoral life, by which the Golden Age may be still visibly represented to the iron one—they delineate full-orbed Age, ripe with the seeds of a second Infancy, which is "the Kingdom of Heaven." The latter half of the volume, comprising the "Songs of Experience," consists, it is true, of darker themes: but they, too, are well and wonderfully sung; and ought to be preserved, because, in contrastive connexion with the "Songs of Innocence," they do convey a powerful impression of "the two contrary states of the Human Soul."

Of the poems that followed *Songs of Innocence,* and of the poet's life as he plunged deeper into the work of building a system, Dr. Wilkinson does not speak so highly. In *The Gates of Paradise* and *The Book of Thel* he felt that Blake "had already departed, in some measure, from that intelligible simplicity which characterizes the Songs of Innocence (*sic*) and fantasies were fast gaining the dominion over him."

That Blake preferred to see truth in mythological forms rather than in the "Divine-Human Embodiment of Christianity" disturbed Wilkinson, for he felt that this had led the poet to divorce imagination from reason and to copy the mere outward form of the past without the inward truth that had made that form meaningful and beautiful in its own right.

"For," he wrote, "the true Inward is one and identical, and if Blake had been disposed to see it, he would have found that it was still (though doubtless under a multitude of wrappages) extant in the present Age."

In drawing the preface to a close, Dr. Wilkinson offered a comparison between Blake and Shelley.

> From the opposite extremes of Christianity and Materialism, they both seem, at length, to have converged towards Pantheism, or natural-spiritualism; and it is probable, that a somewhat similar self-intelligence, or Ego-theism, possessed them both. They agreed in mistaking the forms of Truth for the Truth itself; and consequently, drew the materials of their works, from the Ages of type and shadow which preceded the Christian Revelation. The beauty, chasteness, and clear polish of Shelley's mind, as well as his metaphysical irreligion, took him, naturally enough, to the Philosophy and Theology of the Greeks; where he could at once enjoy the loose dogma of an Impersonal Creator, and have liberty to distribute Personality at will to the beautiful unliving forms of the visible creation. . .The visionary tendencies, the mysticism of Blake, developing themselves, as they did, under the shelter of a religious parentage and education, carried him, on the contrary, to the mythic fountains of an elder time, and his genius

which was too expansive to dwell in classic formalisms, entered into, and inhabited, the Egyptian and Asiatic perversions of an ancient and true Religion. In consequence of these and allied deformities, the works of both are sadly deficient in vital heat, and in substantial or practical Truth, and fail, therefore, to satisfy the common wants, or to appeal to the universal instincts, of Humanity. Self-will in each, was the centre of the Individual, and self-intelligence, the 'Anima Mundi' of the Philosopher, and they both imagined, that they could chop and change the Universe, even to the confounding of Life with Death, to suit their own creative fancies.

In Dr. Wilkinson, Blake and his work found a critic who could at least present intelligently the reasons and beliefs which prevented his acceptance of the later of the poet's writings. His was not the criticism of the ignorant, and his intent in presenting the *Songs of Innocence and of Experience* was admirable from some points of view, even if slightly ambitious in its way, for he hoped that it might serve as an instrument for public interest in the New Church.

The next New Church man to consider Blake at any length was James Spilling, who published a series of two articles on the poet in the May and June issues of the *New Church Magazine* in 1887. His purpose, unlike Wilkinson's was merely to present to the readers of the magazine a better picture of the poet and of the meaning of his work than those which had previously appeared in the church.

> If a man aims at popularity, he must restrict his vision. It is a condition of favoritism with people that a genius must not see too deeply or sing too highly. William Blake did both, and the world, as in the case of Swedenborg, declared him mad."

Blake's apparent lack of concern about whether he was understood or not did not bother Spilling in the least. He saw in the poet's obscurity a deliberate attempt to defy the efforts of reason to penetrate his meaning. For this reason, Spilling divided Blake's poetry into two groups: material for the general reader—*Songs of Innocence, Songs of Experience,* and *The Book of Thel*; and material for the student—the prophetic poems. The latter, he assured the reader, were clear in their meaning to Blake though they might appear like the products of insanity to the ordinary reader of poetry.

Unlike previous New Church writers, Spilling presented his readers with specific examples of Blake's poetry and commented on each of the selections. He chose those poems he considered the most familiar and tried to show how Blake's thought agreed, in part at least, with the teachings of Swedenborg.

He saw in the *Songs of Innocence* the most successful and skillful clothing of the highest truth in forms of sweet simplicity. "The Divine Image" taught that mercy, pity, peace, and love are qualities both Divine and human, and that they are combined in the Divine-Human person of Christ. "The Chimney Sweeper" showed the true nature and relationship of the life of the body to the eternal life of man after death. "Night" treated of angelic ministration to good and evil men alike.

Of *The Book of Thel* he wrote:

> It is an allegory, not strange but familiar; not mystical but crystalline. To understand it, it is only necessary to know that Thel, the mistress of the vales of Har, means beauty that lives for its own sake and seeks no use, but only its own pleasure. . . .This is the teaching of the great poem! The Lily of the Valley, the Cloud, the Worm, the Clod have all their uses and are happy and immortal; but the Daughter of Beauty who lives simply for herself, the shining woman without a use, vanished away to be found no more. Even when taught she is unreclaimed, and flees from the awful voice to pursue her delight in the vales of Har.

This at least is an attempt to look at the poetry affirmatively, and the whole tone of Spilling's commentary is one which marks him as willing to rejoice in what he can understand without condemning that which is obscure to his understanding.

In the same spirit, H. N. Morris included a chapter on Blake in a little work published in 1915 concerning Swedenborg's influence on well-known men of genius. He, too, saw *The Songs of Innocence* as poetic presentations of New Church teachings. "In those beautifully simple lines commencing 'Little lamb, who made thee?' there is the central teaching of the New Church, that God, the Creator of all things, clothed Himself with a human form, came into the world as a little child, and became the Saviour of the world."

Not afraid to disagree with an earlier New Church critic of Blake, Morris wrote:

> Dr. Garth Wilkinson, who was the first to introduce Blake to the public after the latter's death, said that the "Songs of Innocence and Experience" contained nearly all that is excellent in Blake's poetry. No one with the fuller knowledge of Blake we now have would agree with this.
>
> It is true most of his later writings are mystical and incomprehensible to most people, but many volumes have been published during the last few years dealing with these mystical works, and attempting to interpret them. One of the latest writers suggests that the reason so many have failed to understand these later works of Blake is that they have not first studied Swedenborg, and that they would have greater success if they first mastered Swedenborg's system of interpreting the

Scriptures.

We must leave this to be decided by Blake students of the future.

The poet was to come under fire again, however, from an English writer, James S. Pryke, who published an article entitled "William Blake and the Imagination" in the March, 1928, issue of the American monthly, *New Church Life*. Unwilling to accept Blake's own testimony concerning his spiritual experiences as earlier New Church men had, Pryke wrote that the poet's "fancied penetration into the other world persisted throughout Blake's life."

The closing paragraph of the article, a consideration primarily of the functions of the imagination and its relation to other mental faculties, presented this view of Blake:

> Vivid, active, fertile in imagination, he undoubtedly was; but he was also self-centered, with all that that word implies. In bondage to the fixed idea that he must surpass all other men, his imagination was permitted to outrun his intelligence. Knowing, as we do, that Divine help never fails, that he was in contact with the Master of spiritual imagery, Blake's cry, 'I must create a system, or be enslaved by another's,' may be ranked as one of the most tragic to be found in English literature. What monuments in verse and line might Blake have left behind, what beneficent influence might he be exerting even now, had he accepted the new knowledge that was within his grasp!

The feeling of regret over Blake's separation from Swedenborgian thought expressed here is one that has been repeated often since it was first voiced by Dr. Wilkinson in his preface. It certainly was evident in the article on "Swedenborg and Blake" by the Rev. Eric A. Sutton, a British New Church minister, which appeared in the *New Church Magazine* in 1929.

Feeling that the intellectual schism between Blake and Swedenborg was a deep one indeed, Sutton saw the poet's later poems as expressions, though not clear ones, of his conviction about the error of Swedenborg's reliance upon reason as the world's hope of salvation. "At present the New-Churchman is prone to exaggerate Blake's indebtedness to Swedenborg, and those who do not know Swedenborg accept uncritically Blake's interpretation of his teachings. The result is pandemonium. Blake's personality—his unrestrained self-will—his bold, creative genius buttressed with adamantine prejudices, preclude from him the power of sober interpretation. He is poet, not portrait painter—he is creative, not interpretive."

Blake's lack of interpretive ability in his reading of Swedenborg led him to misconstrue his teachings, said Sutton. "While Swedenborg showed that the furniture of earth, the whole pageantry of nature, is the mirror, the embodiment of spiritual things—Blake made that pageantry the mirror of his world of poetic imagination."

Sutton noted, however, that even the severest critics of Swedenborg admitted that Blake's sweetest poetry was written before his rebellion against Swedenborg.

But the rebellion did come, for Blake saw in the religious works he read a tendency to make the church and reason the rulers over those energies in man which he felt to be essential to true manhood. Sutton tried to show the fallacy of Blake's belief. "If man determines to restrain his desire—there is another desire and a stronger desire at the back of his determination. Reason itself is not the restrainer—reason enlightens, and becomes the womb of a new, purified, and more powerful desire—and this, the new born energy, is that which restrains." This, then, was the crux of the problem. Blake misunderstood Swedenborg's emphasis on reason and separated himself from the organized New Church.

Echoing James Pyrke's remarks, Sutton conluded that had Blake been able to understand what Swedenborg had to say, he might have left a richer heritage of poetry than that provided by the prophetic poems of his later years.

A period of twenty years now passed in which nothing of importance concerning Blake appeared in any New Church publication. The latest series of critical appraisals of the poet and his work by literary scholars finally led, in 1949, to the publication by Herbert N. Morris of another consideration of Blake in a series of three articles which appeared in the *New Church Herald* of London. These articles deal primarily with Blake's acquaintance with and attitude toward Swedenborg's writing, and attempt to show evidence of their sustained influence on all of Blake's work.

Morris began by presenting evidence to disprove the idea that few of Swedenborg's works were available in English editions in Blake's day, and discussed briefly the poet's association with the organized church in London. The remainder of the material in the three articles presented the author's view that Blake did not really reject Swedenborg as whole-heartedly as earlier New Church writers and other critics had supposed.

> The one doctrine upon which Blake's entire message, so far as it was consistent, is based, was that of the Last Judgment. In 1757, the year of Blake's birth, according to Swedenborg the Last Judgment, described in symbolic language in the Bible, had already taken place as a spiritual event. It marked the beginning of a new era or dispensation. The Christian Church as known and constituted externally was to begin to pass away and a new and internal church was to take its place. To the end of his life he never varied from the full acceptance of this.

Morris pointed to the poem "Milton" and to the *Descriptive Catalogue*, two of Blake's later works, as evidence that the poet did not continue to reject Swedenborg's ideas. He also noted that Blake never denied two cardinal principles of the Writings: that Jesus Christ is God and that the Bible is the Word of God.

Not questioning the validity of Blake's claims of having had spiritual experiences, Morris wrote: "There is, however, a wide difference in the experiences and claims of the two visionaries." Blake claimed to have received messages from all sorts of spirits, while Swedenborg, the chosen revelator of a new dispensation of Divine truth, attested that he had received the truths of the doctrines of the New Church from God alone. Blake's error, says Morris, lay in opening himself to contact will all spirits, regardless of their nature.

In the last of the three articles in this series, Morris lists the doctrines which Blake accepted wholly or in part from Swedenborg, and concludes with the idea that the things he repudiated were those which he took out of context or those which were confusing because of poor translation from the original Latin in the English editions he possessed.

In many respects, Morris stands at odds with earlier New Church critics of Blake. He persists more firmly than others in seeing the positive and direct influence of the Writings even in the last of Blake's "Prophetic Poems" and seems willing to blame everyone but the poet himself for Blake's failure to understand Swedenborg aright.

These, then, are some of William Blake's New Church critics. Their words reflect a sustained interest in one man and his works which is probably unique in the church except for the interest in Swedenborg himself.

Blake and Swedenborg

H.N. MORRIS

Excerpted from *The New Church Herald* XXX, nos. 1293-4, 1298 (London: The General Conference of the New Church), pp. 157-9, 165-7, 195-7, by permission of the publisher.

I

The popularity and influence of William Blake as a poet has steadily increased in the last few decades and he is today one of the best loved of poets. He was not appreciated in his lifetime except by a small circle of friends. Today [in England] his name is a household word. By the millions he is loved as the author of that new National Anthem, "Jerusalem," taken from a poem written when he was fifty years of age. His *Songs of Innocence and Experience*, written in his early manhood, have been translated and published in different languages, even Japanese, and more than a score of volumes have been published giving details of his life and attempts to interpret his message to the world.

One of the last of these, recently published by the Oxford University Press under the title of *The Theology of William Blake*, by J. D. Davies, attempts "to discover the characteristic doctrines that lie embedded in his books and define his religious views." According to Davies, the writers with whom Blake had most mental affinity were Swedenborg, Paracelsus, and Boehme, and that, of the three, Swedenborg had far the greatest influence on him. . . .

Davies agrees that Blake was greatly influenced by Swedenborg, whom he describes as the founder of a new sect. But Swedenborg founded no sect. He inaugurated no new external order in Church or State. He prescribed no ritual. He stated his expectation that his doctrines would be preached in all churches. That crowning work of his life, *True Christian Religion*, had a subtitle which Blake used, when in his fifty-first year he said in his *"Descriptive Catalogue"* that the subject of his picture "The Spiritual Preceptor" was taken from the "Visions of Emanuel Swedenborg, Universal Theology No. 623," and added, "the works of this visionary are well worthy of the attention of Painters and Poets: *they are the foundations of grand things*" (emphasis mine). (K 581)

No, Swedenborg founded no sect, but what may be called sects have been built upon his doctrines, and the first of these was founded at the Conference in 1789, which Blake and his wife attended, subscribing their names in approval of the doctrines revealed by Swedenborg, and of the desirability of separating themselves from the organized churches of his day. He must have been a wholehearted receiver of the doctrines at that time, when he was thirty years of age. He did not continue to associate with this separated organization after that first meeting, but notwithstanding his occasional sometimes bitter criticism in his later life, what was consistent in his religious views was undoubtedly taken from Swedenborg.

Mark Schorer, however, has given, in his monumental work *William Blake, the Politics of Vision*, a probable explanation for his severance from the organized New Church. He tells how in the same year as the first inaugural Conference "a scandal rocked the community and Blake was surely interested and may well have entered into the controversy. It was a perverted view of Swedenborg's doctrine of concubinage in his work *Conjugial Love."* But the same writer agrees that Swedenborg still remained one of the steadfast influences on Blake's work.

Whatever may have been the cause of the scandal, it alienated Blake from every form of the ecclesiastical or external Christian Church and public worship, though shortly before his death he expressed a wish that the Church of England Service should be used at his funeral. . . .

He did not remain a member of the external organization, but he may be classed as a member of the universal New Church, "that Holy Catholic and Apostolic Church universal, consisting of all men and women and children in the world who acknowledge and love the Lord in His person and in His Word, and are shunning evils of life, private on the smallest scale, and public on the greatest scale, as sins against Him; and doing the works of their calling actively, industrially, honestly and lovingly with all their Might."

This is the internal and real New Church of which Swedenborg wrote.

Figures from *America, a Prophecy* title page

II

Blake's attitude to Swedenborg and the doctrines revealed in his writings varied, but it cannot truly be said that he eventually rejected Swedenborg. In 1787 when he was thirty years of age he subscribed to a full acceptance of the doctrines and to the separation of the receivers of the doctrines of the New Church from the established Church. He had been a devout student of the Bible and of the writings of Swedenborg whose crowning work, a compendium of the Christian faith which he refers to as "The Universal Theology of the New Church" had been published in English since 1781.

The one doctrine upon which Blake's entire message, so far as it was consistent, is based, was that of the Last Judgment. In 1757, the year of Blake's birth, according to Swedenborg the Last Judgment, described in symbolic language in the Bible, had already taken place as a spiritual event. It marked the beginning of a new era or dispensation. The Christian Church as known and constituted externally was to begin to pass away and a new and internal church was to take its place. To the end of his life he never varied from his full acceptance of this. At times he was critical of Swedenborg, charging him with spiritual pride, and that his works were mere compilations such as any man of mechanical talents might produce in thousands, from the works of mystics and poets. He said Swedenborg's conceit made him fit company for angels whereas Blake's particular friend was an angel converted to devildom.

Not long after his withdrawal from the separated New Church organization he said "a new heaven is begun, and it is now thirty-three years since its advent: the Eternal Hell revives. And lo! Swedenborg is the Angel sitting at the tomb; his writings are the linen clothes folded up." (MHH 3) He makes the downright statement of "plain fact" that Swedenborg has not written one new truth. Swedenborg conversed with angels who were all religious and he conversed not with devils who all hate religion, for he was incapable through his conceited notions.

In his annotations to Swedenborg's *Divine Providence* he accused Swedenborg of teaching predestination. But the publisher of the annotations, H. Stanley Redgrove, commented, "it is clear that Swedenborg no more believed in predestination than Blake did," and that Blake misinterpreted Swedenborg's remarks. Where Blake accuses Swedenborg of a contradiction, Redgrove remarks, the contradiction is more apparent than real, for Swedenborg distinguishes between Divine omniscience, in which he believed, and predestination, in which he did not, holding that the former was not incompatible with the principles of human freedom.

His adverse comments may have been influenced by the wording of the Preface which was written by the translator and not by Swedenborg. There is no doctrine of the Old Christian Churches that Swedenborg rejects more vehemently. For example, he said: "Any predestination except to heaven is contrary to Divine Wisdom" (DP 330); "Predestination is a cruel heresy; a monstrous faith" (TCR 487,488); "A detestable error" (TCR 628); "That viper of predestination hatched from the mystical things of faith" (TCR 803), etc.

Blake did not continue to be critical or contemptuous of Swedenborg. In the prophetic poem, *Milton*, written when he was nearly fifty, he called Swedenborg "the strongest of men." (M 24) In the *Descriptive Catalogue* published when he was fifty-two, describing a picture based upon one of Swedenborg's Memorabilia from the *True Christian Religion*, which Blake refers to as "the Universal Theology," he adds, "The works of this visionary are well worth the attention of Artists and Poets; they are the foundation of grand things; the reason they have not been more attended to is because corporeal demons have gained a predominance. Unworthy Men who gain fame among Men continue to govern men after death and in their spiritual bodies oppose the spirits of those who worthily are famous; and, as Swedenborg observes, . . . they possess themselves of the bodies of mortal men and shut the doors of mind and of thought by placing Learning above Inspiration. O Artist! you may disbelieve all this but it shall be at your own peril." (K 581-2)

He is said to have been influenced by Paracelsus and Boehme, but in the prophetic poem *Milton*, Milton is "the awakener" but Swedenborg the strongest of men, while Paracelsus and Boehme are not mentioned.

In his last years such records as we have of conversations with Allingham, Crabb Robinson, Palmer, Tulk and others all indicate his adherence to the beliefs of his younger and what may be called his Swedenborgian days. There can be no doubt that Tatham, into whose hands his manuscripts and papers came after his death, destroyed much evidence that would have thrown light upon the "Mystery of William Blake." One account states that Tatham, who was an active member of what became known as the Irvingite Church and had no sympathy with Blake's religious views, spent two days in destroying the papers. Professor Berger tells specifically of Tatham's barbarous mutilation of Blake's notes on Swedenborg. All the records we have refute the suggestion that he altogether rejected Swedenborg.

Crabb Robinson's reminiscences of interviews in Blake's last two years credit Blake with saying that Swedenborg was "a divine teacher" and that he had done much good, but was wrong in trying to explain to reason what it could not comprehend. The fact that his close friendship with Flaxman, which had been broken by Blake, had been resumed and the two Swedenborgians were again close together is another indication that he eventually rejected Swedenborg. James Spilling, the editor of the *Eastern Daily Press*, in a series of articles on Blake in the *New Church Magazine* in 1887, made this statement: "In a letter which we have now before us, Dr. Garth Wilkinson tells us that Charles Augustus Tulk, one of the most earnest and original New Church thinkers, often conversed with Blake. 'Blake,' says Dr. Wilkinson, 'informed Tulk that he had two different states: one in which he liked Swedenborg's writings and one in which he disliked them. The second was a pride in himself and then they were distasteful to him, but afterwards he knew that he had not been wise and sane. The first was a state of humility in which he received and accepted Swedenborg.' "

We can readily believe this statement, adds Spilling, as it serves to explain much in relation to Blake's attitude towards Swedenborg. In fact, it is the only satisfactory explanation of the mystery of William Blake. The difference in the nature of the inspiration of the two visionaries supports this view.

Blake must have read Swedenborg's *Heaven and Hell* with close attention. It had been published in English when he was twenty-one. It is surprising that no annotated copy has come to light. Berger points out that one sentence of the work applies almost exactly to Blake's experience . . . [:] "The man finds himself," says Swedenborg, "transported into an intermediate state between sleeping and waking, but he has no knowledge of being otherwise than awake. All his senses are as wakeful as they would be if the body were entirely awake. In this state men have seen angels and spirits in all the reality of life, have heard them speak, and still more wonderful have touched them; for at such a time the body scarcely interferes at all." (HH 448)

Many of the expressions used by Swedenborg in that work were substantially incorporated by Blake, such as: "I have spoken at times with spirits recently come from the world"; "I have conversed about this with angels"; "I can affirm this after long experience"; and "in order that I might understand the nature and character of heaven and of heavenly joy, I have often and for long periods been permitted by the Lord to witness its delights. I know them therefore from my own actual experience."

Blake, in a letter to Butts, said, "I am not ashamed, afraid, or averse to tell you what ought to be told: that I am under the direction of Messengers from Heaven, Daily and Nightly."

He claimed to have written one of his prophetic poems from immediate dictation, twelve or sometimes twenty to thirty lines at a time, without premeditation and even against his will; the time taken in the writing being non-existent, and an immense poem that seemed to be the labor of a life-time was all produced without labor or study, he simply acting as the secretary, the author being in eternity. . . .

In his prophetic poem, *Jerusalem*, Blake wrote:

> *I rest not from the great task!*
> *To open the Eternal Worlds, to open the immortal Eyes*
> *Of Man inwards into the Worlds of Thought, into Eternity*
> *Ever expanding in the Bosom of God, the Human Imagination.*

"To open up the eternal world, to open the immortal eyes of man to the world of thought" was also the message of Swedenborg, a message he claimed to be a Divine Revelation, for a new age. . . . Blake had a message to proclaim to the world. "Mark well my words," he said, "they are for your eternal salvation."

> *I give you the end of a golden string*
> *Only wind it into a ball,*
> *It will lead you in at Heaven's Gate,*
> *Built in Jerusalem's wall.*

And the message, so far as it was consistent, was based upon two fundamental truths. The first and most vital was that of the Divinity of Jesus Christ. "Jesus," he said, "was both God and man, for the source of life descends to a weeping child."

Jesus was "the Divine Creator and Redeemer." He was . . . [:] "the image of the invisible God"; "The express image of God"; "He took on sin in the virgin's womb"; "In the Incarnate God, man beholds a human Vision; Human Divine, Jesus the Saviour blesses for ever"; and "God the dear Saviour took on the likeness of man, becoming obedient to death, even death of the Cross."

He prayed to Jesus:

> *O Saviour, pour upon me*
> *Thy spirit of meekness and love*
> *Annihilate the selfhood in me*
> *Be thou all my life.*
>
> *God appears and God is light,*
> *To those poor souls who walk in night*
> *But doth a Human Form display,*
> *To those who dwell in realms of day.*

And in his delightful *Songs of Innocence:*

> *Sweet Babe once like thee*
> *Thy maker lay and wept for me,*
> *Wept for me, for thee and all,*
> *When he was an infant small.*
>
> *Little Lamb who made thee,*
> *Dost thou know who made thee*
>
> *He is called by thy name*
> *For he is called himself a Lamb.*
> *He is meek and he is mild,*
> *He became a little child.*

It was the heart of Blake's religion: One God, Jesus Christ, the Divine Humanity.

The second fundamental was that "the Bible is the Word of God and all truth is to be found in it."

The Bible was "the book of liberty and the sole regenerator of nations"; "The beauty of the Bible is that the most ignorant and simple minds understand it best."

In his annotations on Dr. Watson's Apology for the Bible, Blake makes a very thorough if unorthodox defense of the Bible.

To Crabb Robinson Blake declared that all he knew was in the Bible, but that he understood the Bible in the spiritual sense.

To these two fundamental truths or doctrines may be added other minor doctrines which he held with more or less consistency all through his life. For example: That although the external Church of God is split up into innumerable sects, the real and invisible Church consists of all who live as their conscience directs.

III

Swedenborg's doctrine of Correspondences was the basis of what Blake called his system.

In *Milton* for example he wrote: "Every Natural effect has a Spiritual cause and not a Natural."

In the Vision of the *Last Judgment*: "There exists in the Eternal World the Permanent Realities of Every Thing we see reflected in this Vegetable Glass of Nature."

In *Vala*: "Even I already feel a world within, opening its gates, and in it all the real substances, of which these in the outward world are shadows which pass away."

Davies says that Blake accepted Swedenborg's doctrine of Correspondences all the more readily because it is identical with the "Astranomia" of Paracelsus and with the "Signatures" of Boehme, but it is doubtful whether Paracelsus or Boehme had anything to do with it.

Another doctrine which Blake wholeheartedly accepted was that of the "Grand Man." According to Schorer, Swedenborg's Grand Man became one of Blake's controlling symbols, but he adds that what in Swedenborg is the shape of the literal heaven, is in Blake the symbol of universal humanity.

This is exactly Swedenborg's teaching. "The Lord's kingdom," he says, "is as one man, and is called the *maximus homo*" which has come to be generally translated as "the Grand Man." "All men in the universal world," continues Swedenborg, "have a situation in the Grand Man that is in heaven, or outside of it in hell." *All men in the universal world.* Is this not the universal humanity? Every part of the human body has its use, its members, organs, fibres, nerves, blood vessels, parts within parts, each has its own distinctive shape, character and use. "All these various things," says Swedenborg, "act in man as one, because there is nothing in him which does not contribute something to the common good and perform some use. The whole is of use to the parts and the parts contribute to the whole; thus they act as one."

This is Blake's picture of heaven. It is the picture of the kingdom of heaven on earth, the ideal social state. It is the doctrine of the *maximus homo* of Swedenborg and is the doctrine to guide the world in its present difficulties national and international, the doctrine of interdependence as distinct from independence.

Allied to that of the Grand Man is the doctrine of Uses which Blake also accepted. The allegorical *Book of Thel* is an exposition of Swedenborg's doctrine of Uses. Keeping in view that Thel, the mistress of the vales of Har, is an image of beauty which lives for its own sake and seeks no use, but only its own pleasure, the poem is one of exquisite beauty. The theme is that everything that lives, lives not alone nor for itself. Of Thel it is said: "Without a use this shining woman lived." The humble lily of the valley, the cloud, the worm and the clod all have their uses and are happy and immortal, and they try to teach the self-centred and proud beauty. The lily of the valley though very small and weak says:

> Yet I am visited from heaven and he that smiles on all
> Walks in the valley, and each morn over me spreads His hand
> Saying, rejoice thou humble grass, thou new born lilly flower
> Thou gentle maid of silent valleys and of modest brooks:
> For thou shalt be clothed in light and fed with morning
>   manna.

Even the meanest of all, the clod who speaks also for the cloud and worm, says to her:

O beauty of the vales of Har, we live not for ourselves.
Thou seest me the meanest thing, and so I am indeed,
My bosom of itself is cold, and of itself is dark,
But he that loves the lowly pours his oil upon my head,
And kisses me and binds his nuptial bands around my breast.

Even when taught, Thel is unreclaimed and flees to pursue her delights in the vale of Har. This is Swedenborg's doctrine of uses. "Uses," he says, "are the bonds of Society and their number is infinite." To live for others is to perform uses. To desire the welfare of others for the sake of the common good is to perform a use.

Another doctrine taken from Swedenborg is that of Equilibrium. Blake's idea of the complementary nature of Heaven and Hell, what he called the Marriage of Heaven and Hell, bears a close resemblance to what with Swedenborg is the Equilibrium between Heaven and Hell which makes the freedom of will of man possible.

"Without Contraries," says Blake,"[there] is no progression. Attraction and Repulsion, Reason and Energy, Love and Hate, are necessary to Human existence." (MHH 3) According to Swedenborg everyone is kept in a middle state between heaven and hell so as to be in equilibrium between good and evil and thus in freedom of will in spiritual things. For every human being is attended by spiritual beings, some of them evil or, as Blake calls them, corporeal spirits, and if there was not equilibrium between the good and evil spirits no man would be in freedom. "Every man," says Swedenborg, "has been predestined to heaven, and no one to hell, but a man gives himself over to hell by the abuse of his free will in spiritual things."

The doctrine of Degrees, fully accepted by Blake, is set out by Swedenborg in the treatise on *The Divine Love and Wisdom*, on Blake's copy of which his numerous marginal notes are on the whole favorable. Many of his comments are "mark this," "note this," "excellent," etc. Although commenting on Swedenborg's statement that the whole of charity and faith is in works (the three discrete degrees), Blake observes that the whole of the New Church is in the active life, and not in ceremonies. He made an exception, however, in the ceremonies of Baptism and the Holy Supper, which were the only ceremonies for the new dispensation and were understood by Blake symbolically or in their spiritual sense.

In his *Vision of the Last Judgement* he saw heaven opened and the nature of eternal things displayed, all springing from the Divine Humanity. On each side of the opening of heaven he saw the figure of an apostle; that on the right side representing Baptism, that on the left side the Lord's Supper.

Blake's occasional repudiation of isolated passages from Swedenborg's writings are sometimes due either to misunderstanding of the passages taken apart from their context or to faulty translation of the Latin. . . .

He must have read closely most of Swedenborg's theological writings. His marginal notes on *The Divine Love and Wisdom* and *The Divine Providence* have been published. He certainly possessed copies of *Heaven and Hell*, *The True Christian Religion*, the *Doctrine of the Lord*,of *Life,*, of *Faith*, of the *Sacred Scriptures*, and many others. How many of these he annotated we do not know. If only his copies of these works could be found they would throw a flood of light on his indebtedness to Swedenborg. We can only assume that after Blake's death they came into the hands of Frederick Tatham and were destroyed by him in his wholesale burning of Blake's manuscripts and books.

When Blake joined or expressed his desire to join a separate New Church organization he was no doubt convinced that the truths of the New Dispensation, in which he wholeheartedly believed, needed forms of prayer and worship in harmony with the new doctrines. But whatever was the nature of the controversy which caused him to withdraw from the external New Church, he continued to worship in private and remained to the end of his life a devoutly religious man.

William Blake and the Writings of Swedenborg

PETER M. BUSS

Text of an address given to the Olivet Church of the New Jerusalem, Ontario, 28 January 1984, by permission of the author. Copyright © 1984 by Peter M. Buss.

Introduction

William Blake, unique poet and artist, was also for a time a Swedenborgian. I cannot say, "A New Church man," because perhaps he never was that. He was sporadically an admirer of the doctrines and of Swedenborg himself, but did he ever believe that the books Swedenborg wrote were inspired by God?

How do we account for his initial excitement with its teachings, his doubts and fierce criticisms, and his selective acceptance of some of its tenets? How do we view his wavering interest in his later years, when he seemed to admit that in his better states he liked the Writings, yet continued with his lonely confused mission to recast reality by a resolution of impossible opposites? Who was this William Blake? What kind of man was he?

When we try to understand his life, it must not be against a background of two centuries in which the New Church has grown strong. He didn't live after decades in which the church had explored the Writings and established a settled doctrine, a general body of truth that illumines our personal search for faith. The New Church had not been formed. The books on which it is based were still being written when Blake was born.

We will also want to see the man as he was—a poet, possessed of a rare talent which the world sometimes didn't even bother to scorn. He was a man with an intense, almost fierce love of beauty, struggling with no earthly help to understand the most organized description of beauty that the world has ever known. Could Blake discover the secret joy of the Writings, growing up as he did, an object of pity and rejection at times, at others accorded a grudging respect which by its very transience was an insult? Could this man whose fiery insights were shrugged off, whose beautiful art was disdained, who grew up on the fringes of the artistic world both because of his humble origins and the unique nature of his own talent, find it in himself to reflect in silence and probe the depth of a revelation whose beauty is hidden from the casual sight?

He was born in 1757 of respectable tradespeople and apprenticed to an engraver. As an engraver he worked, and his contribution to art has been as much through that special medium as through his written words. Even as a child he was unusual, and believed he saw visions. He ran home one day to tell his mother that he had seen Ezekiel. He was not only convinced of his deeper sights, but took them for granted, and they apparently stayed with him all his life.

At the age of 26 he met and married Katherine, a woman of a somewhat lower social class than William himself. She was a devoted and biddable wife, never criticizing, always supporting him, even in his wildest imaginings. She accompanied him when he saw visions, and seemed relatively content with the poor circumstances into which his lonely mission and his determined individuality placed them. In return he loved her, and his last act on earth was to sketch her likeness as she sat by his bed.

Blake was a worker all his life, and in 19th century England that put him on the fringes of society. He "was an artisan; an independent journeyman living entirely on the labor of his hands, dependent upon patrons in a luxury trade that was being narrowed down to those who could please most quickly. He lived as near the bottom of the English social pyramid as was possible for someone not sucked into the factories."[1] Engraving was seen more as a trade than an art. He survived largely on commissions which often required of him a conformity of style at which his spirit rebelled; but when he tried to sell works himself he found the public uninterested.

There is a strange paradox in the way he dealt with his poverty. He seemed to have been resigned to it from the first, to have felt that his artistic mission was so great that the acceptance of the world would have amounted almost to insult. "Knowing his superiority to the artists of the time, he was satisfied to be neglected. Feeling the value of his work, he was contented to take pennies when he knew he deserved pounds. Earthly riches he despised. He valued only spiritual gifts."

> Since all the riches of this world
> May be gifts from the devil and earthly kings
> I should suspect that I worshiped the devil
> If I thanked my God for worldly things.

"This was no boast but a settled feeling."[2] Yet there seems to have been some sour grapes in his obsessive vanity with his own powers, and his apparent contempt for the rewards of the world. It produced a man who saw himself very differently from the way he appeared to others. As one chronicler observed, he was in his eyes "the imperial visionary of his meager household, but in the London world a curious and threadbare crank."[3]

It is not surprising therefore that one of his greatest satisfactions was realized when he did engravings for his own books. He claimed to have learned in a vision from his dead brother Robert a special way of engraving. He would "write and draw with a certain liquid on copper, and then pour over the place an acid which ate away those portions of the metal not written upon, leaving the writing and drawing standing up like type."[4] The result was a dramatic presentation of visual and written art. He engraved his poems with the help of his wife, surrounding the words with beautiful drawings. Since his style was then unrestrained the works are valued differently. Some find them untrained and stilted; others are ecstatic. Some are offended by his grotesque and suggestive images; others sense the power with which he used his art to make his points.

His Contact with the Writings

Some have wondered if he met the old Baron himself in 1771, for Swedenborg spent the last months of his life in London. If he did he left no record of the meeting, but that doesn't mean much. His personal effects fell into the hands of a Mr. Tatham whose personal religious beliefs apparently caused him to destroy many records of Blake's dealings with the New Church together with his notes on Swedenborg.[5] What remains are his comments in his works, his reported conversations, and his annotations to *The Divine Love and Wisdom* and *The Divine Providence*. These annotations and his poetry chronicle his early excitement with, and his later estrangement from, the Writings.

The first book he read was probably *Heaven and Hell*. He was intimately acquainted with its teachings, and used them in his own scheme of things. The English version of *Heaven and Hell* was published in 1784, and that of *Divine Love and Wisdom* in 1788. He found many exciting ideas in this latter work too, as his annotations to his copy show. He loved the teaching that God is love itself and life itself; that there is a difference between the spiritual man and the natural man; and that space and time in the spiritual world correspond to spiritual states of mind. He approved of the concept of discrete degrees, and was most impressed with the teaching that our best thoughts come when the human understanding is elevated into spiritual light. (DLW 257). These ideas supported his own conviction that poetic genius is an interior power, often hidden from pedestrian thinkers and therefore scorned by them.

It seems that at first Blake not only felt the ideas in Swedenborg's writings to be in harmony with his own, he was also deeply moved by them. He read these books while writing his most beautiful poems—the *Songs of Innocence*. I don't think it stretches the imagination to say that they are the outpouring of a joyful heart which has found a measure of the Lord's beauty in His Word.

One of the best known of them is "The Lamb."

> *Little Lamb, who made thee?*
> *Dost thou know who made thee?*
> *Gave thee life and bid thee feed*
> *By the stream and o'er the mead;*
> *Gave thee clothing of delight,*
> *Softest clothing, wooly, bright;*
> *Gave thee such a tender voice,*
> *Making all the vales rejoice!*
> *Little Lamb, who made thee?*
> *Dost thou know who made thee?*

> *Little Lamb, I'll tell thee,*
> *Little Lamb, I'll tell thee:*
> *He is called by thy name,*
> *For he calls himself a Lamb.*
> *He is meek and he is mild;*
> *He became a little child.*
> *I a child, and thou a lamb,*
> *We are called by his name.*
> *Little Lamb, God Bless thee!*
> *Little Lamb, God bless thee!*

In "The Chimney Sweep" he speaks of the angel who sets free all the sweeps and lets them run on a great plain, and wash in a river and shine in the Sun. "On Another's Sorrow"

speaks of the Lord's love in coming to earth. Then there is "The Divine Image," which uses words familiar to readers of Swedenborg's Writings: "the human form divine," when speaking of the Lord.

> *To Mercy, Pity, Peace, and Love*
> *All pray in their distress;*
> *And to these virtues of delight*
> *Return their thankfulness.*

> *For Mercy, Pity, Peace and Love*
> *Is God, our father dear,*
> *And Mercy, Pity, Peace, and Love*
> *Is Man, his child and care.*

> *For Mercy has a human heart,*
> *Pity a human face,*
> *and Love, the human form divine,*
> *And Peace, the human dress.*

> *Then every man, of every clime,*
> *That prays in his distress,*
> *Prays to the human form divine,*
> *Love, Mercy, Pity, Peace.*

> *And all must love the human form,*
> *In heathen, turk, or jew;*
> *Where Mercy, Love and Pity dwell*
> *There God is dwelling too.*

In 1789 William and Katherine attended a meeting of New Church people at Great East Cheap in London, and signed the register there. What caused his disillusionment is not certain. There were divisions in the group over some of the teachings in Swedenborg's Writings, and maybe the dissension made him feel that this church was no different from any others. At any rate, his objections to *The Divine Providence* are clearly expressed in his marginalia to that work.

He studied and compared passages, and took particular exception to the teaching that each place in heaven "is opposite to a certain place in hell, for hell is in opposition to heaven." (DP 69) People, the Writings teach, are enrolled in a heaven or a hell according to their life on earth. Blake wrote, "What is enrolling but Predestination every day?" When the Writings taught that a person remains after death as he was in the world, Blake rebelled. "Predestination after this life is more abominable than Calvin's and Swedenborg is such a spiritual Predestinarian witness this number and many others. . . . Cursed folly." (Note to n. 277)

He failed to understand the Writings' resolution of God's foreknowledge with man's freedom of choice. As one chronicler observed, "The contradiction which Blake noted is, I think, more apparent than real, for Swedenborg distinguished between the Divine Omniscience, in which he believed, and Predestination in which he did not, holding that the former was not compatible with the principle of human freedom." Thus n. 329 emphasizes "That any other predestination than predestination to heaven is contrary to the Divine Wisdom and its infinity."[6]

In rejecting the Writings, however, Blake started to develop his own view of the cosmos in his early book, *The Marriage of Heaven and Hell*, and it is both startling and sad. Devils are not devils, he argued. They are people possessed of poetic genius who are wickedly oppressed by those who exalt reason. It is reason, which he personalized as "Urizen," with its attendant restrictive laws, which has stifled poetic genius. By itself poetic genius is meek. Its path is far more difficult than that of people who reason. But when reasoners, who have taken control of the churches, fashion laws which restrain the just and meek man of arts, he becomes angry and rages, and is condemned as a devil.

Blake carried his viewpoint into the spiritual world. Hell is not a place where evil people dwell, he argued, unless you count true goodness as evil. Heaven and its "angels" are those of the false god and the churches. They have stripped the world of its beauty and supplanted insipid law in its place. This greater view of things finds particular expression in his attack on Swedenborg, which we will examine shortly.

His self-ordained system was very much the result of his own nature and experience. He was himself a genius in a world which seemed mildly contemptuous of the talent he prized so highly. He was a man of unrestrained emotions, forced by economic necessity into some semblance of submission to the viewpoints of others whom he considered less able. So he set forth on his mission to free poetic nature, and to resolve the conflict between heaven and hell.

"Blake's spirit was exuberant, passionate, energetic, prodigal, storm-engendering. Life as it is meant to be—life un-spoilt, as it comes from the hands of God—would seem to be something 'fearless, lustful, happy, nestling for delight in laps of pleasure: Innocence! honest, open, seeking the vigorous joys of morning light.' For Blake, there is nothing defiled in the lustfulness he acclaims—it is the sweetness, the limpid purity of exuberant, clean desire. Once this is attained the gates of Eden open to man; his slavery is at an end. . . . Now in Blake's reading of the religious thought of his day, the influence of the Church and Reason and Morality was exercised toward the suppression of man's innate delights—the restraint of his native energy. And it is here that he took leave of Swedenborg. For the human understanding to rise up and exercise authority over the passions and energies of man was a tyrannical usurpation, destructive of real

manhood, leaving the soul 'darken'd and cast out, A solitary shadow wailing on the margin of non-entity.' "[7]

His *Songs of Experience*, published in 1794 but written much earlier, show his other view of life. When he combined them with the *Songs of Innocence* he said that they showed "the two contrary states of the human soul." Indeed they do. Many of the songs of experience are beautiful, expressing the sadness of human life. Others are almost cynical. "Infant Joy" (a song of innocence) told the joy of a newborn baby. What a contrast with "Infant Sorrow."

> *My mother groan'd! my father wept.*
> *Into the dangerous world I leapt:*
> *Helpless, naked, piping loud:*
> *Like a fiend hid in a cloud.*
>
> *Struggling in my father's hands,*
> *Striving against my swadling bands,*
> *Bound and weary I thought best*
> *To sulk upon my mother's breast.*

The imagery is so expressive: the exuberance of the child, its unrestrained emotions, curbed by father's control, clothing's restriction; turned from free delight into a sulking submission. How different from the former song.

> *'I have no name:*
> *I am but two days old.'*
> *What shall I call thee?*
> *'I happy am,*
> *Joy is my name.'*
> *Sweet joy befall thee!*
>
> *Pretty Joy!*
> *Sweet joy but two days old,*
> *Sweet joy I call thee:*
> *Thou dost smile,*
> *I sing the while,*
> *Sweet joy befall thee!*

His parody of the earlier *Nurse's Song* is most cynical. Children waste their unrestrained years in play, and spend their adult life pretending, losing all creative, honest energy.

> *Your spring and your day are wasted in play,*
> *And your winter and night in disguise.*

But the most stark of contrasts appears when "The Tyger" is seen next to "The Lamb."

> *Tyger! Tyger! burning bright*
> *In the forests of the night,*
> *What immortal hand or eye*
> *Could frame thy fearful symmetry?*
>
> *In what distant deeps or skies*
> *Burnt the fire of thine eyes?*
> *On what wings dare he aspire?*
> *What the hand dare seize the fire?*
>
> *And what shoulder, and what art,*
> *Could twist the sinews of thy heart?*
> *And when thy heart began to beat,*
> *What dread hand? and what dread feet?*
>
> *What the hammer? what the chain?*
> *In what furnace was thy brain?*
> *What the anvil? what dread grasp*
> *Dare its deadly terrors clasp?*
>
> *When the stars threw down their spears,*
> *And water'd heaven with their tears,*
> *Did he smile his work to see?*
> *Did he who made the Lamb make thee?*
>
> *Tyger! Tyger! burning bright*
> *In the forests of the night,*
> *What immortal hand or eye*
> *Dare frame thy fearful symmetry?*

How successfully does he present the fearsome, stormy, violent side of life! Is this part of the same creation? In this he harks back to a response he wrote to the last passage in the *Divine Love and Wisdom*: "Heaven and hell were created together." God created both savagery and conformity.

So we come to *The Marriage of Heaven and Hell*. Written around 1790, it is an attack on the Writings, and seems almost blasphemous to a New Church person. Artistically I find it excellent, however much I dislike its thrust.

He starts by explaining how the good people (who are now the devils) got where they did. They were the just, who walked in "perilous paths," and through their goodness made the paths beautiful. But those who exalted reason, who lived in ease, left their comfortable life to oust the just man from his more difficult way. They succeeded, and the just man has become angry in his banishment.

> *Once meek, and in a perilous path,*
> *The just man kept his course along*
> *The vale of death.*
> *Roses are planted where thorns grow,*
> *And on the barren heath*
> *Sing the honey bees.*
>
> . . . .
>
> *Till the villain left the paths of ease,*
> *To walk in perilous paths, and drive*
> *The just man into barren climes.*
>
> *Now the sneaking serpent walks*
> *In mild humility,*
> *And the just man rages in the wilds*
> *Where lions roam.*

He parodies the Last Judgment. "As a new heaven is begun, and it is now thirty-three years since its advent, the Eternal Hell revives. And lo! Swedenborg is the Angel sitting at the tomb: his writings are the linen clothes folded up." He uses this imagery, distasteful to Christian people, to say that true religion is to acknowledge the "energy and passion" of hell; and this can be done only when the restrictive laws in the Writings are cast off.

"Those who restrain desire," he complains, "do so because theirs is weak enough to be restrained; and the restrainer or reason usurps its place and governs the unwilling. And being restrained, it by degrees becomes passive, till it is only the shadow of desire." I would like to quote a response to this point from the Rev. Eric Sutton. "The fallacy of Blake's position, of course, is discernable there—but too many critics miss the point in order that they may join with Blake in belaboring Swedenborg. If man determines to restrain his desire—there is another desire and a stronger desire at the back of his determination. Reason itself is not the restrainer—reason enlightens, and becomes the womb of a new, a purified, and more powerful desire—and this, the new born energy, is that which restrains. If a desire is restrained it is restrained by a stronger one."[8]

Blake speaks on behalf of the devils throughout the poem.

He cites five "Memorable Fancies," which are memorable relations from the devil's point of view, and one of them has to do with an angel who was converted to being a devil. He lists many "Proverbs of Hell," such as "The road of excess leads to the palace of wisdom," "Exuberance is Beauty," "One law for the lion and ox is oppression." Of Milton's poems he says, "The reason Milton wrote in fetters when he wrote of Angels and God, and at liberty when of Devils and Hell, is because he was a true Poet and of the Devil's party without knowing it."

His attacks on Swedenborg are didactic.

> I have always found that Angels have the vanity to speak of themselves as the only wise; this they do with a confident insolence sprouting from systematic reasoning.
> Thus Swedenborg boasts that what he writes is new: tho' it is only the Contents or Index of already publish'd books. . . .
> Swedenborg's writings are a recapitulation of all superficial opinions, and an analysis of the more sublime—but no further. . . . Any man of mechanical talents may, from the writings of Paracelsus or Jacob Behmen, produce ten thousand volumes of equal value with Swedenborg's, and from those of Dante or Shakespeare an infinite number.

A feature of Blake's work is his conviction that he spoke with spirits, and learned from them truths which agreed with his ideas. He would even sketch supposedly well-known people whom he said appeared to him. One cannot help feeling that he had converse with the spiritual world, but that it was very different from what he conceived it to be. In *The Marriage of Heaven and Hell* he would record that he spoke to Isaiah or Ezekiel and asked what they meant in their prophecies; and their answers supported his point of view. The Writings tell us that spirits may put on all the things of a man's memory, thereby counterfeiting a person he has heard of in a most complete manner. They are not allowed to teach, and tend therefore to confirm a man's opinions. At the same time the spirits are seeking to inspire their affections, so they excite in the man's memory such "answers" as will accord with their ideas, and bind the man more firmly to them. This is one reason why the Writings warn us that to seek intercourse with spirits is at the peril of our souls.

Blake probably talked with some people, but it is most

unlikely that they were the prophets, or some famous dignitaries. They were earthbound spirits who spoke to him for their own purposes, and did him no favors.

Blake then set forth on what he considered to be his mission—to restore the balance in the universe between reason and desire. He wrote a set of prophetic poems, using his own method of correspondences. They are most difficult to understand, and have little of the sweetness of his earlier works, although now and then they burst forth into song—witness the stanzas from *Milton*, now popularized in the theme-song of *Chariots of Fire*.

The result was that what little popularity he had faded away and he died in poverty.

An Attempt at Analysis

Was Blake heretic or antiChrist? Did he reject the Writings? People will differ. In a later poem (*Milton*) he lamented Swedenborg's great talent:

> O Swedenborg! strongest of men, the Samson
>   shorn by the Churches,
> Shewing the Transgressors in Hell, the proud
>   Warriors in Heaven,
> Heaven as a punisher, & Hell as One under
>   Punishment.

He is credited with telling Crabb Robinson that Swedenborg was a "Divine teacher," who did wrong "in endeavoring to explain to the *reason* what it could not comprehend." More significantly he is said to have informed C. A. Tulk, an early New Church man, that in his better states he liked the Writings, and only disliked them when he was in a state of pride in himself.[9]

He was very well-read in the Old and New Testaments, and professed a deep faith in Jesus. But it was a faith that created its own parameters. He wrote a rather lovely and lengthy poem called *The Everlasting Gospel*, in which he insisted that Jesus was not humble, He was proud; He was not gentle, He brought a sword to the earth. He was great because He fought those who enslaved others with their moralistic rule. In *The Marriage of Heaven and Hell* he even argued that Jesus did not support the Ten Commandments, rejecting the Sabbath and forgiving the woman taken in adultery.

There certainly seems to have been an arrogance in Blake's works which drove him to formulate rather than to follow another's lead. "I rest not from my great task," he wrote in *Jerusalem*, "To open the Eternal Worlds, to open the immortal Eyes of Man inwards into the Worlds of Thought, into Eternity Ever expanding in the Bosom of God, the Human Imagination. O Saviour pour upon me thy Spirit of meekness and love!"

One reviewer gives us this thoughtful insight, when commenting on Blake's response to *The Divine Love and Wisdom*, that book in which the process of creation is revealed through Swedenborg. "He could never question without desiring to surpass, and the effect on his mind was to project a cosmogony (sic) of his own. He was quite unfitted for the task, for he was not, like Swedenborg, an orderly thinker; and when an opponent of systems determines to create one, we seem to be watching the laborious creation of chaos."[10]

In *Jerusalem* he cried out, "I must Create a System or be enslav'd by another Man's. I will not Reason and Compare: my business is to Create." Perhaps so: but "What monuments in verse and line might Blake have left behind, what beneficent influence might he be exerting even now, had he accepted the new knowledge that was within his grasp!"[11]

Instead he chose to use the mechanisms of the Writings, to establish a set of correspondences of his own. He used the Writings "to plunder them for figures, not for concepts."[12] He wove his own intricate patterns around a strange concept of the universe, and lost a chance to be the first, and to date the finest poet of the New Christian Church.

Yet by itself I feel this would be too harsh a judgment. Our own affection and reverence for the Lord's Word cannot color our awareness that even today the church offers a home for few in this world. The organizations of the Church of the New Jerusalem appeal to a very narrow range of people. Some have blamed us for it; others realize the limitations inherent in all organizations. It is not up to us to reach all people: that is the Lord's prerogative. We must not be judgmental and we must try to broaden our horizons, and welcome those who can find a home in a gentle and understanding organization of the New Church. But we must be content that there are billions of people today who could not worship in comfort within our doors, even though they loved the Writings as deeply as or more fully than we.

Every church will express the truth in accordance with its own sense of what the Lord is saying. In doing so it is merely responding to the heavenly law that societies are bound together by mutual love, and that distances in heaven inevitably exist because of differences in mutual love. The New Church will never be one organization; that would lead to the stifling kind of conformity that Blake abhorred. It will be one in purpose, but many in the ways that purpose is expressed. These distinctions of expression are because of, and express, differences in mutual love.

William Blake looked at the Writings without the benefit of any doctrine, and doctrine, we are told, is a lamp which people use to search the Word. When he thought Swedenborg taught spiritual predestination, who was there to set him straight? When he thought that the understanding can restrain desire, was there an Eric Sutton to point out that this is impossible?—that the Writings teach that only a deeper and purer love, inspired by the Lord, can inspire the understanding with the power to restrain evil desire? Who was there to help him sense the eternal beauty of the new will, whose passions are permissible, or to let him see that heaven is not the anemic place he thought it, but one in which true freedom is to love as our Lord made us to love? The angels in heaven do just what they want. That is full freedom because their *loves*—not just their thoughts but their loves which inspire thoughts—are pure, and pleasing in the sight of their Lord.

And even had he had friends to show him these things, could he have overcome the bitterness he felt that his incredible genius was to be overlooked, that he and his wife must struggle in penury in a world that appeared to love dross better than beauty? Could a nature both independent and oppressed have seen that the Writings were given to alleviate oppression, and set free the creative spirit of man?

Yes, it is sad that Blake didn't embrace the Writings with his whole heart while on earth. As Sutton said, "The world was made poorer when Blake left Swedenborg. Had he read more patiently, he would have found much to purify and adjust his own creed—his storm enveloped genius could have

sung a song free from discord—the song of truth wedded to undying beauty. It was not to be—and on the anvil of his genius Blake forged his own mystic creed, which few can read and none in fullness accept."[13] We can suspect that our church might be much larger and richer in artistic talent had this one disciple held his candle on high for all to see.

But perhaps the lesson New Church people learn from his tryst with the Writings is almost as important. We can look at those who do not respond to the beautiful truths we have seen, and at a world which seems indifferent to them, and draw a more understanding conclusion. To come into the New Church with a whole heart requires not only the willingness to follow the Lord, but also the ability to rise above certain loves and certain ideas which are impressed on us by our environment. Time and again the Writings warn us how difficult it is, for example, for a man raised to love one religious faith to relinquish it. It is not because he is stubborn and narrow-minded. His love of what is good is bound up in his sense that that religious faith is the way to find the Lord. Such holy loves can be redirected only by the gentle hand of the Lord Himself. Perhaps all we can do in such a case is to be wise enough not to interfere with His work in any way that threatens the holiness of his beliefs.

So too people may have suffered enough (perhaps in silent ways) that their affections are not ready to see the beauty hidden beneath the careful prose of the Writings. They may fear institutions. They may not like the steady tone of the books. They may sense a threat to some deep-seated principle; and their rejection is not of the understanding, it is from loves or fears with which they cannot yet deal.

This, it seems, explains Blake's wavering delight in the Word that the Lord sent to earth, and his at least temporary departure from it. Some have put it down to the requirements of his genius. "If a man aims at popularity he must restrict his vision. It is a condition of favoritism with people that a genius must not see too deeply or sing too highly. William Blake did both, and the world, as in the case of Swedenborg, declared him mad."[14] I prefer to think of him fettered by some of the very bonds he sought to destroy. He labored for the freedom of man, but became enslaved by a false principle himself, and could not see that freedom when it shone before his sight. Perhaps today he is free, and singing his songs in the heaven he thought a prison.

And perhaps we might be inspired by his story to appreciate those millions in our world today who are longing for the freedom, the unrestrained joy and the beauty which the Lord has promised in the Writings, and who do not see that the path to such joy comes through "the way of truth." Can we find new ways to speak to the church universal, and help them see the new light which has burst on the earth? Can we respect those who do not see, and understand that in His wisdom our Lord will lead those whom we cannot touch?

Notes

1. Alfred Kazin, Introduction to *The Portable Blake* (New York: Viking Press, 1968), p. 32.

2. James Spilling, "Blake the Visionary," *New Church Magazine* VI (June 1887), p. 207.

3. Ibid. (May, 1887), p. 210.

4. Kazin, p. 37.

5. H. N. Morris, "Blake and Swedenborg," *New Church Herald* XXX (1949), p. 165.

6. H. Stanley Redgrove, "Blake's Annotations on Swedenborg's Divine Providence," *New Church Magazine* XLIV (1925), p. 44.

7. Rev. Eric A. Sutton, "Swedenborg and Blake," *New Church Magazine* XLVIII (April-June 1929), p. 80.

8. Ibid., p. 81.

9. Spilling, p. 210

10. James S. Pyrke, "Blake and the Imagination," *New Church Life* XLVIII (March 1928), p. 141, quoting from Osbert Burdet, *William Blake* (New York: Macmillan Co., 1926).

11. James S. Pryke, "Blake and Swedenborg," *New Church Life* XLVIII (May 1928), p. 151.

12. Mark Schorer, *William Blake* (New York; Holt, 1946), p. 107.

13. Sutton, p. 85.

14. Spilling, p. 205.

Swedenborg Foundation Publications and Films

Books About Swedenborg

A VIEW FROM WITHIN: A Compendium of Swedenborg's Theological Thought

Compiled and Edited By Rev. George F. Dole

A meticulously organized, concise introduction to Swedenborg's philosophical, psychological, and religious concepts, culled from his extensive publications; also includes a brief biography of Swedenborg by Rev. Dole.

THE SWEDENBORG EPIC: The Life and Works of Emanuel Swedenborg

By Cyriel Odhner Sigstedt

The classic biography of Swedenborg.

THE PRESENCE OF OTHER WORLDS: The Psychological/Spiritual Findings of Emanuel Swedenborg

By Wilson Van Dusen

A clinical psychologist's account of Swedenborg's remarkable inward journey, which resulted in Swedenborg's strikingly modern writings about the psyche.

MY RELIGION

By Helen Keller

Helen Keller's inspiring personal account of Swedenborg's writings as the source of her own courage and strength.

Books By Emanuel Swedenborg

HEAVEN AND HELL

A new translation into modern English by Rev. George F. Dole

Swedenborg's revolutionary vision of the afterlife as an extension of the inner realities of the psyche.

Blake, *Jerusalem* 95 (detail)

ARCANA COELESTIA (HEAVENLY SECRETS)

12 volumes

A detailed analysis of the symbolic meanings of the books of Genesis and Exodus as guides to the unfoldment of human consciousness.

APOCALYPSE REVEALED

2 volumes

A similar analysis of the subtext of the enigmatic Book of Revelation.

APOCALYPSE EXPLAINED

6 volumes

A comprehensive examination of passages from the Book of Revelation as they relate to the underlying meanings of other key books of the Bible.

DIVINE LOVE AND WISDOM

A far-reaching philosophical/religious exploration of love as the basis of existence.

DIVINE PROVIDENCE

A celebration of free will as an inherent principle of the divine master-plan.

TRUE CHRISTIAN RELIGION

2 volumes

Swedenborg's own synthesis of his theological writings into a unified vision of a new age with new beliefs predicated on inner realities rather than on outward forms.

JOURNAL OF DREAMS

Only recently available in English translation, Swedenborg's private dream-journal reveals an eighteenth century scientist struggling to interpret his own subconscious in a manner anticipating the works of Freud and Jung.

SPIRITUAL DIARY

5 volumes

Swedenborg's private diary, chronicling over twenty years of his visionary experiences.

Motion Pictures

Available in 16mm, VHS, Beta, U-Matic and other video-formats

SWEDENBORG: The Man Who Had To Know

30 minutes

Featuring Lillian Gish, narrated by Eddie Albert

Award-winning television docu-drama about Swedenborg's life and writings, with a script excerpted from his books, journals and other eighteenth century accounts.

BLAKE: The Marriage of Heaven and Hell

30 minutes

Starring Anne Baxter and George Rose

Academy Award-winner, Anne Baxter, and Tony Award-winner, George Rose, re-create William Blake's inner world and artistic achievements, using Blake's own words, in this award-winning television docu-drama.

IMAGES OF KNOWING

15 minutes

Narrated by Anne Baxter

A highly acclaimed, award-winning, lyrical exploration of the processes of nature as reflections of the processes of mind; written by Rev. George F. Dole.

Many other low-cost books and motion pictures also available. For a free catalog and price-list, please contact the non-profit Swedenborg Foundation:

**The Swedenborg Foundation, Dept. BA
139 East 23rd Street, New York, N.Y. 10010**

Phone: (212) 673-7310